THE

FIRES OF ALCHEMY

A TRANSPERSONAL VIEWPOINT

Dr. Carl Jung

Barbara Somers

The Wisdom of the Transpersonal

Also in this series:

Journey in Depth: A Transpersonal Perspective

Proposed future titles:

The Raincloud of Knowable Things - Ian Gordon-Brown
Symptom as Symbol - Barbara Somers

THE FIRES OF ALCHEMY

A TRANSPERSONAL VIEWPOINT

BARBARA SOMERS

editor
HAZEL MARSHALL

illustrations
IAN THORP

original paintings
FRANCES CRAWFORD

ARCHIVE
publishing

2004

First published in Great Britain by
Archive Publishing
Wren Cottage, Ford Lane, Morton,
Nr. Bourne, Lincolnshire, PE10 0RQ

Designed for Archive Publishing by Ian Thorp

© 2004 Archive Publishing
Text © Hazel Marshall, 2004

Barbara Somers asserts the moral right to be identified
as the author of this work

A CIP Record for this book is available from
the British Cataloguing in Publication data office

ISBN 0-9542712-2-X (Hardback)
ISBN 0-9542712-3-8 (Paperback)

Cover painting: 'The Alchemist's Table' by Frances Crawford.
Also those in the text - all reproduced courtesy of the artist.
Allathumpach, Deskry-Side, Strathdon, Aberdeenshire.
francescrawfordart@yahoo.com
also at www.archivepublishing.co.uk

Printed and bound in England by
The Bath Press

DEDICATION

Dedicated, with love and gratitude to
Sacha, Duchess of Abercorn,
and to all living alchemists
in honour of their heartful work,
courage and persistence.

The Watchers

CONTENTS

PART I
The Alchemy of the West

INTRODUCTION
   An oral tradition

CHAPTER ONE - LIVING ALCHEMY
   Carl Jung
   Caught in the seventeenth century
   Alchemy and individuation
   Life is alchemy

CHAPTER TWO - THE STORY OF WESTERN ALCHEMY
   Egypt, Greece, Persia and Arabia
   The Crusades
   Obscurity
   Heresy
   The dangers of alchemy
   Gold from base metal
   Sympathetic medicine
   Hermes
   The Puffers

CHAPTER THREE - THE OPUS
   The early alchemists
   The alchemist as the *opus*
   Names for the goal

ILLUSTRATIONS

FIGURES

THE OXHERDING PICTURES

SOURCES

PAINTINGS
1-7   Frances Crawford

PLATES
1   Version of *Ripley Scrowle* by James Standysh, 16th C.
(British Museum, London, detail). In Klossowski de Rola 1973, Plate 65.

De summa, 18th C. Bibliotheque de l'Arsenal, Paris, Ms.974, Figs. I-XL:
2   *Calcinatio, Solutio, Fixatio, Sublimatio*. Figs. X, XII, XXXIX, XI.
4   *Putrefactio & Purgatio*. Figs. XIV, XXX.
6   *Fermentatio & Separatio*. Figs. XVII, XVIII & XX.
9   *Coitus & Coniunctio*. Figs. VIII & XXI.
        In Klossowski de Rola ibid., Pp.108-117.
13   *Exaltatio V. Essentiae*. Fig. XXXVII.
14   *V. Essentia Exaltata*. Fig. XXXVIII.
        In Klossowski de Rola ibid., Plates 49 & 50.

Rosarium philosophorum, 16th C. Stadt-bibliothek Vadiana, St. Gallen,
        Ms. 394a, f. 97, 34 64
3   The Green Lion Swallowing the Sun.
10   *Mysterium coniunctionis*.
12   *Hieros gamos*.
        In Klossowski de Rola ibid., Plates 20, 41 & 42.

Philosophia reformata, 1622, Mylius, British Museum, London, i. 7 :
5   Six Alchemical Pictures, Early Stages. Figs. 6, 7, 8, 9, 12, 13.
11   Six Alchemical Pictures, Later Stages. Figs. 13 - 18.
        In Klossowski de Rola ibid., P.107 & 105.

Aurora consurgens.
7   The Sun and the Moon do Battle.
8   Tying the Dragon.
        In Klossowski de Rola ibid., Plates 13 & 14.

FIGURES
1-5   Barabara Somers, various, designed here by Ian Thorp
6-9   The Circulation of the Light : The pictures of Stages One to Four are attributed to Lü Yen. They are taken from 'The Secret of the Golden Flower', and are relevant to the Hui Ming Ching, or 'Book of Consciousness and Life', which follows it (Wilhelm 1931, Pp. 69 ff). The pictures are in Wilhelm 1931, Pages 27, 37, 47, 57, and also in Jung, CW 13, Pp. 30-33.

THE OXHERDING PICTURES
1-10   Painter : Shubun, Zen priest, 15th century (originals in Kyoto). Pictures also in 'Mudra', by Chögyam Trungpa, and 'Zen Flesh, Zen Bones' by Paul Reps, painted by Tomikichiro Tokuriki. Also in Kapleau, painted by Gyokusei Jikihara.

ACKNOWLEDGEMENTS

My deep gratitude to Barbara Somers for the evocation and
inspiration behind this book.
The following are among the many to whom I owe warm thanks:
Anita Somers for her encouragement and unfailing support.
Beata Bishop for proofreading the early manuscript, and for
generously contributing.
Celia M. Gunn for her tireless correction of the final proofs.
Marian Thorp for her patience and for much material help.
Monica Anthony, Pamela Allsop, Dorothy Allen and Peter Merriott
for their steadfast friendship and understanding.
Frances Crawford for doing so much to make the book beautiful.
Hossein Farhadi for his generous ordering of my computer world.

Kathy Smith for much invaluable typing.
My thanks also to Sacha Abercorn, Anne Baring,
Marita Crawley, David Lorimer and Melanie Reinhart,
all of whom read the manuscript and contributed their responses.
Above all, to Ian Thorp, whose enthusiasm, dedication and skill
have enabled this project from the beginning.

Acknowledgement and thanks are due to the following publishers for
the use of passages quoted:
Sarah Bauhan, of William L. Bauhan, Publishers, Inc.,
Dublin, New Hampshire,
for permission to quote 'Fire Hazard', by
Dorsha Hayes, in 'The Bell Branch Rings', 1972.

Thomson Publishing Services, for permission to quote from two of
the letters of Carl Jung.
Collected Letters, Volume 1, Pages 65-66 and 63,
originally published by Routledge & Kegan Paul, 1973.

Care has been taken to protect the identity of anyone whose story
appears in this book.

FOREWORD
Beata Bishop

Alchemy is a strange concept for us today. Although we know that the process of turning base metal into gold truly refers to the deepest and highest transformation within the human psyche, yet Alchemy remains a secret land of the imagination. It is veiled in mystery and inhabited by weird images which seem totally alien but also touch something deep within us; for they invite us into the world of archetypes, full of unexpected meaning.

This book contains a series of talks on Transpersonal Alchemy. They were given by Barbara Somers at workshops held at the London Centre for Transpersonal Psychology which she and Ian Gordon-Brown founded in 1973. The talks, given throughout the 1980's, were originally intended both for the general public and for counsellors and psychotherapists in training. In this book, where they are captured on the printed page and expertly and sensitively edited by Hazel Marshall, their appeal extends greatly to reach a much wider public. For this is a book about a vitally important universal subject: the pursuit of inner development throughout life that Jung mapped out for us, naming it individuation.

Barbara Somers leads us into this world with a sure touch. Those among us who were fortunate enough to hear her in person remember the ease, elegance and wisdom with which she handled the weightiest subjects. Here, too, she guides us into the very centre of the symbolic Alchemist's den and through the phases, trials and tribulations of the inner process that helps us to become what we truly are. It's not an easy journey, it has its risks and dangers, but also its moments of joy and glory. And the gold that eventually manifests in the flask of the psyche is an indestructible treasure.

Let Transpersonal Alchemy do its work through this book and spread its message far and wide. The world is in dire need of the gold that is, paradoxically, not of this world.

Beata Bishop

London
January, 2004

INTRODUCTION
Hazel Marshall

In this book Barbara Somers has opened up, distilled and mapped in her own joyous and unique way the archaic territory of alchemy. Alchemy speaks in a universal language which, far from being dusty and dead, is intensely alive in the twenty-first century. Cutting through all barriers, its ancient wisdom is highly relevant for our time just because of the darkness, of which there is so much. Certainly, many people are keenly aware of the troubles and difficulties in the world. There are no panaceas. Those looking for easy answers have not found them, and they are not in this book.

'The Fires of Alchemy' follows the oral tradition. It is Barbara Somers' spoken word, taken from audio tapes made during courses run in the 1980's in London, Newcastle, Edinburgh and elsewhere. Linking traditions from China and India, the Middle East, Egypt, Europe and the West, her work brings together West and East in a rich blending that may be essential to world survival.

The great psychologist Carl Jung, in the first half of the twentieth century, made alchemy clear, or a great deal clearer than it had been. In turn, Barbara Somers makes Jung clear. Where his writings (themselves fairly obscure, in the view of many) brought unprecedented light, order and scholarship to an almost impossibly arcane and confused esoteric field, she does the same for his work. Her alchemy courses brought yet further heart, soul and inspiration to the subject of alchemy, making its language immediately accessible to us all. Emphasising always the great debt we owe to Jung, and speaking spontaneously from the sketchiest of notes (see example on Page 183), she would often punctuate her own inspired flow with readings from the large white cards on which she had, in longhand, lovingly copied passages from his great works. She introduces a lightheartedness, a humour into the field; however deep the darkness, laughter is never far from the surface.

The book begins in the light; then the early chapters descend into a profound darkness as we begin to explore the stages of Western alchemy.

A consistent drumbeat runs through the dark, reminding us that it is the very repetition that makes the music: each time we hear it, it sounds different because of what has gone before. Many people feel a great depth and heaviness in their lives; this is profoundly *understood* in Barbara's early chapters on the *calcinatio* and *solutio*. For those whose lives are in shadow, much comfort and affirmation lies in knowing that the darkness is acknowledged: 'Yes, it is dark; and that's how things are'. This book is a journey into, and finally out of, that darkness. There is no premature attempt to rise above it. Rather, light is taken down into the deep; we find light through the darkness, our perception changes, and eyes once accustomed can see in the dark. *The gold is there already.*

Hazel Marshall
in her garden at
Rock Bank

For other readers, it may be hard to stay with the fire and the water of the first two stages. For them, the challenge is not to give up on these early chapters. Hang in there! If you want light, there is light, and if you would like to jump to the light without going through the darkness, you may turn straight away to the later stages. However, if you would dare the alchemical process, then stay with the 'nice cooking heat' of the earlier chapters, travelling lightly, but also acknowledging the darkness. Going through it to be transformed, soon we shall be coming home to our earth in the *coagulatio*; and then the feeling rises till it soars into the airy dawn of the fourth stage, the *sublimatio*, carrying us on into the alchemy of the East. It's worth waiting for. Here, Barbara Somers 'walks in snow without leaving footprints'.

Today, people in therapy spontaneously turn up the images of alchemy in their dreams and drawings, undergoing the process at the hands of the great Alchemist of their lives. The pictures and phrases you will find in this book are universal and ancient, and they speak to us now. The process is mysterious, yet mystery is the more vital the more it is squeezed out of our modern lives. Many present-day books on 'spirituality' are so much 'candy-floss of the spirit' - chew and there's nothing there. But 'The Fires of Alchemy' points to the Stone, the turning of the tin or lead or dross of our lives to gold. In denseness we may discover the spirit. Here is an account of the transforming of dead, dense matter into a spark of purity. Once that spark takes hold, once enough people see the flame, the true alchemy of the spirit may enter the world and the human heart.

Hazel Marshall

Rock Bank
February 2004

The Seven Seeds

PART I

The Alchemy of the West

INTRODUCTION

An oral tradition

Let me say first of all that nobody really knows much about alchemy. It is a subject that we can talk around, but we can't really talk *about* it, because it is such a totally individual thing. I can describe it but I can't define it, and neither can anybody else. I've studied it for about thirty-five years, and am still barely on the edge of the mystery. The alchemic tradition doesn't make things concrete, tie them up too neatly nor define them too clearly. Indeed it is said that it's dangerous to talk too clearly on this very interior, subtle subject. There's the risk of calcifying it, of killing the living spirit and turning it into a dead stone. It was the *living* stone that the true alchemist sought - and still seeks. We need to free the spirit of alchemy or we block the living stream of the great tradition, the golden hermetic chain from which alchemy springs and in which all alchemists have worked for centuries. Even today those who work with true alchemy are members of the great tradition.

For many alchemists, the goal of their endless lapidary process was the Philosophers' Stone that finally brings the *lapis*, the touchstone, into being.[1] Of all the names alchemists have given to what they are pursuing, 'the Stone' is one of the major ones - the simple, grey stone. Whatever it touches will be turned to pure gold, become immortal and everlasting. It is the touchstone of something greater than our own lives.

There are very many endless recondite texts on alchemy. I do not intend to amplify them theoretically, but rather to look at the whole

---

[1] Philosophers' Stone: a substance believed by the alchemists to turn base metals to gold. The search for it led, *inter alia,* to the invention of porcelain and gunpowder, and the discovery of acids, gases and salts.

subject humanly, critically, clinically, talking about it particularly in its relation to counselling and therapeutic practice, asking what bearing it has on our everyday lives. So I refer to the texts as we go, for those who feel excited enough to want to explore them. If the reader should become enthusiastic enough to go directly to the books and treatises I recommend, they'll open themselves up in a different way. However, alchemy has been mainly an oral tradition. Many of the treatises that came out of it were put there to confuse as much as to explain, and I hope to have you in a happy state of confusion quite a lot of the time. I offer you here an affectionate warning: if this approach works for you, you will be in the flask. And people who get into the alchemic flask are generally lifted up and put down, burned and cooked and washed, pulled apart and put together again. So, be prepared!

I will begin by going through the processes of Western alchemy and (with the reader perhaps living in the flask in the meantime) will open with a bit about its back history, then about its four varying stages, relating them to clinical material, to therapy, to modern life. At last, with joy and delight, I shall come to Chinese and Japanese alchemy, ending in the East.

CHAPTER ONE

LIVING ALCHEMY

The art requires the whole person

We are dealing with *living* alchemy. It's 'living' because it's still so vividly alive in the human psyche, totally relevant to ordinary factual, practical, pragmatic living, as well as being one of the most obscure and recondite of subjects. Someone came to see me recently, wondering whether she wanted to be in therapy with a man or with a woman. She hoped and expected to become my client, and was quite shirty when I told her I wasn't at all sure that it was a woman that she needed. We talked about this. She went away and had a dream: 'I'm renting a flat. A man shows me into a circular room made entirely of glass. I'm unsure, but cold, and tired of searching. I say, "OK I'll take it." He says, "Then I'll go and stoke the boiler," and turns away. I ask, "Oh, by the way - what's the rent?" and he says, "You are." He goes out and locks the door. "Let me out!" I scream and wake in panic, thinking, "Must go to a woman, if this is what's going to happen!" '

As we worked on it together, the dreamer came to recognise that in fact she needed to go to a man, since he would hold her in the flask. She did, and told me it was an appropriate choice. That is a most beautiful statement of the whole process of alchemy, suddenly alive and vivid in the modern psyche of a thirty-four-year-old woman. She had never heard of alchemy, but suddenly the answer was there for her. What was that dream about? 'What is the rent?' 'You are,' and the locking, the sealing of the flask. An alchemist would recognise that. The art of alchemy requires the whole person. There's nothing left out. The price of being truly in the flask is the whole of ourselves.

Carl Jung

I can talk about alchemy neither as it is today nor as it was without making reference to the monumental work done by Carl Jung in this

whole area. It is his major works that have made alchemy accessible even to the degree that it is, and for this we owe him a tremendous debt. Jung was an empiricist, and thus true to the tradition of alchemy. He used the substance of his empirical work to bring about the theory, rather than the other way round. He had done an enormous amount of work on his own case-material - his dreams and symptoms and those of his clients - before he came around to alchemy. He mugged up his Greek and his Latin in order to be able to translate ancient texts for himself - endless hours of grinding work, hours and hours of translation - to produce his own understanding of the subject. For this we must be intensely grateful.

Plate 1. The Ripley Scroll - opposite

Wherever Jung looked in alchemy he saw the motifs that he also saw in his patients' material. He came to recognise, as he said, that alchemy was a great projection-canvas, a way of putting 'out there' what was already within here. Marie Louise von Franz, in her highly recommended book 'Alchemy',[2] tells how Jung discovered it absolutely empirically. Searching in old books, he began to see a connection between alchemy and certain frequent but hitherto incomprehensible motifs in the dreams of his patients. One woman dreamt of an eagle: it flew up into the sky, then, dropping back to the earth, began to eat its own wings. Jung understood this to be a 'thought bird', symbolising the high soaring spirit and indicating an *enantiodromia*, the reversal of a psychic situation.[3] Knowing this was an archetypal symbol he was led to feel that it was touching on something collective, the nature of which he didn't understand. So when in 1923 he came across an illustration out of the Ripley Scroll dating back to the fourteenth century, of an eagle with a king's head turning back and biting its own wings, he realised he was into an area that he was going to have to explore. Pictures are frequently found in Western alchemy of the pelican, the bird biting, pecking into its own breast for the blood to flow to nourish its young. This is also linked with the image of Christ.

---

[2]   Von Franz 1959, 'Alchemy: an Introduction to the Symbolism and the Psychology'. And see Pp. 21-22 below.

[3]   '*Enantiodromia*' is when one energy goes on to the point where it turns round and becomes its opposite.

Of all who have written about alchemy in modern times, it is Jung who most recognised and made clear the degree to which it was an *inner* process that the alchemists were about: that they precipitated what was inner on to the outer flask. Although it was a science 'out there' - a chemical process, and seen as such by a lot of the alchemists - it was in some way a precipitation of psychic reality, psychic experience on to the external flask; a grand 'projection-canvas', as we've seen. In fact, many of the alchemists did act as scientists and chemists, creating a flask, setting up the furnace. But whereas the less noble of them thought it *was* a scientific process, not recognising that it was also internal, the true ones recognised that they were doing no more than creating outwardly what was an internal process.

Caught in the seventeenth century

Jung was, of course, also led by his own dreams, a crucial one of which anticipated his encounter with alchemy.[4] He dreamed that he was on the Italian front in the South Tyrol during the First World War. He was driving back from the front line in a horse-drawn wagon with a little peasant man and shells were exploding dangerously all around them. They must push on quickly. Now, this was 1926, the war was over, but Jung himself felt that these missiles from the other side were shells being lobbed by his own unconscious. He believed that solutions needed to be found in the inner rather than the outer world. He described how they crossed a bridge, went through a tunnel and arrived at a sunny landscape which he knew to be the region around Verona, a city where the seventeenth-century alchemists had gathered. It lay radiant below, in full sunlight. 'I felt relieved!' said Jung. Driving on, they passed the vineyards, rice-fields and olive groves of the lovely springtime countryside, finally arriving at a large manor house with many outbuildings. They drove in through the main gate, from which they saw another gate across the courtyard.

Then, all unexpectedly, both gates flew shut with a dull clang. The dreamer and the little coachman were caught in front of the house in the middle of the courtyard. 'It's the seventeenth century and we're trapped!' cried the peasant. Though the chances were they would be

---

4   See Jung 1961, 'Memories, Dreams, Reflections', Pp. 228-9.

caught for years, Jung felt resigned; there was nothing they could do about it. He consoled himself with the thought that one day he would get out again, even if it took many years. Waking, he went on to plough through 'ponderous tomes' on philosophy, religion and history, but found no explanation for the dream. However, realising that it was during the seventeenth century that the science of alchemy reached its height, he later came to see its relevance.

In 1928, after Jung had done a great deal of work on Western alchemy, Richard Wilhelm, who later became his close friend, sent him a manuscript from China. It was Wilhelm's translation of one of the great texts of Eastern alchemy, now called 'The Secret of the Golden Flower'. I think some of Jung's best writing went into his remarkable commentary on it.[5] From that manuscript he realised the extraordinary cross-connection and cross-fertilisation between Eastern and Western alchemy. It certainly lured him further into trying to discover all he could about alchemists and the alchemic process. His dear friend had triggered for him much that was latent and in a kind of *plenum*,[6] waiting for him.

Alchemy and individuation

Jung saw alchemy's quest for the *lapis* as being extraordinarily coincident with the idea he had come to of this life as being a quest for Selfhood. He brought out the whole conception of the progression of the ego, or small everyday self, around the Self, the Self with a large S, the great Self, the Self that has us. The search for the Self is a spiral movement from the periphery, a circumambulation around the centre, bearing in towards it; and this is the work of alchemy. It starts with external materials and by degrees, following the labyrinthine ways of the work, comes to the centre. Certainly Jung held that the divinity and the Self are there in the beginning. The most - or perhaps the least - one can hope for is that that is going to be revealed within the process.

So the more he worked, the more Jung recognised how much within the old texts was what he was already discovering in very many

---

[5] In Wilhelm 1931, 'The Secret of the Golden Flower'. Also in Jung 1967, 'Alchemical Studies', CW 13, Section I.

[6] *Plenum*, a space filled with matter, (OED); a fulness, a wholeness.

individuals. By degrees, he was beginning to call it the 'individuation' process: the movement from the unconscious towards consciousness, from the ego towards the Self. He found themes common both to alchemy and to the experience of clients going through the therapeutic process: the endless work involved; timeless, archaic images, such as the one we have seen of the eagle eating its own wings.[7] Later, when he began to use the terminology of the 'collective unconscious', he realised that these must be shared images, and that the alchemists had been getting in touch with them from at least the first century AD. Here was the whole idea that God and man are not separate but that God is within man, that man is divine, that *God needs man*. And, most particularly, that the gold that is being sought is already there - it is immanent within the process right from the start and has to be rediscovered, 're-membered' back into consciousness. These things were very close to him.

Life is alchemy

Life is the great alchemist: this is exactly what the alchemists believed. For certain people (though not all), life is about being in the flask, and the many burnings of the flask. In his own work on the *mysterium coniunctionis* (the mysterious marriage of the contra-sexual opposites within each person), Jung saw how much the whole process of alchemy is about the marriage and then the transcendence of those opposites. It's the mysterious marriage of the struggling elements within ourselves, the effort to bring about a resolution between all those opposing pairs in our lives: masculine and feminine, inner and outer, heaven and earth, good and evil, spirit and matter. It's the need to bring them into some kind of resolution - and then to transcend them. In therapy, much of the work has to be in helping people to take their projections back, own them as their own, and stop putting inner stuff on to the environment.

So let's dive into this combination of study and experience. The true alchemists recognised that, although they might have started theoretically, what they were working on was ultimately their whole

---

[7] Although the Ripley Scroll was published in the late 1500's or early 1600's, it would already have been drawing on earlier motifs.

life. In a very real sense the alchemist *was* the flask, *was* what is in the flask, *was* the furnace, as well as being the practitioner sitting outside the process. There is a famous statement by a mediæval alchemist: *'Rend the books, lest your heart be rent asunder'*. It's experience, not books, that leads to understanding. This is Jung's continuous theme: life is alchemy.

Adrift

CHAPTER TWO

The Story of
WESTERN ALCHEMY

A secret and dangerous art

Here is a very quick run-down on the history of Western alchemy insofar as we know it. We have seen how Jung in his vast *opus* translated and opened up for us a lot of the ancient texts. They tend, with some few exceptions, to show that the birth of Christ was roughly concurrent with the birth of Western alchemy, or at least with its written recording. However, being an oral tradition, it might well have pre-dated the first known text.

Egypt, Greece, Persia and Arabia

Like so many of these esoteric, internal matters, alchemy is very like an underground stream; it comes up and strikes the surface, goes down under, strikes surface again with the in-breathings and out-breathings of history. From what we know of its beginnings, it emerged in Egypt at around the time of Christ - alchemy and Christ were born at roughly the same time. There is a famous Egyptian papyrus from the first century BC with a story about the goddess Isis [8] and her son Horus; though the first and only known text from this particular time that may be alchemical, it suggests that already in the first century BC the Egyptians were drawing on some previous tradition. It has very clear alchemical motifs, taken up later. That was the first big flourishing.

By the second and third centuries AD there were a number of written texts in Greek. Alchemy had come out of Egypt into Greece, Arabia and Persia. After the third century it went into decline but, like the underground river, it rose again, with many Persian texts flowering in the

---

[8] Isis was the wife of Osiris, who features prominently in Jung's 'Psychology and Alchemy' (Jung 1953, CW 12). She is sometimes confused with Maria Prophetissa, see below P. 16; and see Jung CW 12, para 209 n.

Arabic languages in about the seventh and eighth centuries AD. Then it went under the surface once more.

The Crusades

Around the tenth century came the Crusades and a whole alchemical resurgence. There are Persian, Islamic and Arabic sources from around this time. The true crusading tradition (concerned with the living blood of the living Christ, going out to protect Jerusalem) meant that a number of the crusaders from Europe were able to (and plainly did) get in touch with Far Eastern alchemy from China and Japan, as well as with the Persian and Arabic traditions. We know that the Warriors of the Cross and the Templar tradition had a great deal of alchemic admixture. These crusaders brought back into Europe various texts and books, and whatever they could pick up of the oral tradition. Translation began into many European languages, particularly Latin, and there was a great interaction and cross-fertilisation with the Western approaches. The bringing back of that knowledge into Europe meant that alchemy became pretty widespread, coming to its full flowering in Europe in the seventeenth century, particularly in Italy. This is the period that Jung was writing about.

Obscurity

The whole field is full of misunderstandings and muddles. With so profound, so subtle a subject being picked up here and there and put into so many languages, the number of compilations and translations and mistranslations that were made must have led to even more confusion, obscurity and paradox. In the texts we find contradictions and parallels and the widely variant images and insights of different cultures all being overlaid on the tapestry of alchemy.

Not only that, but this is an extremely personal, individual science and art. Different people - different ways of looking at things. Think of the translating of the Bible. We can imagine how it must have been for those trying, through their own understanding, to translate the highly paradoxical, imaginative substance of alchemy. If it's a precipitation of the inner substance on to the outer, people will naturally see it in different ways and their own language, their own ideograms will be overlain on the common themes that run through.

Also, they themselves deliberately obscured the language, in the belief that a secret that can be told is not a secret. It was highly dangerous to be an alchemist, in many cultures at many times. Many of them were being treated as heretics, as we shall see. So there was naturally a great deal of wilful misleading, a distinct blurring and fudging of issues, to protect and keep hidden the ancient art. Like most secret traditions, it was kept secret also because it was ineffable and could not by definition be expressed. How put words to an ineffable experience? There are certain insights, certain 'Aha's' we may have in our lives that *cannot* be put into words. So many of these big breakthroughs and understandings are like *remembering*. It's as though we always knew it, or heard it somewhere as an echo a long time back, and are now hearing it again. Profound and inner, unique to every individual alchemist, how can it be put into words - most of all, for people who haven't had the same experience?

However, the alchemists quite often confused matters *without* meaning to. What with the widely variant images and insights and all the misleadings - well! The psychologist Kenneth Rexroth [9] invites us to imagine textbooks on pharmacology, gymnastics, chemistry and mining engineering, together with breathing exercises, sex manuals and treatises on transcendental mysticism, all being torn up, mixed together and fused into a completely new 'chemical compound of thought'. Which roughly describes alchemy!

We plunge in and try to bring some clarity, attempting to get a ravel-end in the middle of all this, acknowledging some of the basic principles. It's fascinating that the word 'gibberish' we use so freely - 'Oh, it's all gibberish!' - comes from the name of Al Gebir, one of the leading seventh century Arab alchemists.

Heresy

Alchemy, particularly in the Middle Ages, was called 'the secret and dangerous art' - and secret and dangerous it was. A master of alchemy could, after a period of time, allow some of the secrets to come out, but

[9]   See Rexroth, quoted in Stern 1976, 'C.G. Jung: the Haunted Prophet', P. 194.

he would not pass on his knowledge and wisdom to his apprentice (who would one day become an alchemist himself) unless that apprentice were sworn to secrecy. He would warn, 'Don't speak of it because - literally! - your tongue will be cut out.' Of course in the Middle Ages alchemy was heresy, especially in the Western world. Think of mediæval Europe. The tradition is that man is *fallen*, fallen from grace, fallen into original sin. Through a process of discipline and behaviour, he has to take himself, or herself, back to God through the threshold of Christ, but only through that door - and then only through the priest of Christ.

It was religious heresy to practise alchemy for two particular reasons. Firstly, the alchemists believed not that God was transcendent and had to be worked towards in that way, but that God was already immanent within matter, already in man! They held that, in the *prima materia*, the stuff, the basic material on which they were working, the gold was already in existence. That was an enormous statement: God, the divinity, already within the person! The spiritual, immanent within earth. Not that man needed to be saved, was fallen and struggling to be taken up and translated into heaven by a forgiving God, but that God was already within man. A completely different viewpoint. The alchemists held that the whole *opus* of life and of the work was for the *internal* divinity ultimately to unite with the external divinity. Man and God were one and the same thing.

Secondly, and a short step from that, the alchemists came round to an even worse heresy: not only is man (and woman, of course) divine, but God *needs* man. God is not perfect and complete, God is not transcendent, 'out there'. God is immanent within every human being, within all nature, within every plant and planet, within everything that is created, within the creation which God is in the process of becoming. God is not a static God. 'God needs man as much as man needs God.'

Well, if ever you wanted a heresy, that's it! That really would have put the Pope and the bishops and all the angels out of business! And the poor old alchemists knew it. Part of the work, the *opus*, was to make apparent that divinity which is in man. Put man in the alchemical flask, put him through a number of burnings, and what will emerge is the divinity that is already within him - Boom! To say this became very, very dangerous stuff. This is why so many were burned. It became extremely dangerous to be around an alchemist. 'Heretic, heretic!' was the cry. So they did their work in silence and privacy, in danger if people got wind that an alchemist was in their midst. Because they were saying 'Man is divine', they were tortured, flagellated, skinned and boned, stripped apart, opened up, had their guts taken out and wrapped round their necks, were garrotted with them - to mention but one or two small things that happened to alchemists!

The dangers of alchemy

Alchemy was dangerous not only because of the heresy of it but also because, if you were thought to be creating (or trying to create) actual, profane gold, the dukes and the emperors and the kings were going to be after you as well. If the Church didn't get you, all the rest of them would. Just think - you'd set up somewhere and in no time at all the news would get around that you're making gold. Hearing this, your local kalif or princeling or baron wanting to fight one of his wars would haul you in. He'd ask you - or try to bribe you - for your secrets. It wasn't that your secret formulæ were *seduced* from you - you were being spied on for them. Ultimately, you'd be tortured for them.

So, God willing, a secret and dangerous art. In Greece, Egypt, Turkey, Arabia, Europe, wherever an alchemist's work was going on a sign was put up - carved on walls, scratched on the pavements, put down in the catacombs. It meant 'the work of alchemy is in process - within this place is an alchemist'. It was their secret symbol to each other, put there so that others could be drawn into the oral tradition of alchemy - though masters of alchemy also took the right to say, 'Go away'. Such signs were necessary since the art was not written down till much later. I believe the sign to have included the six-pointed star which, for the alchemist, came out of the interaction between God and the personality. Paradoxically, the art of alchemy is often known as 'squaring the circle'. Everything is held within the circle of God, and the process is intended to bring *spirit* out of the triangle of the body, mind and feelings of man. Thus, to the love, wisdom and penetrating spirit that form the trilogy of God, is added in the devil. So it was brought to the fourfold out of the threefold and a square put around it. Very simple stuff, very difficult to live by, very difficult to work on - and highly heretical!

One woman alchemist, Maria Prophetissa (and it's certain there were female alchemists, though not too many are mentioned in the texts), came up with a profound formula: '*One becomes two, two becomes three, and out of the third comes the One as the fourth.*' [10] 'The one becomes two' - out of the mass emerges the pair of opposites; 'the two becomes three' - out of the two, the tension of the opposites emerges as the third, the transcendent function; [11] 'and out of the third comes the One as the fourth' - out of the transcendent function comes the One - the *lapis* - as the spirit, the pure stone.

As an early alchemist, caught neither as heretic nor as maker of gold, you were liable to be asphyxiated by the noxious airs in your own laboratory. Toxic fumes came out when you experimented, putting a whole load of stuff into a flask. And, since you were experimenting on yourself, it was your own flask, your own experimenting. If you weren't poisoned you might get blown up, or be driven mad. You might go into inflation, hallucination, dementia, sickness, every known physical problem. And obsession, that continuous obsessive burning. Obsessionals of the world, unite! Seeing clients troubled in that way, I wonder how many of them are also working with the alchemical process in their struggle to ritualise the chaos of their lives.

So, alchemy was dangerous and it was secret - ineffable because when experienced it cannot be voiced. But also it was isolated: the non-contact with people year in year out; not being able to talk to others of your ilk; every work being done alone and lonely except for God. And whom can you trust in all this area? Working alone, ultimately you had to rely on others not to pass on what they had discovered to those who were not ready for the experience. And the hours of study, and

---

[10]   See Jung, CW 12, para 209. Maria Prophetissa was very famous. Her dates are unknown, though she was fairly early. To this day her name is linked with putting something into a dish of water and slowly subjecting it to 'a nice cooking heat'.

[11] We work between a pair of intractable opposites to go to a third position, the transcendent function, and out of that transcendent function comes the fourth. See Somers & Gordon-Brown 2002, 'Journey in Depth', Chapter 10, especially P. 175.

endlessly having to do it again, start the work again - all these things: ...danger, isolation, non-contact. Some of us might recognise that we too have been in this process for a long time.

Gold from base metal

In alchemy we're looking at the beginnings of the sciences of metallurgy and chemistry. The art of pottery also re-enacts the alchemic process, as does the work of the blacksmith, the wheelwright and the sword-maker. The alchemists knew a great deal about astrology too. Astrology was a vast subject and its language paralleled that of the alchemists. Where alchemy was seen as an *external* art or science it was primarily about the transformation of metals. The idea was that you could draw gold from other minerals and metals: *you could actually change lead to gold* . This very logical hypothesis grew out of the familiar belief of those times which had, of course, been current for centuries. The understanding was that the energies from the celestial planets struck into the Earth and the metals in the ground were precipitations of those energies. It was a small step from there to the belief that certain astrological configurations would also coincide with the metals which interacted with the planets. The alchemists believed that all the ores and minerals found within the Earth were the children of the primary metals, and that the Earth gave birth to these metals. They thought that the energy and action of the Sun, by precipitation being rayed down on to the Earth, impregnating the Earth, being taken into gestation within her womb, would bring forth gold. That accounted for the mines of gold in the Earth: the Sun's energy had been precipitated and solidified into gold. If they could somehow trap the energy of the Sun they would have gold in their flasks. They also believed that the precipitation of energies from the celestial Moon coming into the womb of the Earth created silver; the precipitation of Saturn on to the Earth produced lead; that of Jupiter produced tin; that of Venus, copper; the precipitation of Mars' energies to Earth produced iron; and those of Mercury resulted in quicksilver.

It doesn't take too much of an active imagination to see that, with this understanding, alchemy could become an experimental process to bring gold into being. The idea was that you could start with metals, or various substances related to each of the deities (including wood, in the Chinese traditions), put them together and they would bring you back to the king of metals. You could create gold by bringing together say lead, copper and quicksilver in every kind of combination and putting them through a burning process. Ultimately, the divine gold was imminent in matter, so if you had all those things held and working together in a flask, you might come up with gold. And - well, good luck to you!

There's a wonderful esoteric tradition of mining; the initiatory rites were very close to what later became the alchemic rites. Miners, particularly in the Eastern countries, were prepared and shriven and cleansed before they went into the dark womb of Earth to bring out these metals in which they felt the deities. And one had to be very, very careful with the furnace and the smelting. If the reader is interested in the early rites of mining, Mircea Eliade has written some superb books.[12]

Sympathetic medicine

The naturopathic, homoeopathic approaches are deeply rooted in the alchemic tradition. Homoeopaths will be familiar with the basic principle or belief that the metals and chemical substances found in the earth are precipitations of the planets. Certain plants and herbs, minerals and metals came to be seen as related to each of the planetary configurations and to the four elements. This led to the emerging of a sympathetic medicine. A whole pharmacology was growing up here. If people lacked particular qualities within themselves, they would be given the minerals and by degrees the plant essences - very often, the metals themselves! God knows how they ever survived - although gold and other metals are used now as remedies and people can deal with them.

Hermes

We're talking about metals here, but also we are talking about the gods. Prancing joyfully through it all is Mercury, sometimes called by his Greek name, Hermes. In the Greek tradition out of Egypt, alchemy is hermetic and Hermes is the messenger of the gods. To honour what was in the flask, the alchemists said that wisdom came via Hermes

---

[12]   Mircea Eliade, eg. 'The Myth of the Eternal Return' 1949.

from God to man, through the underworld and back again, in a continuous process within the 'hermetic chain'. Hermes moves back and forth between heaven and hell, heaven and earth, continuously bringing about the visitation of the gods through the planetary energies, all of which can at some point be focused on and used in the flask. As Mercury, quicksilver, he is present throughout the whole of alchemy, the link between God and man. 'As in life, so in alchemy.' He is the flask and what is in the flask, the seal and the fire under the work. He is the catalyst, the third that comes wherever there's a pair of opposites. He is said to *be* the transformative process. He's there in the beginning in the *prima materia*, trapping us in the flask for the *calcinatio*; he's there as Eros in the *solutio* stage. When the *coagulatio* begins to come together he appears as the winged messenger of the Gods, Mercury, both tempter and friend. And he's there at the end as divine Mercury, the Philosophers' Son, the Divine Child that's born out of the whole process.[13] As Hermes, he is also the guide of souls, both upward and downward, providing a link between heaven, humanity and the underworld. Thus, through all the stages and under his *aegis*, man would eventually be able to communicate with God and God with man.[14]

The Puffers

So, you could actually change lead into gold. Certainly a great number of the old alchemists believed that as a basic fact, until it began to dawn on them that it wasn't the external gold that was being talked about. Some mediaeval alchemists, as in the East at a much earlier stage, were already making very clear distinctions between mundane, profane gold - 'ignoble gold' as they called it - and the true gold, the 'noble gold'. If someone's aspiration were not true, if he wanted this process in order to produce the gold of the market-place, then he would be called a 'puffer'. Puffer - I love that! A lot of wind is used to blow the bellows, creating and claiming false gold. Aspiring to an ignoble end, your puffer would work on the furnace to create a substance inferior in the view of the true alchemists. He wanted mortal longevity. An awful lot of them ended by being puffed up and burned

---

[13] This is the 'golden child', archetype of the Divine Child, whose master workman is Mercurius. See Jung, CW 12, para 215.

[14] For the many roles played by Mercury, see Jung, CW 12, para 84.

on the fire themselves.

It's so close, isn't it, to what happens to us in therapy, as well as to our clients? the puffers - inflation - *hubris:* 'I have the elixir, I have the gold!' We take straight off and leave the ground, rushing around saving the world, huffing and puffing till we explode.

That is the pattern. I've given a resumé of the story; you can see that we're dealing with an obscure, esoteric, recondite way of working. It's an inner process running through all those languages, with each alchemist using and seeing things in terms of their own imagery, just as happens in dreams and workshops in the modern psyche.

CHAPTER THREE

THE OPUS

The decision to begin must be carried out
with a whole heart and the result not sought for.
The result will come of itself

Whether from the scientific angle, seeing the whole system as one of research, openness and patient application, or with mystical vision, at a certain point in the work those alchemists with a scientific mind found they had to bring in their hearts and go into their research with openness and patient application. Those who naturally followed their mystical hearts were also required and honoured in this. The two are now polarised and set apart - left-brain *or* right-brain, head or heart; but then, in the whole work, both the scientific mind and the religious mind, the scientific heart and the mystical heart were required. Our highest scientists still work on that basis: the two coming together, using the heart as vessel.

The early alchemists

For a very well-done brief history of the emergence of alchemy I again recommend 'Alchemy' by Marie Louise von Franz;[15] and also her lovely 'Alchemical Active Imagination'[16] where there's a wonderful, exciting description in her inimitable style of the sheerly[17] practical matters involved in being one of those early alchemists, and the difficulties of just such an ordinary chap starting up. I think you'll love it. She tells how an alchemist might have been someone who had asked himself from early boyhood, as Jung had, 'What *is* a stone? Does it have a soul?' He might have tried to get information on chemistry, but in earlier centuries, outside Rome and certain other cities where there

---

15 See von Franz 1959, particularly Lecture Two, P. 39.

16 See von Franz 1969, 'Alchemical Active Imagination', Lecture One, Pp. 1-20.

17 'Sheerly' (sic): word I believe is coined here by Barbara Somers. (Ed.)

were bookshops and libraries, it was very difficult to get hold of books. Indeed, it would often have been a ruinous adventure to find and buy them. Then, the language! *Mix the divine, 3 pounds of it, with the arsenic, 2 pounds of it; and look out that the Astrological Constellation is right. Then, if you pray to God and have purified your house you may be patient, for the great union will occur.* This is just one example.

Excavations at Ostia, continues von Franz, show us the kind of holes in the towns and cities in which an alchemist might have lived and worked. The neighbours, understandably, wouldn't have liked his having a furnace and setting the place on fire, so he would have had to acquire a clearing in the forest outside and build his furnace there. Then spies would arrive. He would hope that his apprentices would honour their oaths not to tell about what he was doing. Rumours would be rife: 'He is an evil Magician, he's conjuring demons. Set the police on him, or he'll destroy the place!' If he still had any money left, he would have had to try to corrupt the local ruler or priest to get them to leave him alone for his experiments.

He would also have needed to get the *prima materia*. Where would he acquire the necessary gold, or whatever, to start the process off? To build the flask would require a potter to make a vessel that could withstand great heat. Such vessels were simple thermoses and they had to be heated day and night with wood or charcoal. Bellows were necessary to get a high enough temperature, so he would have had to find 'some simpleton' who could not only learn how to blow air into the fire but could stay awake night and day to do it; and 'if the chap went off for a beer' his experiment was ruined and he must start again. And this is no fantasy, comments von Franz; it's in the alchemical books. 'See that your fire never goes out ... otherwise you can start again.' The fact that so many of them stuck with it is, I think, lovely.

The alchemist as the *opus*

True alchemists wanted passionately to discover the mystery of the nature and transmutation of metals. In the process they began to realise that the work of alchemy was something 'other': the alchemist was also distilled. The *opus* from a very early stage was seen to be a chemistry of the psyche, an externalisation of the complex distillations within the alchemists themselves. The message of the Bhagavad Gita, which I also see as an alchemic tradition and treatise (though it isn't always read as that), is not to look for the fruits but only to work from the total man.

Difficult, dangerous and secret art as it was, a great number of spirits continued the process. Inevitably, though he might fall away or end up being crucified upside down, the true alchemist realised it was he that must change, must become that which is sought, become the crucible. The alchemic statement was *Ars totum requirat hominem* - 'the Art requires the whole man'. It was an internal process. The sense is that inevitably he was changed. The *alchemist* became the crucible, the *alembic*; it was he who was put into the flask and became the process and ultimately it was he who became the inner gold, or whatever the thing sought came to be called.

Names for the goal

For the true alchemists, work was to do with the spiritual gold, the noble, true gold. It was *not* about ordinary, mundane gold. That which at the end came out of the flask was called by multiple names, depending on their culture, their background, their own vision of the goal. They were looking not just for gold, but for eternal life. It was called the *Lapis* or Stone; the Golden Pill; the Universal Panacea or Panacea for All Ills (aren't we still looking for that?); the Golden Door; the Golden Ball. See how these things come up in story, myth, legend, folklore, fairy tale. It has been known as the Diamond Body, the Pearl of Great Price, the Holy of Holies; it is the Holy Grail, the Holy Sepulchre, the Heavenly Heart, the New Jerusalem, Paradise Regained - terms never defined, each from its own culture describing the end that was sought. In the Eastern tradition, as we shall see, it has been called the Elixir of Life, the Elixir of Immortality, the Purple Hall in the City of Jade. All these are names for the grey stone, or ordinary gold - ordinary in the sense that it was extraordinary - the *lapis* of the alchemist. The true alchemists recognised that the gold could not be given away, it could not be bought; the end of the process was an emergence from the flask with a totally new understanding. Something would come out which would raise him from mortality into immortality, from linear time into eternity. It would give the transmutation of body into spirit and, over and above everything, the release of the God within matter.

Beginning the *opus*

So what did the alchemists actually do? Let's have a look at the *opus* itself and what was required to set it up. It was quite a complex business one way or the other. Both scientifically and inwardly it required the laboratory or oratory; the container, flask or *alembic*; the furnace or *athanor*; the fire; the *soror*, the mystical sister or soulmate; and the *prima materia* or *massa confusa* with which to begin. It required the *temenos*, the sacred precinct set up around the work.

'The decision to begin must be carried out with a whole heart and the result not sought for. The result will come of itself.'

Here is an absolutely alchemical statement from Lao Tsu, speaking out of the Chinese tradition on the process of the Tao (the Tao Te Ching is of course an alchemical treatise). In the main mode in which the alchemists worked, everything was under the will of God. Many of them were also astrologers, as we have seen. They agreed that the best time to start the alchemical process was in the spring. The *opus* was begun usually when the Sun was in Aries - the most favourable sign - or in Taurus or Gemini, but no later than that. If they couldn't begin by then, they would wait until the following year. Preferred phases of the moon varied; at one time they nearly all began at the new moon, but later took to waiting for the full moon.

Laboratory as oratory

Most of the true alchemists worked in places where labour and prayer went together: *laborare et orare*. The scientific laboratory would also be an oratory - a place of prayer *and* science. As a true alchemist, you would recognise more and more that yours was a priestly art, and it needed to be a combination - of heavenly prayer with damned hard work. You worked from head *and* heart. What's different, I ask myself, in therapy and counselling?

The flask

First you needed a hermetically-sealed container, the *vas*, also known as the *alembic* or flask. Everything had to be mixed in with everything else in this flask or crucible. It took various shapes, usually an egg or a sphere, sometimes the body of a bird with a beak, which is why it was often called the 'pelican'. It was made of clay, or later of glass. The glass ones were created by an old method, first blown and then sealed - 'hermetically'. The hermetic seal isn't the sealing *of* Hermes, it's the sealing *by* Hermes. The name means that Hermes is present, aware, part of the process of sealing you in. Look upon alchemy as an inner process and the human body is the flask. The early images show it as womb-shaped; you go into a lower womb but, through the transformation of the four stages, you pass from the lower to the higher. Hermes won't remove the seal until you are in the higher womb, part of the whole creative process, and purified enough to be led into the presence of God.

The furnace

Then you had to have an *athanor*, which was the word for the furnace. To the true alchemist that would surely be the furnace of aspiration and fervour, continuously giving the firing that would cool only to allow the process to come to a gentle, lenient heat - and even then the aspiration went on. 'Never let your fire go out' - the fire of the illumined will and the imagination. Perhaps where the will-power gave out only the imagination could carry it forward.

The fire

And the fire itself, for the various heats of the many firings? Aspiration, prayer, patience, contemplation…and imagination. How could you keep going without imagination? The various spiritual disciplines of all peoples bring this fire about: the yoga and meditation systems; prayer; the art of staying with the process; giving an increasing commitment to it; being tempered within it.

Soror mystica

Many of the illustrations show a woman working with the male alchemist. He needed the accompanying feminine principle, his soulmate, his *soror mystica*, and the spiritual sister is very familiar in both the Western and the Eastern traditions. She might have been an actual woman; she might have been his own soul. The two of them would work together in research and openness and patient application, saying always, *'Deo volente, Deo concedente'*, God willing, God conceding. Everything they did was acceptance, 'God agreeing'. They realised that God is in the work. And love. As the great alchemist Paracelsus (fairly modern by contrast with some of these earlier ones) said, 'Love is the agent'. The agent that finally brings about the gold in the flask is love.

Temenos

Around the work would be set up the *temenos*, the sacred area or precinct within the laboratory. This is the protected and protective environment that is created between two people around the work of therapy, too. A lot of it was done in order to help the world, as well as the individual.

Prima materia

The first thing to go into the flask was the *prima materia*, the first material out of which it was hoped the gold would be distilled. It was sometimes called the *massa confusa*, the confused mass, or as someone said, 'the confused mess' of one's life - chaos. The books really get going here as to what it was. Nobody really knew; it depended what sort of alchemical text and what sort of translation you got hold of. The belief was that from the outset it contained gold, and the account of it seems to go on for ever. Usually the old alchemists put some dark, ignored, reviled substance in the flask. Among many descriptions, it is the magically fecund earth or soil that Adam took with him from Paradise, also called *antimony* and described as black blacker than black, *nigrum nigrious nigro*. Jung says that it is the black earth in which the *lapis* or the gold is sown like a grain of corn.[18]

---

18   See Jung, CW 12, para 433. His footnote refers to Maier, *Symbola aureae mensae*, Pp. 379 f.

When Paracelsus started his major teaching at the university, he put a stinking pot of human excrement hot on the table and said, 'This is what the work is about, this is all life, this is God.' And they got him off the platform. It's a very big issue, I think, cranking open our beliefs that there is any place where God is not. Perhaps it depends how you've been pottie-trained! You may remember the dream-like thought Jung had as a boy, where the big turd came down on the cathedral roof?[19] This was Jung's thought, not God's! Jung was very young when it came to him and, don't forget, his father was a pastor. I suspect that he was looking at what for him was not the living spirit of the Church but the empty doctrine, and that the cathedral of Basel stood for that doctrine. Jung was trying to get his father to give him meaning and purpose out of that doctrine, but also the young alchemist, Jung, was standing there as any alchemist would, asking, 'What is the difference between the heavenly throne of God and a turd?'

A disciple said to the Buddha, 'What is enlightenment ?' And Buddha picked a rose, a single flower, and held it up. A rather more comely and acceptable thing - but he could just as easily have picked up a piece of dung, or the turd on the cathedral. If we believe we understand the nature of the mystery of God and start sticking labels on it, we have no doubt killed the living spirit. I can't recall this being in any of the alchemical texts I've read, but I think implicit in it is, 'Don't label, don't narrow'. Yes, we're put into a flask, but it's a flask that widens us. We are rendered down till we don't know what we are, taken down to the essence of bone, getting rid of all sorts of rigidities and limitations on God. It's crank, crank - open, open. The trouble was that when people came out and said such things, they were put on the rack and - 'crank, crank' - wrenched apart for their mystery. It was also because they dared say *something*. In those times only the Pope was allowed to say things like that.

We read how all sorts of things went into the *alembic*: mud, excrement, dragons' teeth, dragons' milk, frogs' legs, bats' wings; a toad, a bear, a wolf, a green dragon; Saturn; Mercurius, crude original man…put that lot together! Chaos was put into the flask, and all to be transmuted into pure spirit. Some said, 'Add the urine of a mare'; others said, 'No, of

[19] Jung 1961, 'Memories, Dreams, Reflections', Pp. 52-56.

a virgin boy' - or virgin girl - you name it. And every alchemist had to find out for himself. Occasionally he would put ordinary everyday gold in the flask, hoping that, by adding a lot of minerals and other things, the eternal gold would come out. You see how very easily alchemy got muddled with witchcraft and wizardry, particularly in the Middle Ages, the Inquisition time when the religious came out hunting. But the idea was that the primal Mercurius - the original, crude man - was to be translated into pure spirit; a finer, a spiritual gold.

So, the *massa confusa*; and so too for us. Into the flask go our earth, air, fire and water and everything they represent - our minds, our bodies, our feelings, our intuition, our heat and cold, our dry and moist - all go into the flask.[20] And through the many firings they are all whizzed round and round and round, mixed together to become a confusion of elements until we don't know where or what we are; until at last, by degrees, they are again polarised and married together. And finally there arises out of it something which is a combination of these and greater than all of them, that will take us through to the Self at the centre of the Individuation process. For the alchemist would bring us back to the divinity that was in us, the divinity which manifests through all creation, through all of these modes, these multiple forms. The idea was that one could bring them together through the act of creation, through the powers of imagination and love and will, to recreate the divinity within us. Pairs of opposites are put in and muddled together and confused again, until they come up not as polarised opposites, but as a square, the square of a new creation, of a new world, a new understanding that will eventually link the underworld, the middleworld and heaven. Divinity and humanity will be made into one and the same thing.

It was quite a complex business one way or another.

---

[20] The earlier mediaeval elements - the dry, the moist, the warm and the cold (as well as air, fire, earth and water) - were emphasised in both Eastern and Western alchemy. Many of the heating and cooling processes had to do with the pairs; the dry and the moist must move together, and so must the warm and the cold. The reconciliation of opposites became absolutely major in the work.

Therapy as alchemy

As in alchemy, so in analysis or therapy or counselling. There are some outstanding parallels: the patience, the constant repetitions, the regressions and the progressions; all are here, endlessly. The many burnings and cleansings, the meltings and hardenings and dissolvings of alchemy are very close to the processes of therapy. *Solve et coagula* (dissolve and coagulate) is one of the great alchemic commands; and the therapeutic process is also to dissolve and then to regather. It's hard work. 'Seventy times seven' for each process, said the alchemists - 'seven hundred times seventy - seven thousand times seven hundred'!

Then there's the circumambulation around a theme, the continuous moving in, the deepening that takes a person off the wheel of external experience and inward by a circular or a spiral movement (an upward or a downward spiral or both) towards the hub of meaning and purpose in their lives. It's to be hoped that the therapist will sense, as did the alchemist, that the divinity of the Self is there from the beginning within the personality and that the work is to help render out the gold already immanent within the individual. It's highly alchemical.

Alchemy is again very close to the therapeutic process in that there are the two people working together. We've seen how the alchemist nearly always had a partner or assistant, his so-called *soror mystica*, his spiritual sister, his soul-mate. The alchemist and his feminine soul were working together on the process. You needed your soul, you needed your heart in this work. I don't think it would be stretching it too far to say she could nowadays be seen as the *anima*. In therapy too at some point we work alongside our *animus*, our *anima*, in that conjunction of two people working together on a process.

The *alembic* that the alchemist set up, the hermetically-sealed flask of alchemy, is also paralleled where two people are working within the flask of therapy, which gives containment of the analytic process. Traditional, classical Jungians may say, 'When you come into analysis, don't use other disciplines, other therapies - you may leak the flask.' I think this can be taken quite a long way too far, but one sees the point: the analysis is a contained thing. 'Don't talk about it to people outside,' they say. And that does create the hermetic seal, as in alchemy. The *alembic* contains the work; too much cross-contamination between the external and the internal worlds might make it leak. This can work both ways: 'leaking the flask' can too easily bring in an added extra from outside; or something can leak away into the environment.

The flask is in the *temenos*, the sacred space or precinct that is set up between the two people around the work. It is a protective environment: the client can come to the therapist and the therapist honours confidentiality and honours the process, and is to a very great degree always there. The two are working together in this place to bring about something which is greater than either of them.

In the *temenos* there's the furnace or *athanor*, and the fire that burns. The many firings are very like the continuous burning processes of therapy and counselling - the coolings and the heatings, coolings and heatings, over and over and over. In the therapeutic process we have to go *back*, with the client and with ourselves, again and again over the same thing. We just get the fire to cook us nicely, and then, dammit, we're being barbecued and grilled and all the rest of it! It's the fire that burns again. And it isn't just the client, as we well know, when that happens. We've seen how the alchemists needed the fire of aspiration and prayer and will, of patience, meditation, contemplation, imagination, the commitment of staying with the process. How true this is of the therapeutic process too: the idea that we are tempered within it, that we enter the flask, we *become* the alchemic work, the *opus*. We become what is in the flask.

We've also seen how the eight elements were seen as essential in the alchemical process. They are very important in Jung's work too, and in the modern typology of the thinking, feeling, intuiting and sensation functions. At times they will be confused or thrust into one another, but eventually we'll begin to bring them together into a harmony, a marriage, till they create the One and are no longer opposites. Finally, we hope that we'll come out able to manifest the essence of them, neither polarising them in ourselves nor projecting them on to other people.

Stages of the work

The alchemists worked in stages. Books on the process nearly always give only three, but I'm going back to the much earlier tradition, linked with Eastern alchemy, of its being a *four*-stage process. We will look, turn by turn, at *calcinatio, solutio, coagulatio* and *sublimatio*, going into deep detail on each of them. They seem to me to come in that order, but we have to go many times through each (remember the seventy times seven). In a sense there is no order, and I can't emphasise too much that they come in a different order for different people. Each is drawn in the round within the flask in these illustrations, a classic and comely shape given simply to extrapolate out a rhythm and a pattern. Their implications are very relevant to the whole of our experience and our therapeutic practices.

Plate 2. The Four Stages within the Alembic - overleaf

The alchemical drawings that follow illustrate these stages:

Plate 2a. Calcinatio - The Darkening

First we're cooked and divided, separated out. This is the *nigredo*, also known as the *calcinatio*, the scientific, chemical name for the process of calcining. The alchemical image, again, is 'black blacker than black',[21] and the element is fire.

---

[21] The alchemists call their *nigredo* melancholia, night, an affliction of the soul, confusion, etc. Also, 'the black raven', see Jung 1963, "*Mysterium Coniunctionis*", CW 14, para 37.

Plate 2b. Solutio - The Washing

Next we're plunged into a bath for forcible washing in the *solutio,* or *albedo*, the 'whitening' process. This is the dissolving of a thing into infinite solution; the element is water.

Plate 2c. Coagulatio - The Fixing

At last a new Sun arises which renders the material fixed and adamant. It is the bringing together, the coagulating process, also named *citrinitas*, the yellow-white stage. I've taken the illustration *'Fixatio'* (a very old term) for the *coagulatio*. Its colour is more yellow than gold - a yellow tending to gold. Its element is earth.

Plate 2d. Sublimatio - The Consummation

Finally, an eternal, loving bondage with the larger Self takes place, the *sublimatio* or raising process. This stage was also called the *rubedo*, the 'reddening', a red not so much of blood as of gold. The element here is air.

Those four are the main key stages of the opus, giving the four colours *nigredo, albedo, citrinitas* and *rubedo*. So the movement of the stages is from black to white to yellow - and to gold. A lot of the traditions from, say, the seventeenth century in Europe, left out altogether the yellow stage and spoke only of the black, the white and the red. But in colour-illustrations over and over you'll see black - white - *yellow* gold - red gold. The secret sign left outside the doors when the work of alchemy was going on was in those colours and you'll often see the harlequin quartered in them when alchemy is at work. The red-gold, the final process, is the colour of the eternal Sun and also of the blood of life.

Cauda pavonis

Other Latin terms are mentioned. One is the *cauda pavonis*, the peacock's tail shot through with all the colours of the rainbow, which begins to come out after the black and again after the white stages. It's a starry, flickery flash of colour referred to by a great number of alchemists. Its place varies according to the text. It may follow the black stage, which breaks up into this rainbow of colour before coming into the whiteness of the second stage. Sometimes, on the other hand, there's said to be a peacock's tail of colour later, where the white begins to move to the yellow-white as the Sun returns. [22]

Stages in therapy

Sitting in therapy with the endless rounds of the alchemic process can be most important. One person dreamt she was at a party. A woman wanted to get her attention and she felt uncomfortable because she was with the men. Later, she was faced with this woman who was wearing a white dress with red and black in it. The dreamer hit out at her, and she fell to the floor. As she did so, other people jumped out of a cupboard and she woke up terrified because they were in such a rage with her. The dreamer had had a great deal of violence from her mother, and a father who was also extremely violent and angry, yet very weak. In imaging, she asked the dream woman who she was. 'I am your mother and your father,' came the reply.

---

[22] See below, *cauda pavonis* P. 101 and note.

The dream woman spoke very positively and this seemed a crucial dream. It was important to watch that the dreamer didn't kill either aspect within herself. Some people have dreams like that years and years before the process comes through. It gives the therapist confidence that they are within the alchemic flask. We don't have to say so (I rarely talk in terms of alchemy to people for whom it is an unknown language) but the knowledge we bear in our own hearts can enormously pervade the process. With this person it did just that, and what had been stuck began to flow.

In therapy, we don't totally complete one stage and then move into the next. Our modern Western minds expect due order, one thing leading to another; but, as our own alchemists, we have to be prepared for one *not* to lead to the next. Rather they overlap, one filtering across another with a wave movement running through. Somebody can already be having experience of the *sublimatio* and the end stages while still dabbling around in the deep waters of the *solutio*. So although I treat each stage as though it were clear-cut, yet there is a continuous interplay throughout a person's life.

Figure 1 - Mercurius within the Pelican - overleaf

The illustration shows the flask as a bird, with Hermes in the centre and the four stages circling round him. As we saw above and will see again with the *sublimatio*, the pelican pecks its own breast; sometimes seen as a phoenix, it is letting its blood flow to nourish the world. In therapy, we may tend to major in one of the stages, going through minor forms of it a number of times and not much resonating to the others. A whole life may be lived along that particular alchemical line, which will ring bells right deep down inside us because it is absolutely our line.

But more usually we go many times through these overlapping stages. There are many burnings and washings and coagulations before the true *sublimatio*. Then the whole area comes together in the *coniunctio*, the bringing together at the end; the mysterious marriage, the reconciliation and then the transcendence of those opposites which have been separated out, and the re-joining to become one. We also

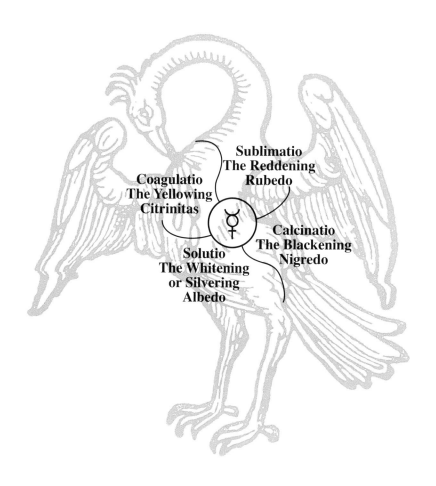

Figure 1 - Mercurius within the Pelican

have minor *sublimatios* at those moments of insight and peak experience that come in the few days or weeks or months that we walk alongside the Self; and then we lose it again. It is a continuously repetitive process.

Vertigo

I studied this subject for many, many years and always strongly resisted talking about it. Then I had a dream: a lion that I recognised as the alchemic lion came into my life and said, 'And now the work will proceed.' And I thought, 'Oh God, now I've got to do it!' I realised I'd been resisting because I had a strange, swoony feeling every single time I began to address the work. Even though I loved alchemy more than almost any other subject, I still had this tremendous resistance. However, the excitement and the loveliness of the subject would get to me again and I'd be able to deal with it.

I'm aware that some readers may be experiencing this resistance as well. It's very odd. I have asked groups, 'Do you feel melancholic now - do any of you have that peculiar, queasy, "Oh-my-God"-ness, while we're on this subject?' And, yes, they do. The stomach is where I register it. A lot of people feel that awful quease - that vertigo and sickness. Alchemy is one of the most unconscious of processes. It is very powerful, and it is beautiful - and the ego dislikes it! Once at a workshop somebody erupted. She stood up: 'Barbara, I've trusted you all this time, and now you've let me down! This stuff might as well be all about witches' cats and frogs' feet, and I didn't think it would be and I'm leaving!' And she went! Quite a lot of clients, too, feel this way: 'Oh, I'd never go into therapy!' They back off - the ego backs off. After all, I suppose it's taken many, many aeons for the personality to be able to abstract itself out of the unconscious, and not everyone is prepared to go back into it again.

Nigredo

CHAPTER FOUR

CALCINATIO

Ordeal by fire is necessary for the proving of a substance
Love is the agent

Fire of Fire

The stage I want to introduce now is the *nigredo*, the blackening, the *calcinatio*. This name comes from the chemical process of the burning of energy, the intense heating of a solid to drive off water and volatile constituents. What remains after that is dry powder and ash. The word *calcinatio* may remind us of the calcium in our bones, of being stripped down to the bare bones, all that is not totally essential being burnt away until we're left with the most indestructible substance - more or less. That might not be true in the first *calcinatio*, but by repeated cookings we will be rendered down to our essence. Once the *prima materia* has gone in, the flask is hermetically-sealed, as we have seen. The process puts the fire below the flask. This is the test by fire. They are all by fire, but this is the 'fire of fire'.

Since fire is its element, the original tradition said that the god overseeing this stage was Vulcan, the ancient Italian fire god.[23] More recently the residing, presiding gods, the deities of it, were held to be Pluto - it's extremely Plutonic, as we shall see - and Saturn. 'Poison' and 'venom' were two of the alchemists' words for the *calcinatio* - the poison and venom of the ego-personality's suddenly having its desire-life shoved into a flask and suffocated. Frustration of ego-will is very toxic. Paracelsus said that ordeal by fire is necessary for the proving of a substance. All that is unpurified is destroyed and removed, and that which is volatile and fugitive is separated from that which is fixed and constant. [24]

---

[23]   Vulcan was linked with the Greek smith-god Hephaistos.

[24]   See A.E. Waite, Ed. 1989, 'Lives of the Alchemystical Philosophers'.

Alchemist as cook

At this *nigredo* stage the alchemist is a cook, and don't we know it! Roasted, barbecued, grilled, poached - the lot! The alchemical images are of death and rebirth: the dead bird, the dead dragon, the dead king, old fire dead in order that a new fire shall come, everything rendered down. As Yahweh said to his chosen people in the book of Isaiah, *'I will turn my hand against you, I will smelt away your dross in the furnace, I will remove all your base metal from you.'* [25]

People dream alchemically all the time. One man had many dreams where things were burning. He said, 'I feel as though I am the vegetables in the cooking pot and the heat is being turned up and up, and I'm trapped and I can't get out.' Mostly we're only half-baked. Now the juices are really brought out of us. We go round and round in the baking process but it's not a dead round, it's a spiral. 'Oh no, not that again!' Enormous help lies in recognising that this *calcinatio* is part of a process, and only one of four stages at that. Then it begins to take on a different meaning, even when we are in the heart of it.

Plate 3. The Green Lion swallowing the Sun - opposite

One of the loveliest characters in it is the Green Lion, *leo viridis*, lion of the unconscious. In the Egyptian tradition from which alchemy derives he is Ruti, the great implacable lion-god of Egypt who takes all human beings into death.[26] He usually has a head turned in each direction, one back and one forward; the present is going into the body of the past and of the future. Here he is in Plate 3, green and black, gold and red, swallowing down the Sun of the ego and causing blood to flow. This is a typical alchemic illustration. At the start of the process the ego is going into the flask, into chaos, into confusion. Green is the colour of transformation, the colour of earth in both Eastern and Western traditions. This is about ingestion and disgorging, the whole process of dismemberment and being re-membered. We see the blood flowing out from the Sun; the blood of the heart has to pour from the

---

[25] See Isaiah 1, 25.

[26] In Phoenician mythology, the son of the Sun-god Ra was the god Ruti, that is to say, 'He who resembles a Lion'. Graves 1959, P. 74.

Plate 3. The Green Lion swallowing the Sun

ego. In dreams, never be fearful of blood flowing; where blood is, there is life.

One way to see the lion, king of the instinctual world, is that he is the flask or *vas*, and the bright Sun of our own ego-darkness is being devoured by him. The light we as personalities have lived by, the sun of our nature, is becoming dimmed, being taken down into the darkness, the dark sun, *sol niger*, black blacker than black.

Yet again, we could see it as if the ego were the lion king in us, the ruling principle, and it is being put out. It is the dimming of everything that we have believed in and stood by. Not many people would opt to do that. Some do - some initiates of the spirit. But usually we're plunged into this by accident; tripping over by mistake, we find ourselves in the flask. The picture is about the beginning of the separation process that forces us to leave home. It can feel like the loss of absolutely everything, but it's an essential stage in individuation and it's only afterwards that we recognise how important it was.

The Green Lion is also linked with the Green Man, the wild man, 'natural nature'. He'd be seen here as the 'wild ravening beast' of our lower nature, all that in modern jargon would be called the shadow, the inferior, instinctual stuff. Some people find it very difficult to contemplate incorporating their own shadow and shit and sexuality and evil into God. The possibility of *all* being God gives them a sense of extreme discomfort, even horror. I understand that feeling of vertigo. Alchemists were tortured and put to the fire for saying that there are both light and dark in us. But we are talking about incorporation. Candles cast shadows. Light and shadow belong together. It's not so much about negative and positive; the ego-will that is trying to cleanse itself, purify itself, redeem itself at its own level revolts against the negative. However, most philosophies, most religions, most disciplines including alchemy have incorporated light and shadow as one and the same thing: where there is light there will be dark, where there is dark there will be light. We need dark to see light; we wouldn't see a greater light if there were nothing but light.

Paradox of alchemy

There is a tremendous paradox in the old images of alchemy: one image can be both a beginning and an end at the same time. This very same outstanding picture is used again at the end of the process but the other way round.[27] There again is *leo viridis*. At the beginning he swallows the Sun; at the end, as flask, he regurgitates the new Sun, the great, golden, eternal Sun. Then he has become the celestial lion, often with stars on him, the immortal God regurgitating the eternal son, the Philosophers' Son, which is what has come out of the personality.

The lion is the *vas* at the beginning of the process and the lion is the *vas* at the end of the process. These alchemical pictures are sometimes described as 'impregnable', and our modern brains can find this sort of pun and paradox mind-boggling.[28] I don't think anybody in the Middle Ages would have been particularly baffled. Alchemy is a language of paradox. Learning it, the old alchemists would look at a picture like this and read it all. They knew of the paradox of nature, and of the right-brain dream function. Certainly they had to use pictures as part of their secret language, but they'd have chosen pictures anyway, because there simply are not words for so much of this.

In the flask

What goes into the flask? The *prima materia* is where we start. Psychologically speaking, we've seen how this first material is our life's experience, all that we have been and are to this date, which is put into a flask and hermetically-sealed - Hermes, sealed by heat, by the god. And the prime stuff, all that we thought we were, is going to be suffocated to death in the sealed flask. The *putrefactio* process will occur later. Bitter and harsh, to pass through this valley of the shadow, as Jung comments. We've seen how it's here that the brightness of the ego is darkened and becomes *sol niger*. Everything that has ever meant anything to us is put into the flask and pulled apart; all we have served, or that we felt served us, rendered meaningless. This is where a lot of our assumptions about the world go to cock and are taken down into the

27 See Plate 11f, P. 113 below.
28 Another paradox is brought out in Jung, CW 12, 'Psychology and Alchemy', para 338, where *filius philosophorum* is translated as 'the miraculous *stone*'.

darkness. Things that our ego had thought it was in control of are pulled apart so that it will give up that control. Not willingly - oh no, none of us does that! It's prior to the advent of another meaning, but that which we thought was our father and our mother ceases to be. If we have never left home, are still dependent on our parents or their environment, then the separation process is going to begin at some point, and it usually starts here. We are forced to let go of the supports. Those to whom we've turned as parents and substitute parents, as well as the authority we've taken upon ourselves when we don't have the authenticity to use it, all have to be stripped away.

The alchemical term is *separatio*, the separating out of the pairs of opposites - light and dark, heat and cold, gain and loss, love and hate - in order to bring them together in a new way. Our good and our ill, our inner and our outer, our head and our heart, our masculine and our feminine - all in conflict! The only way we can handle it is by saying, 'It's obvious; either it's this, or else it's that!' Yet a thing is neither this nor that, and the *nigredo* brings the two together till they merge into a grey ash. So there takes place a loosening of old, narrow, cramped attitudes, helping us out of the tight confines of our nature. Very few people who are truly coming into the round can avoid this stage. When it is the true process we are there by right, though it's a privilege most of us would certainly wish to be without. I don't think any alchemist ever promised that it was comfortable, but we hope, when baked, to be transmuted and see things in a different way. It's part of the process that will take us eventually from dependency to responsibility, from yoked bondage to the greatest kind of freedom, but it can feel most un-funny while it's going on. It will indeed test whether we are true to ourselves. Will the gold that eventually comes out ring true, or will it be somebody else's gold? If it's somebody else's then we haven't paid the price to be in the flask.

If all this is anything more than words on a page, we can't be unchanged by it. That's why we need to treat it with care and with caution. We are dealing with archetypal material here. If it is the actual process, this is our own ego-personality going down into the flask; I give the reader warning! However, I assure you that it gets better as it goes along.

Plate 4. Putrefactio, Purgatio - overleaf

The great alchemist, the cook, could equally well be seen here as the dustbin man taking away the refuse in rubbish-bags. This is the *putrefactio*. Until this happens, nothing has happened. It's the decay, the putrefaction of all that has been: dark material, dark substance. Here's all our blood and guts, and heart and will and imagination and hope - everything. It is the burning-off of dross, of anything no longer relevant. There's no fat left after this. Here, certainly, one is down to the bare bones - yes, they're going to be put together again, re-articulated in some new way, but first are death and loss, *purgatio*, hell-fire and suffocation, the agony in the flask, darkening, dying, immolation - a different kind of confusion.

The unity of chaos

In the death and putrefaction of that which is put into the flask, we are moving away from the oneness that we believed we were, away from the unity of chaos. That's a strange, a very alchemic phrase: 'the unity of chaos'. Chaos is diffuse and - well - chaotic. A lot of us say we don't want chaos, we're frightened of it; what we want is order. On the other hand the familiar chaos we know does have a certain unity to it. Within that unity of chaos, the original womb of life, is there not a certain comfort by contrast with the chaos that we recognise when we get into the flask? As when the client says, 'I was all right until I paid you to get me into this mess!' When the heat goes on, up comes the resistance: 'I wish I hadn't started this!' The ego thinks it's free. It demands free will, but actually has no conception of it. The freedom we thought we had is not the freedom we come to when we are brought out of the flask. This alchemy will bring us to a different understanding, but it is extraordinary how later, when true freedom does begin to be born in us, we don't want it, grabbing tightly to the nipple of the known and sucking furiously. Kafka surely knew something about this alchemical process. In his short story, 'The Great Wall of China', [29]

---

[29] Kafka 1915, in 'Metamorphosis and Other Stories'.

Plate 4a. Putrefactio

...He feels imprisoned on this earth, he feels constricted; the melancholy, the impotence, the sicknesses, the feverish fancies of the captive, afflict him. No comfort can comfort him, since it is merely comfort, gentle,

Plate 4b. Purgatio

head-splitting comfort, glossing the brutal fact of the imprisonment. But if he is asked what he actually wants he cannot reply, for that is one of his strongest proofs - he has no conception of freedom.

Nigredo in myth

'Inexorable, punitive, harsh' are words used by the alchemists for the *nigredo* process. People say: 'When I was in *that place*, I couldn't hear the voices coming to me.' Here are Saturn and Pluto, intent upon bringing this that is in the flask to the firing. Mythically, we're in the realm of Hades, hell; Persephone, through experience raped of her innocence and taken into the underworld; Hecate, the dark side of the Moon. Here are Inanna and Ereshkigal.[30] We're talking about dismemberment, about an instinctual tearing apart and cannibalisation. It's the necessary separation that has to come about before we can move towards any later and further stages of re-membering, re-gathering. Osiris, Wotan, Attis in myth are symbolic of dismemberment - the Christ, dismembered. Christ went down to hell, too.

So this is the *putrefactio* process, purging off any flesh or fat, rendering everything down to its essentials. And, my God, it does reduce us to essentials! Ultimately it brings us down to a different sense of perspective, brings in something else: the cross of the crucifixion is rendered into a pile of broken sticks, before being lifted and raised and turned into a square.

Perhaps human history, certainly in the twentieth century, has itself gone through and is going through a kind of *nigredo*. What sort of philosophy do we have behind us? I believe that we *have experienced* elsewhere. When we are drawn or called, voluntarily or involuntarily, to go into the flask for the true process to occur, we are the sum total of our experience. We come from somewhere, we go to somewhere, we've had many experiences in other times, other places (whether other lives is probably neither here nor there). We need to recognise this as an old process, part of the profundity of human experience, known in the East for four thousand years. The earliest alchemists in Egypt were talking about it. Many artists and writers and poets know it very well, speaking of it out of their own experience.

[30]   See Sylvia Brinton Perera 1932, 'Descent to the Goddess'.
[31]   See Klossowski de Rola, P. 98.

Plate 5. Six Alchemical Pictures, Early Stages

These six pictures give some of the marvellous images that come up
for the *calcinatio*. [31] Klossowski de Rola points out that they are from
a very fine collection of alchemical engravings, many of which were

used to illustrate the work of other alchemists. They illustrate the words often used to describe it, which are certainly not particularly creative: destruction, repression, *melancholia*, frustration; being eaten, devoured, dead. A lot of people are very aware of this parched, arid state, this dark night, withdrawal of libido, loss of soul. It's an *oubliette*. We've been dropped into nothingness.

Plate 5a - The Alchemist in The Split

The first drawing, where the alchemist is sitting in the crack, the abyss between two land-masses, is a very, very important one. He's sitting in the pit of the split, he's in the flask, he can't get out. The death raven of the underworld is beside him, the stars are overhead, the wind is blowing - the *pneuma*, wind of the spirit. There are 'wet' depressions and 'dry' depressions, and this is the dry kind. It's the melancholia of the alchemists and it's the pits. (I like the term 'melancholia' much more than the modern 'depression'. It's not the same.) We talk about loss of soul, withdrawal of libido - our interest in things that used to interest us runs out. In the Eastern tradition, it's 'dying to the ten-thousand-and-one things'. This is the true alchemist at work. He would have been urged to practise contemplation, to sit in the split, to stay with it, patiently waiting upon the process. *Meditatio, contemplatio*; he's meditating through the abyss, holding the split together, acquiescing in it, breathing his way through it - or trying to and then discovering that he can't. All celestial, divine things are present, but he feels a long way from them. What had once been firm ground for the ego has opened out and given access to the lower realms. This is what yoga systems and disciplines are all about: staying with it; not thinking why, but staying with the split. Slow the pace! There's nothing we can do about it. We can't shift it. We don't have to try and get out. People think, 'Must get on and *do* something, keep pushing.' But we can't push - or not effectively. The alchemist of life just looks at what's happening in the flask and turns the burners up. It's not funny, is it? It's the earth-darkness of the underworld. In darkness, in melancholy, we learn to be underground.

Other pictures may show dead bodies and skeletons, but here we start with the alchemist himself, knowing it's a process, being able to turn the raven into a future angel. The real alchemists knew that they would do their work well if they stayed true to the process, letting what happened happen. The art of staying with it has held the mystics through the dark night of the soul. Whatever our religion, somehow we need to do what the alchemist within the split is doing: contemplating and meditating to hold it together, to transform and transmute the situation. We stay in the split and meditate through. Already there are angelic figures and *pneuma*, pure spirit, is blowing through.

'Let me out!'

There are lovely mediæval pictures from Italy showing tiny, tiny people inside the flask, delightful little figures banging on its sides, bouncing out from the bottom yelling, 'Let me out, I didn't mean it. Why can't I be the nice chaotic cabbage I was, why am I in this trouble?' And the alchemist is sitting there in profound meditation, with the hermetic seal firmly in place and the fire building up underneath! And, my God, isn't that typical of us? We want consciousness, we want to go into therapy, we want to grow, we want to be individuated, but when the heat is turned up and the flask is closed: 'I didn't mean it!' And we try to bribe the gaoler, bribe the alchemist: 'Let me out, I'll give you anything you want, let me out!' We've seen how it's Hermes who is the catalyst. As Mercury, quicksilver, he is tricky and unfixed and volatile. He is present within the prime substance at the beginning of things, saying, 'Don't let it happen to you, get out of the flask!' and at the same time, 'but you're not going to be able to make it, you are now trapped within the *calcinatio*.'

However, we may indeed be let out at this stage if we can't take the heat, if we've been tested as much as we can handle. Certainly, a lot of clients do pull out of therapy, take themselves out of that particular flask at this stage and that's the end of it. They've started counselling, even getting into analysis - and they *didn't* really mean it. Slowly finding that they're precipitated into the process, it's, 'Let me out!' I don't think we're ever taken into the true flask unless the powers that understand these matters allow it. If the gold in us is to come out, then we are held there and there is no letting out. We are being cooked by life itself and if the great alchemist of life hears us yelling, 'Let me out!' why, we'll stay in the flask and be heated some more.

Thank heavens that the alchemists said a creative process lay behind all this! Only those capable of it, only the strong, are tested. Only the sword that has been very carefully shaped and moulded and layer upon layer upon layer of metal put on it will be put to the fire by the great sword-maker. Only the pot that looks as though it's going to withstand the heat will be put into the kiln. There's some sort of special grace by which life puts in only those liable to withstand the fire and to be transformed. It's ultimately a very benign process; those who go in can come out of the flask at the end.

Active imagination can be very valuable here. People talk about the abyss: 'I'm falling into the pit, the abyss, the underworld!' Sometimes, when dreams and images are being worked through and a client has enough returning ego-strength to be able to take it, it helps them in active imagination to go into the underworld. Then they may come up with something completely different. One person said, 'I landed on a pile of dead leaves and beside me was a fox, asleep.' However, we don't know. There is also a void which is like the dome of heaven, the fullness or *plenum* of the higher womb. That is another issue altogether, another experience, the *sublimatio*, one of the later stages. But here in the *nigredo* the void is seen as Pluto's realm, Hades. It's the abyss that lies under our feet when everything that was under our feet is wiped out from under us. Here, people describe it as hell, not heaven. The void *is* abyss, unquestionably, and people may leap from worse to worse in the process, from frying pan to fire: 'I fell into the snake pit!'

Celebrating sorrow and melancholy

As therapists we need the ability to stay with it even if the client can't, to hold the edges of the crack together and to know and trust that wings will somehow emerge out of the *nigredo*. And that is *not* to deny the darkness. It's not to say, 'Come on, it isn't as bad as all that!' That's blasphemous. That is taking the experience from the client. We need to honour their experience of the true *calcinatio*, true burning, the black blacker than black, and yet, at the same time, to have that winged heart. To be with someone in this deep place calls out everything we've got. Though they may not respond at all, yet there may be some unconscious, unspoken, secret part of them that is listening and incorporating something from it. It may go somewhere. And that secret life that listens can perhaps be seen in those winged figures, those angelic birds in the picture. The alchemist is keeping in touch with it. In one of Samuel Beckett's novels there's a little bit where the hero, crawling on his face and hands, says 'I can't go on, I can't go on'. And he crawls on! That's very close to the apparently endless process of the *nigredo*. Here is a colleague's story:

'I have a client very much into this sense of utterly losing everything - not in the outer world; it's in her interior journey. She feels that she's totally lost all she had thought right for her: "What is the point of it all?" She's in utter despair. She cries a tremendous amount, not just in the sessions but outside them. She's reached a point of almost complete inertia. When I'm with her, I experience my own inertia as well as hers. And yet at the same time there is a curious feeling that we both know there is a point to it all, even though it's pointless. It's a contradiction in terms; but when we've talked about it enough, clarified it - we almost experience the meaning of the meaninglessness.' As described, it sounds like Hades, like the 'great' *nigredo*, that black blacker than black . . . .

Is it that in our melancholy the psyche is *honouring* something, celebrating an old sorrow? I use the word 'celebrating' appropriately. If we look back, we may find that our psyche remembers something we don't, which needs to be celebrated in this way. We may need to honour some appropriate grief or joyfulness. It's not depression, it's something different - quiet, and with low energy: 'By the waters of Babylon I sat down and wept.' Modern psychology has done us a great disservice by calling it 'depression'; it's such an ineffective word. As I said before, I so much prefer 'melancholy', *melancholia*. There is a time to be in the melancholy of life, in the mists, to feel the heartbreak at the heart of things. For quite a few years now I've been using that word and it's amazing how often people respond.

And if we're really in it, if it's very deep, no-one else can get us out of it, though I think a number of people might have a go! In the true depths of the real *nigredo* (and there are many levels of this; people do have mini-*nigredos*), we cannot hear the voices. We have to stay there till some time-clock of eternity has sounded, we've become aware of it and it's possible to move on. Then the art is in not allowing a person to stay in the flask but encouraging them to come out. But we can't push the process.

The next picture is a very famous one. It shows the old king sitting on his throne and he's being clubbed to death. He's looking very calm about it. It's a calmness which has to be, a submission to the inexorable moment. There's an inevitability to it. Notice the astrological starry heavens with the eternal Sun and Moon presiding over the process. The ego, the personality, is in the flask. The images have shown it being first devoured (the Green Lion eating the Sun) and now the king is being beaten over the head, having all his head-ideas clubbed out of him. His ruling principle is being flattened, severely bashed.

It's the old Adam that's being clubbed to death. It's the frustration of our ego-will, our ego-desire. Everything that we had thought was personal, our own, all that the ego has lived by, all the consciousness of the ego

Plate 5b - The King Being Clubbed

as personality, is taken into the flask and frustrated. All the scripts, stereotypes, assumptions and illusions that we normally mask within ourselves are put through this 'painful corrective', as Jung called it. All the complacency and pretentiousness and fanaticism have to be burned out. Degree by degree, stage by stage under these multiple heatings, all that we believed in, stood for, thought was our ruling principle, is melted down, rendered to a dry ash. It's impotence, dissolution of the ego. We can't *think* ourselves through this, we can't feel through it, we can't use our physical strength to break out of it, we can't intuit our way through. We're just stuck with it. The death of the old king!

Yet the king's feet are placed as if he's almost inviting, even welcoming, what is happening to him. There is a sense in which all this is a self-chosen process. Someone enters the flask or is called into it (and how the choice is made I don't know) and we meet them in the inexorable alchemic movement from matter to spirit and from spirit back to matter again. We have to take back into ourselves that which we have projected into the environment. Thus we accept responsibility for the flask and for the process, and ultimately begin to discover the true gold that was always in us.

Pondered on, these pictures render up a lot of meaning. This one had a considerable effect on one man; it grabbed him and therefore it became *his* picture. He said: 'I'm just incorporating, just allowing that there's a wonderful thing happening in this picture. It's the interaction. It's like a group or team fulfilling a purpose without knowing what they're doing; and they're doing it together. Yes, he's going to have a sore head and more, but it's as if the king *needs* what's going on. It's as if you're part of everything: you're the king *and* you're the group doing the clubbing, and you're the club - the whole thing. I get struck with a sense of absolute wonder at what's going on.' When is a club a club and when is it a Zen master's stick, about to give the person an 'Aha!'? The picture led this man to the realisation that we are taken out of the mass to become the individual; and then ultimately we learn to work with the group. It is about the extraction (the *separatio* again) from mass-consciousness. Yes, we do get beaten up in a group when it has a mass mind and of course this can be extremely *mal*ign; but it can be very *ben*ign. A paradox!

Many of us might identify with the next picture, the skulls and the rising and falling birds. 'Dem bones, dem bones, dem dry bones.' You see one of the skeletons hanging over the grave, and the abyss, and the ravens pecking off any meat that is left. It's like the embalmer's process, or the putting of the guts and brain and heart into the canopic jars of Egypt. The Egyptian religion had a lot to do with this particular stage. They honoured, were in love with, the *mortificatio* process. Their culture stood on its head from where we stand - or we stand on our heads from where they stood. They believed that the underworld is the entry to eternal life. A person went down into the underworld with nothing left of them but a bag of bones; if they were carrying anything non-essential when they approached the portals of everlasting life, they had to go through fire again and have it burned off. In the realm of the underworld the soul was weighed against the single feather of truth.

Plate 5c - Dry Bones

Those who measured exactly went into the overworld. However, those who weighed heavier than that feather were sent back again. [32] It's like the Bardo process within Tibetan Buddhism: you go back again and again and again until you're rendered down to essence.

Even among the skeletons and the absolutely bare bones there are rising as well as dark descending ravens.[33] The skeletons have the ravens above; already the birds of spirit are involved. This is the time when we may rally the 'talisman', the memory of past strength or past light, an inner figure of wisdom, in preparation for some other light to come in.

---

[32] After death, the soul was led into the underworld on the solar barque of the god Ra, for the meeting with Anubis and Thoth, great gods of Egypt, who would weigh the soul against the feather of truth. Any disparity and the soul would go back on to the wheel of rebirth and be born again, to repeat the process.

[33] In some of the earlier pictures the descending birds are white and the rising ones black.

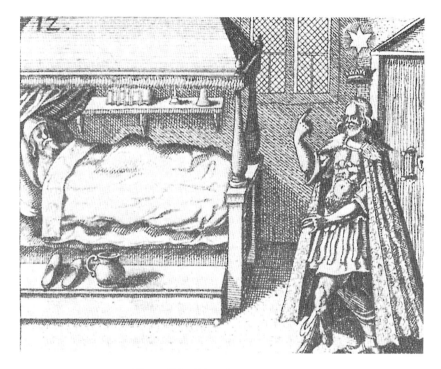

Plate 5d - The Old King Dies

So, the Green Lion swallows the Sun; the alchemist sits in the split; the king is clubbed to death; and now, here's the dying king.[34] This picture is a truly lovely one, for already the new king with the crown, and the star of accomplishment and wholeness above, is entering the death-chamber of the old king. As the old king dies, the new king comes in at the door! If one can stay true to the process, the beginning and the end will start to come together, as always in alchemy. The old king is lying in his bed with his nightcap on and his slippers and his pisspot beside him, and here's the new king with the eternal crown of immortality, the spiritual star over his head. Even in the putrefaction process of the *nigredo* it is the gold that we are about.

However, the gold comes later; it's not apparent in these early stages,

---

[34] There are also *nigredo* stage alchemic pictures of the old king lying there being eaten. Sometimes it's a wolf that's swallowing him. Sometimes there's a fire behind and the wolf is being fed into it. It is often a serpent or a salamander eating its own tail, devouring itself in the flames; or two salamanders or dragons, one in a flask.

which lead to separation and dismemberment. We've seen how, in therapy, we need to stay in with our clients, walk alongside them, help them to stay with what *is*; not what may be, not what has been, but the reality of what is. Yet somehow, through ourselves if we can, though not denying the reality of the abyss we also have to keep the crown and the star there. Already, as the ruling principle dies, implicit within it is the appearance of a new king. One man said, 'In meditation, suddenly I found myself on a rocky plain and out of the rock was a twin flame, and I knew I had to step inside it. I stepped inside the flame, and the fat went and the flesh went and left the skeleton, and the bones of the skeleton were rendered down to powder, until around the hole was just the white ash. After the meditation ended I was absolutely bereft, because it seemed as though I'd been torn away from other people. And then I stepped back into a much bigger life'. These extraordinary motifs came to him absolutely bang on target: he changed his career and his life. 'Definitely it's been quite a big flask,' he commented, 'and a pretty hot fire, too!'

So even now the fire is put on to bring the work to dry ash and powder. The term *mortificatio* means what it says: mortification. 'Oh God, not even *more!*' A person seems to have gone through just about everything - and the heat's put on *again*. Each phase often includes this at its end, because new birth requires the death of the old stages. 'Rebirth requires prior mortification', and if that isn't a therapeutic statement, what is? Part of the experience within the flask is that we *cannot* come up all sunny from the old place; we cannot make the old adaptations. This is what the ash is about. We have been rendered down, not yet to the essence but to the essential nature of ourselves and of life. Those of us who tend to rise above things, keeping up the happy, beautiful smile everywhere, may feel desperately frustrated at being unable to stay bright through this.

Symptom as symbol

I suspect that in quite a lot of illness people are undergoing something of the *mortificato* - the death-bringing, the *putrefactio*. Looking at symptoms as symbols, we know that, because Saturn is at work here, it's the structural stuff, the actual bony structure of our lives, that's often attacked during this stage of calcification - rheumatic or arthritic hips, backs going out. There may be illnesses that go with each of the alchemical stages. Though we don't necessarily use alchemic language, it can be very helpful to know that we're going through something that has a profounder meaning than we might ever have thought. For a lot of people, cancer is a distinctly calcining process. It is a flask in itself. People with cancer, unaware of the flask, will often go to a healing centre with the idea of recovering, getting out of it. Their relatives also may see such a centre as a place that makes you well immediately. But the point is to try to help the client stay with it, stay in the flask. Experiencing its meaning with creative imagination, they begin to look upon the crisis as opportunity, seeing the gold in the crisis. Also, the relatives begin to understand their own flask. One cancer patient said, 'I've felt, from the physical point of view too, as though I'd been grabbed and held. I've been in a cage, pinned down by some "jaws" or other. All my ways of knowing how to do something about it aren't terribly good, so I've learnt a lot; and I've learnt a lot about pain. I'm still in it but - it's not necessarily about getting better. It's about something deeper…'

The shadow

And certainly, the more we stay in the *calcinatio* the deeper we go. The deeper the therapeutic and analytic process, the more it becomes a descent into the shadow stuff in the flask, the really primitive stuff of ourselves, that which is most unacceptable to us, that which we most repress or suppress. The ego, of course, would come out of this. It doesn't like it. It feels un-proud, humiliated, flattened, very unsure of its own erstwhile certainties. It dislikes it. Yet very often in the shadow is the most vivid, alive, creative part of ourselves, and it has to be taken back from others and returned to us. The whole approach of therapy is that unless we know what we're dealing with, unless we take back the shadow, stop putting it 'out there', unless we begin to take responsibility for the mass of confusion, the mess and the divinity of our lives, we remain children and don't deserve to be in the flask. If we undertake this alchemic process, then the flask will be heated and all those ego-drives - our lust, our greed, abuse of power, our complacency, pretentiousness, fanaticism - all will have to be subjected to Jung's 'painful correctives', taken back, reassessed, revalued and made part of the process.

The disillusioned ego is impotent here. It won't help. It can't. We may be in the habit of dealing with situations with a great deal of deviousness and manipulation and collusion - yet all the time looking good! We may justify ourselves, blaming and projecting out on to others, manipulating to reach our own ends. But we cannot think our way through this with an ego. We can't pretend it's not happening. We have to honour it. The trickery of the mind doesn't help, for all its knowledge and wisdom and wit. The trickster we are is shown up, the Mercurius within ourselves; the way we bribe life, con other people, seduce them, use and misuse and abuse them. For the mind, quicksilver, compromising and buying its way out, paying the gaoler, paying the alchemist to open up the hermetic seal, nothing is of avail. We are in the flask, the heat is on and we have to honour it.

So the extra heatings really bring us into our primitive shadow stuff. 'Bestiality' is not a good word for the lust, greed, rapacious appetites, destructiveness, murderousness, which are all to be confronted and owned within the process; the animals are higher than that. But what a lot of human beings find in themselves, both collectively and individually, is the instinctive and sexual desire for power over others. Whoopee for sexuality! But not when it's lust and desire and rape; not when it projects out on to the environment, going against rather than with life. The process of primitive, instinctual purification is often personified in our dreams and images. Half-animal, half-human, demonic figures come up, titanic, plutonic; dwarfed or giant beasts; the raging, the damaged, the wounded; all appear until we have to say, 'That is me, it's mine, its darkness is my life!' If we can accept that that possibility is within *us*, then we can see that justification and blaming are beside the point. Our own actions all have to be confronted and owned within the process. 'It's nothing to do with *me!*' says our ego. '*I* couldn't possibly be like that!' But then we're living out of only a part of ourselves. We need to say not, 'Out there is the murderer!' but, 'In here is the murderer. I am both raped and rapist, I am both victim and torturer.' We have to know that that which is out there is also within us, and make decisions of choice as to how we handle that. And what we choose to do with it becomes primary. It is part of the process of growing up and of responsibility, helping us to purify, to come back to life in a different way.

Dangers of the nigredo

People don't have to come into counselling in order to get into the flask, or to get out of it. Life itself will put us in the flask if we are of the quality of the true gold. Life is the therapist. But if we are taken into the flask of therapy, the *calcinatio* may be in the murderous, destructive feelings that we have towards our analyst or therapist. And as therapists at the other end of that process, that's what we'll be receiving! We recognise, in our clients and probably in ourselves, the sense of being trapped in an alien element. None of us wishes to stay in fire because at this stage we are flammable. 'I used to know what to do and now I don't - I don't know how to handle it.' Intense anxiety goes with this - angst, frustration, rage. Here are the self-destructive impulses, the fury that mustn't get out but there's danger in turning it in. Here's the violence we feel against life, or against the person in whom we'd invested our trust who's suddenly let us down. Here's the feeling of total impotency and the fear of annihilation that goes with it, the sense of abandonment and betrayal, of pressure and death. 'My God, my God, why hast Thou forsaken me?'

Honouring the darkness

I don't know how we can handle this intractable state that the client (let alone ourselves) is in, unless we have some point of attraction outside the situation. How does it raise our own material as counsellors and therapists? It would be dreadful to be caught in it ourselves and have no sense of transpersonal meaning over and beyond the personal situation; that's two of you in the flask. Maybe that's what does happen in certain forms of therapy where there is a great deal of transference and counter-transference; and then that bleak, hopeless state within the unconscious begins to contaminate and cross-contaminate. We need only to be able to stay with somebody through this, holding on to the possibility that meaning will emerge out of the totally meaningless. 'Let me out!' There's nothing we can do; we just have to wait on time. This is the abyss of despair, the *melancholia* deep in a true *nigredo*. The person can't hear the voices from outside. 'It's like listening from inside a glass box,' they say. 'People are talking to me from outer space.' And while this can come first, it can come anywhere *en route*.

Too many on the transpersonal line try to rush people far too quickly through to their coming out of the darkness. To honour the darkness, to find the light within it while yet *in* the darkness, is the art of true transpersonal therapy. Push people towards the bright and the light and out of what they are experiencing - which is one way of blaspheming against and dishonouring the experience of the client - and we deepen the very split that the alchemists were trying so hard to pull together. As therapists, we help to hold the split and remind the client of what might be growing out of the darkness, all the while not denying the darkness.

Dark poetry

Today we recognise much of the old language used by the alchemists to illustrate this cooking stage, because it describes our own feelings. Just listen to the words of modern people's similes, the dark poetry out of their life-experience:

'I'm falling into a pit and I can't climb up the sides.'
'It's poisonous; the poison erupts out of me.'
'I'm poisoning myself with my own venom; everything that's anti-life is being drawn out of me by the heat.'
'I'm thwarted, impotent.' (It's the ego that's impotent; it swoons into this and struggles to keep control, stay in power, grab on to anything of the known and familiar, the safe and secure.)
'I'm cut off from my corner-stones, encased, bereft; the light is turned out.'
Someone said, 'When I came out of the grave, I wandered like a cadaver; it was strangulation, valley of the shadow of death.'
Someone else, graphically: 'Like a flattened cat, done for,' (and she made a wonderful drawing of a squashed animal, spread-eagled flat on the floor with a huge steamroller running over it).
Yet another: 'It's anorexia, fasting, reducing time.' (Fascinating, this: anorexia into *calcinatio*; a lot of people with anorexia speak of similar feelings.)
'Burning with nervous tension, every nerve-end twanging and raw.'

'Charred, refined, reduced; like a cigarette squashed out under a great heel on the ground.'

And anger, rage, fury; yes, that's part of it too. We don't want this to happen to us. Here is the therapeutic process in action. The list goes on: 'Implosion, no way out but in - chasing my own tail and eating it - like an empty house - loss of bearings, losing all hold, heavy, stuck - sullying of reputation - relinquishing all life-supports.' Guilt, numbness, frost, hell, crucifixion, strangulated despair - these are words that people use. Life does this to us at times and this is what it can feel like. Many of us have found ourselves plunged willy-nilly into stages like this, when everything we had believed in seems to go out from under us. What we had thought was our gold, our ego, our personality, everything we had felt to be 'our values' - all taken down into the fire. It's right to acknowledge the pain of this stage. Later on, of course, it will be submitted to another process and sublimated, lifted, made to render a greater value. But that's later on; at this point it doesn't feel as if anything else will ever come in. 'Let me out!' we yell. But, because the gold is already present within the *prima materia*, something else that may be very important will come along: a dream, a meeting, a book. That's why I ask two key questions right at the start: 'What makes your heart sing?' and 'What, at your darkest points, has carried you through?' Then there is some motif to hold on to when, later, the dark sets in.

Nigredo dreams

People who know nothing whatsoever about alchemy often dream in alchemical ways. Frances Wickes [35] quotes a man who had a problem with his mother. His dream is extraordinarily of the *calcinatio*: the old king is irrationally cruel, and must be killed by his own bent and rusty sword. Then a flame springs from the body, it is burned to ashes and in the flame appears a new and gleaming sword. Such dreams appear frequently, though they don't always bring such archaic images.

One man, entirely unaware of the alchemical process, gave me this dream of his father, who was still alive at the time: 'My father has been cremated. I'm not sure if it has just happened - or is it a past event? I

[35] See Frances Wickes 1963, 'The Inner World of Choice', Pp. 114 -116.

go to one of those chest-of-drawers-in-the-wall type cemeteries you find in Mediterranean countries. The wall is crumbling - faded flowers - my father's picture is torn and faded on the ground. He's of Italian stock. I look inside the small vault, feeling sick and yet somehow excited. There's nothing but grey ash and what looks like a few teeth. One of them has a gold filling, strangely bright and glowing in the darkness. I awake deeply moved, and knowing something important has happened in my relationship with my father.' To say the least!

A woman dreamt: 'I was in our vegetable garden and the rows of vegetables had transformed themselves into hedges, a bit like a maze. I heard a blackbird's clucking sound and turned to my six-year-old son. "Have you got any food in your pockets - the bird is hungry and wants feeding?" And he pulled out of his pocket a bunch of grapes. All the grapes had been eaten but one. "Give that one to the bird," I said, "It'll be something." And he offered up the grape to the bird. The bird was enormous, a very large, black bird with a curved beak.' There's something very Dionysian, as we shall see, about the grape feeding the bird. And the blackbird would be associated with the *nigredo*. They are birds of the underworld carrying the black blacker than black on their wings. The bird is a great alchemic symbol and motif. Birds come in all shapes and forms; they're interchangeable. We've seen how the alchemists very often called their flask 'the pelican'. We've seen the pelican, sometimes a peacock or a swan, pecking its own breast so that the blood will fall and feed its young. As Christ did, and as all the Sun gods have done, we pierce our own breast. It needs to be pierced to free the blood to flow to nourish the earth, to make it fecund, to bring about the emancipation and marriage of earth and spirit, so that earth can be fertilised and raised to heaven.

One very powerful person, working on an image of an enormous split in a rock, dreamt that she was down in that split, sitting on a fairly safe ledge by a reservoir. She could see both the sun and the moon. A figure appeared in the water of the reservoir - a female figure, half submerged on a sun-bed. The water and the sun were playing on her, making her all the colours of the rainbow. The dreamer expressed the dream by painting it, saying her need was to be patient, sit in the split and hold it. Yet the peacock's tail, *cauda pavonis*, seemed to be coming in here, heralding the next stage. Although the *solutio* has a very different feeling-tone from the *calcinatio*, being watery and about relationships, the separation and the coming together, yet it's already here. The dark is already moving into light and the light and the dark are swimming together. It's certainly to be hoped that even in the blackest or the whitest or the yellowest of times - even in the redness - we do have moments shot through with some other colouring.

Another person, who later became a writer, told me this dream: 'I find a wounded black swan, and there's also a huge *white* swan with a jewel of many colours in its head. They have to be joined. There is a journey. The black swan becomes one with the white swan and they twine around me. The dream set me on to a path of being creative in a different way - or it came from a different place. I've turned it into a story, and it's that which started me writing.' The swan is a water bird - it isn't really a land bird although it walks on land - so this dream is almost certainly about the passage from the *nigredo* to the *solutio*, and the peacock's tail is coming in with the many-coloured jewel. The interaction of the black swan and the white swan is essential, and the release of creativity helps to produce the bridge between them. To sit there and turn something dark into a story is again the alchemist sitting in the split. After the intertwining of the swans, the dreamer was set on a path of being creative in a different way or - a nice alchemical statement - 'it came from a different place'.

It is rare to find any true artist who hasn't gone through a great many of these processes to produce their art. There's a price paid for that heavy privilege, and if, like Mozart, they produce it early, they still have to live it through. Perhaps some of the poets and artists die young because their egos are hardly more than an approximation, a roughly-cast candle or lantern, trying to hold a flame too great for them. They are overwhelmed by their own souls. But great writers then leave behind them flaming words that touch the human heart. I found a poem by Dorsha Hayes, an American poet. Written by somebody who I think really knew their life experience, it speaks directly to this stage. It's called 'Fire Hazard'.

Filled with the clutter of unsorted stuff,
A spark can set a man ablaze.

What's there heaped high among stored rubbish,
At a puff will burst in flame.
No man can be aware of how inflammable he is,
How prone to what can rage beyond control,
Unless the piled up litter of his life
Is known to him, and he is able to assess
What hazard he is in, what could ignite.
A man disordered and undisciplined
Lives in the peril of a panic flight
Before the onrush of a flaming wind.
Does it now seem I seek to be profound?
I stand on smoking ash and blackened ground. [36]

Reducing of the fire

I have to resist the urge - with which I am very familiar - to plunge on too quickly out of the *calcinatio* to the next stage. However, it's said that if we've taken the message of the burning and are truly cooked rather than just half-baked, the fire can be reduced. The wise alchemist turns it down for a little and the burning eases. The *mortificato*, the *putrefactio*, have been fully and totally completed, there has been enough firing and nothing is left at the bottom of the flask except some grey powder. The alchemists said that that which was, no longer is and that which has to come into being has not yet arrived; but the gold is being processed. The Bible has this:

'You tested us, God, you refined us like silver, you let us fall into the net, you laid heavy burdens on our backs, you let people drive over our heads; but now the ordeal by fire and water is over, and you allow us once more to draw breath.' [37]

According to the various texts, the peacock's tail, the *cauda pavonis*, comes at different stages. The majority of the alchemists placed it here, between the *calcinatio* and the *solutio*, where it's sometimes said to be like the dark rainbow you see when there is oil in a puddle. The dark is beginning to break up into a different kind of light, as the colour-spectrum will spin to give white light.

[36] Dorsha Hayes 1972, 'Fire Hazard', from 'The Bell Branch Rings', P. 26.
[37] Psalm 66, 10-12.

*Nigredo **into** solutio*

So, what's left at the base of the flask at the end of this process? Grey ash, the fag-ends of our life. 'All those years of wastage!' But it's not wasted; it's necessary expenditure, which is rather different. Without that process, that firing, without the benign work of Pluto and Saturn, painful though we feel it, we do not recognise hell and the underworld, and tend to grow without roots. But to go into our underworld, to know the other side of the face of sunlit reality, to learn to move in the Stygian darkness - that is what makes us truly human. It gives us eyes that can see in the dark.

A lot of people have been through the sense of abandonment, betrayal, depression and death. It's very, very real. It's to be hoped that alchemy and the processes of therapy are helping people not to be slain by it. Lovingly we have to be alongside our clients in the work and in the process; as we hope some day, when we are going through it ourselves, the Great Alchemist will be alongside us. One person said, 'I've always thought that I had to find my own solution, whatever it is; and somewhere it appears.' She used the phrase 'find my own solution'. Usually in the *calcinatio* we're more aware of problems than of any solutions. Things feel rigid, tight, restrictive, constrictive and dry; there's just that grey-white ash in the flask after we've been in the hands of the *cordon bleu* cook that life is. But then in the *solutio* we begin to come up with a few solutions.

We've been looking at the fiery stage, where the alchemist is the great cook at work. I've explained that I don't think any of us, unless peculiarly blessed or peculiarly cursed, stay all the time in any one of these stages. There are days when we do hear the birds of summer! But then, whichever the process, it's back again. But in this darkness of the *calcinatio* the gold is already beginning to shine through. Later it will become the golden thread of the hermetic chain leading us ultimately to the *sublimatio*.

I would say to the reader, if you thought the *nigredo* was problematic, wait till you get to the *solutio*! For next we meet the washerwoman, and it's about tears and the water of our lives. So, God bless you and go with you.

CHAPTER FIVE

SOLUTIO

Vision and understanding come
through the portal of a broken heart

Fire of Water

As we've seen, people can enter the alchemical flask through different stages. The *solutio* is not necessarily the next, though for me it follows here. We've seen how in the *calcinatio* we were being dried out. The *separatio* took place, the pairs of opposites were divided and there were just bare bones, the essence, the essential, left cooling there. There was the death of the ego. Nothing is left now but grey ash at the bottom of the flask. The colour - or lack of colour - within the flask (milky, cloudy, *albedo* white and silvery) indicates that among the presiding deities are the Moon and Neptune; Venus as well, for here is her copper colour, already heralding the red-gold.[38]

Alchemist as washerwoman

We've seen how in the *nigredo* the alchemist was cook. Here, pictures and illustrations often show her dressed rather differently. In whatever order the stages come, sooner or later we're going to meet life as the alchemist in charge of the eternal round, the 'centrifugal force', the up-down of the cosmic washing machine in which many of us find ourselves. Just as we think we're through the process, something clicks and we're churning about in the water again. Life in the launderette! Once more the heat is increased and we are in the hands of the eternal washerwoman. She gives us many patient washings to cleanse us, make us aware of our own dirt, adhesions, the stuff we get rid of by dumping it on other people's doorsteps. She helps us become aware of our contamination of ourselves and other people, our projections on to them.

---

[38] The balance of copper and iron in the body is said to be different for men and for women. They go together: in women there's more copper, which is the Venus element, and in men more iron, the Mars. It's said there's even more copper in women during pregnancy.

The *solutio* is said to be a baptism process. There are alchemical pictures showing a seated Christ-figure being boiled in a baptismal font. The motif is of 'being taken into the river', into the stream. Most of our great experiences, great motifs, are part of these 'many washings', until head and heart finally begin to work together.

In the *calcinatio* the motto was 'stay with it'; now it's 'go with the flow'. Alchemical images for the *solutio* are the fountain, the bath, the sea, the lake, the pool, a great fish. Dreams and images of river or stream, sprinkler or shower, melting or flowing, may arise. A lot of very useful work can be done by defining this melting process: art, imagery and imagination, dance, music, sculpting, anything that will help to loosen the dry, arid soil, melt the ice in us, start the flow.

Plate 5e - Lion and Bear

The sixth illustration belongs with the *solutio*. It shows the Moon goddess, whomever she represents in any culture, dividing off the Green Lion and the bear into the flask (here the Green Lion is masculine and the bear is feminine), and the birds are being driven out again. This stage is very much about the feminine principle. Once, the ability to melt and to be gentle was seen as a noble quality, more fluid, more flexible, dissolving some of our polarities, solving our 'head' problems by bringing in our hearts; both-and, not either-or; *solve et coagula* - healing the split.

The Moon

We'll look at the Moon goddess, Luna, in terms of the moon's phases and how they have been seen from time immemorial. The alchemical work begins at the new moon, which is still only a mere slip of a girl, the little silver wedge that we see in the sky while the moon herself is still mainly dark. This is the underside of the moon. It is where the dark side of consciousness begins to come out. The alchemists say that at the new moon, Sol, the sun, the old principle, descends into dissolution and darkness and is killed by the poison of the mother - or of the beloved. That's another way of saying that if we stay around too long on the umbilicus of our original mother, trying for that incest, then the womb-fluid, nutritive when we were children, is going to become toxic to us. If we are to move from dependency to responsibility, then it becomes straight poison.

As she begins to increase to the half and then the three-quarter moon, Luna becomes the maiden, the pregnant maiden. The mythic images are of copulation and ecstasy. Here are the seductress, the temptress - Circe, Calypso, the Nymph, the Lorelei. At last in the time of the full moon we have the totality. This is the great Moon goddess, Blessed Virgin as well as original mother, wise woman, Sophia, Kuan-Yin. It's said that the king, the new Sol, makes Mother Luna visible, whereas before she'd been in the unconscious, in the dark and in the flask. People have dreamt dreams where sun and moon have been close together and glowing at the same time. Now the process has brought her out and she emerges to stand coequal with the king's son, reigning with the new king.

Confusion

If we thought we were confused in the *nigredo* stage, we are certainly confused in the *albedo*! However, here it's a different kind of confusion: a fragmentation and disintegration, yet also a dissolving, a diffusion, a melting. As we are taken down, the opposites merge and everything is chaotic again; not the original chaos of the *massa confusa*, but a different chaos where we don't know whether we're coming or going, up or down. The turning of the solid ash into a liquid, a 'solution', is experienced in at least one of two ways, or both at the same time: on the one hand it can feel very difficult, like drowning; on the other, as we shall see, it may be felt as ecstatic bliss. [39]

Drowning in *solutio*

There are pictures where the old king is in the water crying out for help as he goes under. At the same time the new king is coming in, washed clean and looking for the new land, the New Jerusalem. These alchemic pictures do not leave out the instincts, but honour them, reminding us of the wonderful story of Noah and the ark, all the animals of the instinct contained in one place. Seeking land again, a white dove (*pneuma*, spirit, soul) is sent out to find new territory - 'There must be some other way!' Again, it's Jonah being carried in the belly of a great fish, or Hercules swallowed, carried into the waters of

---

[39] The person who wrote about the alchemical laundrette realised that it was to do with the *solutio* - amazing what the process gets going!
   '*Spinning and whirling from empty to dry,*
   Banging and clanging from 'normal' to 'high',
   Rushing around from pillar to post,
   Boiling and sizzling from oven to roast.
   Thrashing about like a billowing sail,
   Massaged and pummelled in wintery hail;
   Never a clue as to which way to turn,
   Never a lesson we're willing to learn;
   Over and over and over again
   We shrink the same garments exactly the same.
   One day, perhaps, we'll buy a new washer,
   Stop messing around with the splishy-splosh splosher;
   Push the blue button and pull up the pail,
   Cast off all ropes and hoist up the sail,
   Shake the old compass to action again,
   Use a new powder and not the brand name!'

the underworld and then regurgitated; the fish, the barge, the *nekyia*, the night-sea journey in a boat.

Although it is about a new baptism, about being reborn from the amniotic fluid of the higher mother, a lot of us find it extremely difficult to go through this drowning, this going under and disintegrating in the flow and flux. It all seemed so clear - even in the *calcinatio* stage things tended to be black and white, though that was mainly about our relationship to the outside world and external authority. Now we're into feeling, affect, relatedness; the heart has to be broken open, drained, crying, bleeding, rent, before it can come back to be a different kind of heart. The greater engulfs the lesser: the Self begins to engulf the ego.

Relationship

It is very often in the heart of *relationship* that we come to this absolutely major experience. Our great life-transitions are nearly always in relation to others or to the collective. They are very deeply *solutio* experiences - the joy and the tears of it and the birth of it. Birth, puberty, partnership, children, divorce, bereavement, ageing, death, rebirth - it's they that cause us to weep and to laugh, till eventually we come to value the heart. Extracting our true feelings from the false, our true gold from the profane, they first split and then re-mate the pairs of opposites, the inner and the outer, the heart and the head. An old alchemic saying has it that new vision and understanding come through the portal of a broken heart.

However, while for some of us it is a heartbreaking, heart-rending process, for others the *solutio* is a mysterious transformation, through love and through desire, towards some different mode of being. It helps to free us from being lost in the mass, making us more individual so that one day we'll be able to work with the group. It's a movement towards a less self-absorbed, less narcissistic kind of loving. That which causes us to lose boundaries, lose control and become fluid can also get rid of the final vestiges of the old king. At last we re-shape ourselves, re-define our boundaries and find ourselves a new identity. We are seeking a new land and a new foothold, battling to breathe again. So we learn by degrees to bring flesh and spirit together. If the flesh is without spirit, then all is venal and lustful; if the spirit is without flesh, then all is air and no substance. These wonderful affairs ('affairs' indeed! - these experiences that cause us so to weep and to laugh) help us also to value the heart and to value feeling in others and in ourselves. Issues of the flesh can also be of the spirit!

There are many stories from literature and the Bible about lust and its transformation. Remember how it is told in the second book of Samuel that David saw Bathsheba and lost his integrity? Lusting after her as she was bathing, he was led to go against his high principles and make sure that her husband was sent to the front line of battle to get killed so that he could possess her. We have many stories of the interaction between the lusting desire-body still fighting it out within us, and the higher body of love - the passion in the beginning that will turn to *com*passion in the end. In the flask everything is mixing, and it's very difficult to know where one begins and the other ends. The following dreams (and dreams often come up at this stage) talk particularly about the crossover between *nigredo* and *albedo*. Although neither the dreamers nor I knew it at the time, it became apparent later.

Albedo **dreams**

This dream is from a thirty-seven year old man, a computer analyst, emerging from a very profound depression. This had been labelled 'clinical', but when he came to me we treated it as being alchemical. 'I come to an underground pool. In the depths of dark water I can see an unspeakable *something*, amorphous, with tentacles curving and flowing, unshaping and reshaping, first dark then cloudy. It forms up and a young girl of about sixteen, moony white and ethereally beautiful, almost intangible, with closed eyes - maybe blind - steps from the pool and begins to dry her long, yellowish hair.'

This is a 'crossover' dream, and very beautiful. Just as the dreamer is emerging from his *melancholia*, here is the underground pool, the 'unspeakable something' - the amorphous underwater octopus (his mother, as he said). Then emerges the young girl, 'about sixteen, moony white ('moony' is very close to 'milky') and ethereally beautiful'. He has broken away from the deadly pull of the undersea octopus and this is the first emergence of his soul. He has moved from the dark stage of the *nigredo* through into the *albedo*. In fact his soul is already moving towards the *citrinitas* with this first vision of his young anima appearing there, drying out her long yellowish hair (the yellow of the third stage). Here is the first intimation of gold coming through all the darkness of his depression. Moments like that make my heart full of awe and full of tears and full of love for the process. I didn't say to the dreamer, 'Ho ho, that's the *solutio*!' I just thought, 'Thank God,' and held it at the back of my consciousness while he went through the issues that he needed to go through. It was only later that it became apparent to *him*, and then he did a double-take!

People often do that when they recognise how universal is their profoundly personal work. The parental, personal, archetypal scriptings of the *nigredo* stage lead here to the projections and introjections going on in relatedness. All those stereotypes from the old king principle (if there are any left!) are being taken down into the creative ocean to be reborn. Here is the amniotic fluid of the original womb. There have been many washings in this water, for most of us through relationship. Now we're moving into baptismal waters, the seminal and vaginal fluids of the orgasms of love. They are the waters of purification, the waters of love, the waters of our own lives.

However, we still need to remember the dark sun, *Sol niger*. We remember how, in the confrontation with the opposites of the *calcinatio* stage, the ego was dimmed in our personality, and all that it represented and had lived by was suffocated. As the Sun of consciousness is taken down into the unconscious, it meets its dark opposite, the shadow of the sun, which at this stage is the Moon. The original mother and father traditions and stereotypes have come down into the flask. These are not the personal mother and father, but at the moment they are muddled and merged deep within the *alembic*. They will eventually emerge as Sol and Luna, but now the conscious ego is going down. In modern terms it's the 'descent into the unconscious', where the underlying factors begin to come out.

Plate 5f - Sol et Luna Separated

So, to the last of the pictures in Plate 5; we can see the king again, now with Sun and Moon held apart. Separated out in the *calcinatio*, soon in the *solutio* they're to be melded together again as the heat is reapplied. Soon, Sol is to merge with Luna, the great feminine goddess. But, while the conscious, bright side of it all is indeed about relatedness, that which synthesises, now we're about separation. And so we meet the dark forces of *un*relatedness and cold-bloodedness. As we explore the dark opposite, the Sun's shadow - witchcraft, destruction - out come all the dark images of the struggle: the dragon, serpent, octopus, indicative of the original mother. Here are the sea-crab, the dark spider, scorpion, basilisk, toad; cold-blooded, unrelated. The old ruling principle that the ego stood by is being poisoned and killed by the mother. This is the dark side of the feminine principle.

SEPARATIO

Ignis

Aqua

Aer

Terra

Plate 6. Separatio and Fermentatio - **6a. Separatio**

It's incredible what animals and creatures appear in the *vas*! Do you remember the image of a cat flattened out on the road, having been run over by a steamroller? That's exactly what the frog or salamander looks like in the flask, doesn't it? (see 6b and 6c overleaf). Well and truly flattened out. The Ripley Scroll has a marvellous text describing the vision of a great toad. [40] One woman told me how, for her, it was the little frog of fairy story and legend, the frog of transformation with its green colour that appeared in her dreams. She had a house near the coast with the sea at the end of the garden, and a pond, and the place was full of frogs. They would come right into the kitchen, and there'd be a mass of them hopping all over the place. We see what we like in the flask; if you see a frog, then you can bet your life for you it's a frog!

The flask is rotating, setting the ash whirling; fermentation begins in the bottom until in the end the solution is formed (see Plate 6c. Fermentatio - overleaf). And through the dissolving process the images, in alchemy, in myth and in our lives, are transformed from the cold-blooded, unrelated side of ourselves. At last, in come the lion, the bear, the she-wolf, the dog, the bitch. They are still struggling with each other, still predators, still part of the eating and dissolving process, but now they're warm-blooded.[41] These are pictures and mythic images, but also human experiences of the dark side of the Moon. The presiding deities of this stage, who also arise here in image and myth, include Kali, Hecate and Demeter.

Agony and ecstasy

In the language of the alchemists the *solutio* is the return to the creative womb of ocean to be reborn. How we experience it depends very much on our temperament, possibly on our astrological make-up. For some people it is an exquisite ecstasy. Artefius, a very early Greek alchemist, describes this stage as an overwhelming, drowning, orgasmic rapture. For him, it's about passive bliss, half swooning back to the original womb and half moving in the ecstasy of love towards the higher womb.

Just read his poetry - it doesn't matter if you understand it!

> *Dissolve then Sol and Luna in our dissolving water, which is familiar and friendly and the next in nature unto them and as it were a womb, a mother, an original, the beginning and the end of their life. Thus it behooves you to join consanguinity, or sameness of kind [like attracts like, the attraction of pairs of opposites].*

---

40 See Klossowski de Rola, Pp. 23 ff., for full text and exposition.
41 See Jung, CW 13, para 172.

SEPARATIO

Ignis
Aër
Aqua

Terra

Plate 6b. Separatio

And because Sol and Luna have their origin from this water, their mother, it is necessary therefore that they enter into it again, to wit, into their mother's womb that they may be regenerate, or born again, and made more healthy, more noble and more strong. [42]

---

[42] Artefius: *'Clavis majoris sapientiae'*. In A.E. Waite 1888, Pp. 145-146.

That's Artefius talking about the friendly and familiar return, as the process moves out of the head and into the feeling level, as Sol is dissolved in Luna and Luna melts into Sol.

So, Artefius was into the ecstasy of it all. But it isn't like that for everyone, not in the least! For these people it's a terrific power-struggle, exquisite agony. There is a terrible tension between the opposites, a locked battle between their masculine and feminine sides. They are caught in the attempt to break away from the parent, usually the mother, in order to discover *soul*. The alchemical illustrations are very variable, but the pictures quite often show a dog and a bitch fighting it out in the flask, green and red dragons in mortal conflict, white and black birds fighting together - tearing, rending, devouring. This is the battling.

The words of the *Turba* are very different from those of Artefius. Here is a strange and beautiful passage from this fourteenth century text of the Persian/Arabic tradition, describing the struggle between the masculine and the feminine (within ourselves of course) as they are mixed there in the same womb:

> *The body of that woman who slays her husbands...is full of weapons and poison. Let a grave be dug for that dragon, and let that woman be buried with him, he being chained fast to that woman; and the more he winds and coils himself about her, the more will he be cut to pieces by the female weapons which are fashioned in the body of the woman. And when he sees that he is mingled with the limbs of the woman, he will be certain of death and will be changed wholly into blood.* [43]

The pair feel they are devouring each other, or trying to; it's a rending - somebody has to be torn. Here's where the rapist comes in, the fear of the womb, the vagina with teeth. How many times have men dreamt about the *vagina dentata* and being cut open, castrated? And women have castration dreams about the male, too. This being cut apart is the underbelly of sexuality and ecstasy. He coils himself around her and she around him, but the cutting weapons within her nature cut him open and out flows his blood. The idea is that, with the rampant,

---

[43] *Turba philosophorum*, Sermo LIX, P. 162. In Jung, CW 14, para 15.

Plate 6c. Fermentatio

rapacious, Venusian sexual appetites, as he coils and winds around the woman he will be chained and cut and severed and torn in the processes of love, until he is rendered 'wholly into blood'. When we are still struggling backwards to hold on to the known and the familiar, we tend to see the dark side of the Moon as the shadow of the Sun.

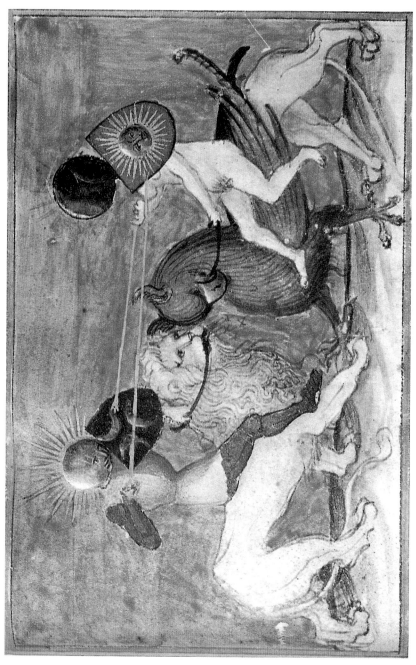

Plate 7. The Sun and the Moon do Battle

Certainly, Sol being dissolved in Luna feels like death to Sol. It's as
though he's being trapped in water, drowned. Our minds swoon. We
think we have a mental grip on the subject, but then, when we're into
a relationship, everything is overwhelmed by the waters. The
masculine in us all is wounded, cut open to let the blood flow, to put
us in touch with our feeling-nature. It's a heart-opening. Of course, it's
an alchemical picture, too. The Turba goes on:

> But when the Philosophers [the alchemists] see him changed into
> blood, they leave him a few days in the sun, until his softness is
> consumed, and the blood dries, and they find [and remove] that
> poison. [44]

That was written by an alchemist with a strong fighting temperament,
who saw it in those terms. The language sounds very impregnable
until, working with it, we realise it isn't so impregnable after all.
Neither is it trying to exclude the sexual; it's about the movement
through and alongside the sexual, from sexual to compassionate, to
become a different form of love.

Plate 7. The Sun and the Moon do Battle - opposite

Here, the lion and the griffin are going to tear each other to pieces if
they can get at each other. The male is astride the lion; the Sun is his
head and the Moon is on his shield. The female figure rides the griffin,
with the Moon as her head but the Sun on her shield. They're opposed,
they're against each other. That is after all how we work, in therapy as
in life. We don't really become aware of the opposites until they are
brought up out of the unconscious and set against each other as a pair
of polarities. Jung said that the opposites cannot be reconciled until
they are made conscious. The whole art lies in bringing them out.

I have an extraordinary guided imagery from a man in his forties. His
father had been a Seventh Day Adventist and he'd been brought up in a
very heavy religious atmosphere. Deeply religious himself, he was also
vegetarian - these don't always go together but in this case it was
important. In the imaging he went through a mirror and was shocked and
horrified at what came up: 'I'm in a jungly place, animal - violence and

---

[44] *Turba philosophorum*, ibid., P. 247.

killing, lots of flesh...' he says, with a look as though he'd walked over a bad-smelling drain, '...flesh, and hermaphroditic figures, some with sexual organs of the opposite gender, some with both male and female organs. There's lots of...' (now, this is horrifying to him but it takes him back to sado-masochistic fantasies he'd had when he was eleven, twelve, fourteen) '...rape, cannibalism, men and women, children and animals fucking, being fucked...' (these are his words) 'eating, being eaten, biting off penises.' And then he said: 'And I whipped Christ and nailed him to the cross. I had an erection throughout, he bled and I revelled in it, and I said to him as I raised the cross, "You, the world of light, keep me down." ' (That's absolutely straight out of the alchemic flask.) 'And Christ from the cross said to me, "In me, dark and light are mingled. You look up and down and don't see the combined depths and heights. I am everywhere and I will not particularise." '

Boom! into his search this came as crudely, as abruptly as that: straight into the middle of every one of his rigidities. Fortunately he'd taped what he'd said, otherwise I think he'd have denied it. The fact that it could come out of *him*, out of his own imagery, blew him up from below - or from above. Then, in active imagination, a wise person said to him, 'Know God as Himself, as crucified Christ *and* as incestuous cannibalism. What else is the Mass?' This man, vegetarian that he was, later said, 'Oh this is terrible - but do you know, I have the most appalling desire for some steak *tartar!*' I said, 'Good, go ahead! For a vegetarian, a new experience.'

Dionysus

That waking dream from a very religious man is a good example of an *enantiodromia*: take something too far in one direction, press it and you'll get into the other side of it. Become too rigidly lopsided and you'll reach the opposite; too far towards heaven and you'll come to hell; too far with hell and there's heaven. There's no point at which agony and ecstasy aren't very close together. And this is Dionysus! The god of ecstasy and wine, madness and orgies, the great lord Dionysus became one of the most important of the Greek gods. King and lord of the dance, of *mardi gras* and festival, he is in the depths of this experience. In myth and legend Dionysus is both the server and the mate of the mother. Whether he is daemonic or ecstatic depends how we experience him. Here is the ecstasy of our mystique, or the mystery of orgasmic sexual glory, or however we wish to see it.

In the 'Inferno', Dante, accompanied by Virgil, goes down into the seven levels of hell. And then he discovers that the journey down has become the journey up - he realises he is coming up again out of hell. It's a spiral process, a double helix. We go 'in the round'. Some people are by nature and tendency more aware of the rising out of the circle; others by nature and tendency are more aware of the descending. We go down to go up; down into earth and water where, fighting for air, we find fire. And, yes, through each of these stages a person may go into a sublime ecstasy, a swooning, orgasmic, overwhelming drowning. This is passive rapture, bliss - very close to the symbiotic merging back into the original mother. Know the ecstasy of it! Caught here, we are looking to become again the original *puer* or *puella*, seeking the child's experience of being taken over and inundated, becoming so much one with the mother that we're lost and don't have to take personal responsibility.[45] It's intensity of experience, of feeling or instinct and it flows all over the place. Nothing is clear or structured, there's no exact meaning in it; it is experience for the sake of experience.

To dissolve boundaries and limits, to let life in, Dionysus is *required*. The idea of the need to incorporate Dionysus is very, very important. The church threw out the devil, putting him down into the underworld and raising God up to heaven. This created tremendous schism and split. Certainly, by the Middle Ages, and later with the Inquisition, the whole feminine principle was pushed down and relegated to the devil. Adam was tempted by Eve: 'It was the woman who gave me the apple to eat - it was not I, Lord - it was she who tempted me!' Sin - the devil - the whole world of the senses! Christ, thin and attenuated in his appearances in icons and paintings of that period, is pure, non-sexual; in a lot of pictures he's still his mother's boy. However, the alchemists' idea is very different. For them, the sixth point of the six-pointed star is the devil's tail. It comes, as we saw, out of the interaction between God and the personality. The alchemists said, 'How can you leave the devil out? If God isn't out there alone but is within, then the devil is

45   The bliss of the infant. See Somers & Gordon-Brown 2002, 'Journey in Depth', P. 81.

also within and must be brought out of the underworld. He is part of human experience.'

Dangers of the *solutio*

Obviously we cannot concentrate only on that venal, lustful side, or we'll keep Dionysus in hell. We can raise earth to heaven, but we must also bring heaven down to earth. Certainly, in the Dionysian picture of the wild, irrational, mad, orgiastic, boundless breaking of all conventional rules and laws and order, the extremes can overwhelm people. Those swooning into alcoholism and drugs are very often struggling through this whole *solutio* process. They can be overwhelmed and taken down (or up) into suicide and death. And at the same time it can lead them to the place which is irrigated, fertilised, enlivened, the place of the spirit. We need to know if somebody is getting blissed out in order to swoon into a regressive oblivion and escape responsibility, or whether, following the same journey, they're looking for new vision, for a new spirit, a new meaning in their lives. Many people I've worked with for alcoholism or drug addiction are in my view undergoing the *solutio* experience; we have to know the depth of it.

Suicide can happen in all the stages, and particularly in the *solutio*. However, we have to know our suicide. Again, is somebody swooning away into the unconscious in order to opt out, because they can't face the process? Or are they going through another threshold into a different level of meaning? Socrates also, under sentence of death, drank the hemlock. In these areas we can never know better, and never know first. The feeling can be disintegration, going under, swooning and drowning, but also, and maybe at the same time, cleansing and purification and baptism. We have to hold that in our hearts as therapists. The greater engulfs the lesser. If the ego is greater than the Self, it will engulf the Self at this stage, and if the Self is greater than the ego, then the Self will do the engulfing. Although the experience may feel the same, the outcome is completely different. We human beings have the struggle and the joy and the ecstasy and the privilege to be part of the creation dance that will help God to proceed with more creation. For God requires humanity.

You see how heretical alchemy is? The water and the wine and the blood are all very close together. Quite frequently you'll see pictures of Christ hanging on a cross, but with a great cluster of grapes below him; or hanging like a serpent on a great bunch of grapes; or a snake will be coiled around a tree with grapes hanging on it. Although a lot of Christians thought such pictures satanic, Dionysus was in fact often placed alongside the image of Christ on the cross: Dionysus, the one who dealt with the feminine principle, being reunited with the figure of Christ - Dionysus and Christ seen as one and the same figure! The alchemists saw Dionysus as the other side of Christ, Christ as the other side of Dionysus. They saw no difference between the transcendent God and God immanent. God is in sexual ecstasy, as in the ecstasy of the orgasmic heart, as in the basis of tantric yoga and the Upanishads - Shakti and Shiva copulating. Whatever tradition we turn to - where is God not? In all our ecstasies, there is God.

And if the masculine principle in us all when first it goes down into the flask should see the feminine principle (the cutting edge, the teeth, the castrating womb) as 'down there', to be used and abused, if in that ecstasy we abuse the other, then we have split it all apart again. Different temperaments will experience the *solutio* differently. The feminine diffusion and wateriness is given outline and definition in the struggle with the masculine. Your strong, gritty person will fight the movement towards the unconscious, struggling for ego-assertion and to hold on to that which the mind knows. The less strong individual will be only too happy to let someone else take over the process and do it for them. If they can get away with it, they'll 'go with it', regress, swoon, fall into the flask and plunge precipitately into the unconscious.

Plate 8. Tying the Dragon - overleaf

The second picture, overleaf, shows the two of them again, but now they're working together. They are holding down the earth dragon of the instincts. They're not *killing* the dragon but tying its feet in favour of love. They're working 'venally', erotically with each other, although they're in opposition. It's a beautiful alchemic statement of the whole process. He's got a golden face, she's dark - dark and light have come together. They are neither killing nor denying their lustfulness, but tying it and turning it into a higher love. So now, in the return of the *solutio*, the battle between the Sun and the Moon is laid to rest and peace. The two are working together in a different way. An individual who reaches this holds it in preparation for what later belongs to the world. The heart of courage, the heart of feeling, the heart of joy and the heart of pain - this is what all the great esoteric traditions mean, the way to understanding is through the doorway of a broken heart. 'Impregnate me with the spirit that I may give birth to the child of love' is a summation of that experience, both alchemically and mystically true.

Drowning in therapy

The *solutio* is to do with our relationship with the collective unconscious. Many of us are lost in the mass, and at this stage it is necessary that we should be. This is the time when we go round looking for people to provide answers for us. We want dependency; we want to be devoted to the guru or to the therapist. The flow of transference and counter-transference is, after all, about *relating*. It's not only about projection as between parent and child, it is the interaction, the relatedness between the therapist and the client. On the one hand, it's the desire to blend: 'I want to be an analyst just like you!' On the other, it's the pulling apart, the trying to separate. 'You're confusing me, disturbing me - upsetting - seducing - overwhelming me! I can't bear you, you're leading me into places I don't understand!' People in the *solutio* may indeed feel drowned in the therapeutic process, submerged in the relationship with the therapist. As Jung would say, if you're drowning, don't just cry out for help. Learn to swim, to become a diver. Out of it then you can bring the pearl of relationship. However, they quite often drift away. 'I can't swim and I don't want to dive. Sorry I came - didn't mean it - going out to find somebody else.' They drift on, drift out, can't take it any longer, float out of the flask.

In our relationships, both we and our clients risk losing our space and boundaries. This is the devouring, the invading, it's the attempted symbiosis, the eating into another person's soul. We're drowning in affect, unconsciously swamped by and swamping another. In terms of the ego, the agent is lust. It's the desire and lust of the ego to consume and claim as its own, to annex the other person. There's all the

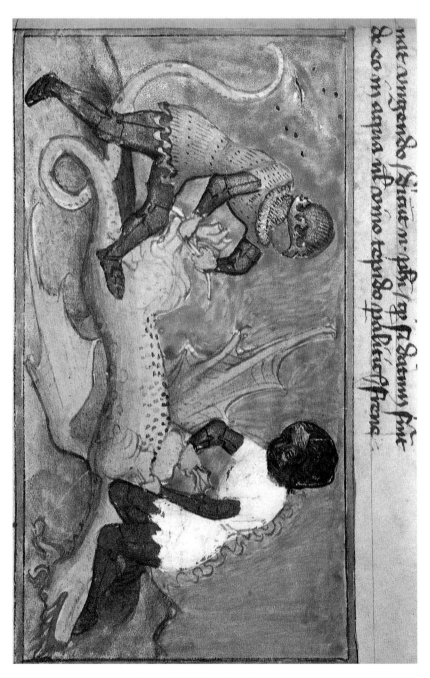

Plate 8. Tying the Dragon

difference in the world between an orgiastic swoon into the original mother, and the separation and dissolving into *samadhi* or *nirvana*. It's the difference between lust and love.

The therapy is tremendously important now as containment, a flask to help hold us in this disintegrating, overwhelming flux. As the flow of tears and of life begins and we lose control, we are walked alongside and held until such time as our boundaries begin to form up again and we come at last to the reintegration. 'Many patient washings!' As in alchemy, so in therapy; the washerwoman has to have a great deal of patience to be there when tears fall, when semen, blood, the liquids of our nature begin to flow; till we can bleed and piss and joy and laugh. Very many clients were told as children, 'Dirty!' (mustn't masturbate!); so all their natural expression of self and selfhood was put on to a fantasy level. Such people are unearthed and so go on treating life at that fantastical, masturbatory level. And that's but one of the things that emerges here. So the therapy can help to hold a shape while a person goes through the ups and downs of relationships and the reintegrating of them. Here is not only the longing, the ecstasy of relationship, but also the terrible fear and horror of - and yearning for - commitment. Commitment is much involved in this. We can mistake the whole Don Juan thing - venal love without commitment - for the process, taking love and life as it passes, like fancy. That's a stage we all need to go through at some point - but not as a way of life.

The therapist sits in quietly through it all and holds a steady centre, a little point of new land in that ocean of flux and flow. It is true in all areas, but especially in the *solutio*, that as therapists we help enormously by encouraging artwork, imagination, dance, music, sculpting. All help to loosen the dry, arid parts, melt the ice and snow within and get the person in flow. Imagery is particularly useful here, and to work with dreams. Dreams come out of the unconscious, and their very fluidity, their moonlit, lunar, non-substantial settings and landscapes, help people to get a grip on earth, to recognise its relevance to their life. The aim is to help the client make a creative penetration, a more individual defining of themselves, an outline, rather than the regressive, incestuous intent to ooze away and climb back into the original womb. It's helping them to free themselves from the collective, to become individual, to meet with and to recognise the transpersonal

COITVS

Virtutes

Plate 9a. Coitus

aspects of the Self within them. It's the Green Lion doing the creative *coitus* (Plate 9a above), defining and outlining the individual, which also honours the other person out there. It's extracting their true feelings from among the false, helping them to be more true to themselves, to the heart of gold, the lion-heart, the heart of courage that begins to emerge out of this combination of masculine and feminine.

Plate 9a. Coitus - **previous page**

This is a glorious drawing of the lion going down into the flask. Look at his tail! In a straight line, zoom! Down, joyfully to penetrate the Moon in the flask. Whoopee! I think this has to be my favourite picture of the lion. A very beautiful thing about the alchemic process is, as we saw, that it's not saying, 'Don't be lustful'. It must have seemed so heretical, from the point of view of Christians of that period, not to say 'You must *deny* Venus!' The alchemist is saying, rather, '*Transform* Venus.' Through the understanding of love and the use of the senses we open up to a deeper kind of loving. There's as important a difference between the passive oblivion of Dionysus and positive new vision, as there is between a swooning back into the original mother and the dissolving into a true *samadhi*. To come to such new vision usually means that we have to be blinded. A 'hoodwink', as it was called, was put on the initiate before initiation. Our eyes are dimmed by the blindfold. People quite often have eye problems at this stage; we can no longer see by the bright light of the sun. It's through our relationships that the ego's eyes are dimmed; we have to learn to see by lunar light, see under water.

Myths of the solutio

The image of the beautiful beloved who is also 'soul' is the *solutio's* development of the masculine. Here are the fire and clarity of the Sun coming down into the cool, dim waters of the Moon, and the feminine takes on her fire so that Sol and Luna dissolve in each other. We know from legend about both the seduction and the ecstasy. Remember Anthony and Cleopatra, the beautiful Serpent of the Nile - that power-struggle? The maiden Circe, Calypso, the nymph, the Lorelei - they too are all about the *solutio*. The music of Wagner is extraordinarily so. Some of it is highly embattled stuff; [46] but also, in comes the beauty of the love-senses; all that drifting, dreaming, melting - 'I merge, I swoon, I long to die'. The last great epic song of Tristan and Isolde burning through their passion is very much of this process. And so the heart of the masculine is opened up. The movement is from Faust and Helen, a venal, Venusian love, to Petrarch and Laura. Abelard and

---

[46] At the beginning of Wagner's opera Tannhåuser, in the Mountain of Venus, the masculine principle shouts, 'Oh Queen, Oh Goddess, let me flee !'

CONIVNCTIO

Plate 9b. Coniunctio

Heloise first came together as lovers; they then became brother and sister, not only because Abelard was castrated but because the nature of their passion turned to something wider than themselves. Something else grew out of the flask and they became more like the alchemist and his *soror mystica*, his soul's sister. The young Dante never touched, probably never spoke to, Beatrice, but she became the beautiful principle out of which his creativity flowed, staying with him as an image of his soul for the rest of his life.

People finding themselves in *solutio* relationships where there is a lot of eroticism or poison may be striving towards a different level or octave. They are discovering the baptismal waters of a new beginning, being cleansed and purified for what is to follow. This baptism is about being immersed in the waters of a very major experience which washes away all the flow of their lives until, later, the higher octaves are reached. It's then that they begin to know both the agony and the ecstasy.

Plate 9b. Coniunctio - **previous page**

So to the first beginnings of the mysterious marriage. This is the coming together of the elements of air, earth, fire and water and their merging in the new womb. A *white* bird flies down; the bird of the soul is beginning to move, entering the process in the flask. The soul and the waters are beginning to come together. The white bird, like the dove, is very often to do with the feminine principle, but later it becomes the bird of pure spirit, the firebird descending with fire on its breast. I'd invite you also to look back to Page 33, where we saw the white bird of the *solutio* once more going down into the dark water in which Sun and Moon are coming together. Remember, everything in the flask is rotating; the fermentation in the bottom in the beginning, as they struggle to come together, has set the ash moving around, and in the whirling it has begun to bring out its own solution, the tears and the ecstasy.

Plate 10. The First Conjunction - **opposite**

At last the king and the queen begin to emerge. They haven't got there yet - it's still a struggle! This beautiful, beautiful picture of the *mysterium coniunctionis* from the *'Rosarium philosophorum'* shows the stages in which venal love, lust, is converted in the flask, so that the *two* of them are being reborn through their mutual love and understanding of the battle. It's the higher womb. The green and gold are beginning to show through. Sol and Luna are together; the Sun's above and the Moon is down in the fluid. She's underneath with a silver crown on her head and he's on top with a golden crown - all he

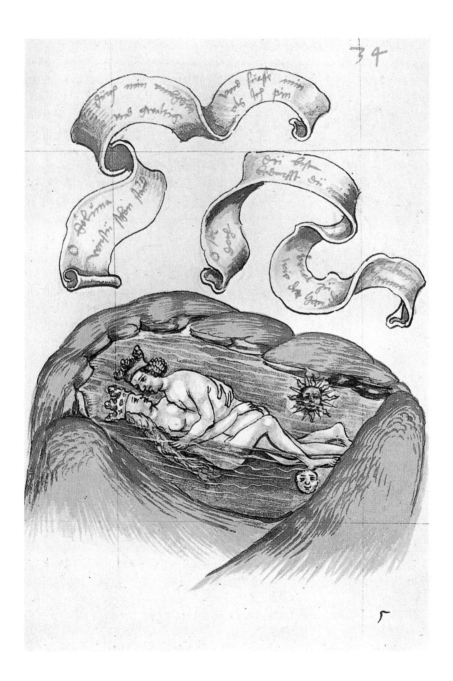

Plate 10. The First Conjunction - *Mysterium coniunctionis*

is wearing. However, this is not yet the fixed, true marriage, the *hieros gamos*. This picture implies the coming together of the alchemist with his *soror mystica*. It is the linking of masculine and feminine at the horizontal level, leading towards the mating of brother and sister, not as incest but as friendship. Out of what had once been possession and lust and desire for each other, *friendship* begins to emerge. This beginning of their working together is the finishing of the old incestuous urge towards the mother or the father. It is the movement towards the full Moon, towards the Blessed Virgin, towards Sophia the wise woman, Tara, Kuan-Yin. It is the totality of hope and redemption as the emergent new Sol becomes king regnant. Soon he will be married; soon the nuptials will take place, the mysterious conjunction with the queen. However, this is still not the goal; this is fairy gold, the beautiful gold which (pray God) we all experience. The copper colour of Venus is coming through, but it is not the final, absolute gold, not yet the sacred marriage of Father Creator and Mother Earth, Mother Water. Still, this *mysterium coniunctionis* is quite a good stage to reach! All that painful *separatio*, drowning and being overwhelmed, feeling dissolved, unfixed, alone, has helped us through. It has led us towards a new and greater understanding and acceptance of our instinctual, feeling, Venus-like side. Now we recognise in it not just the organ of sexuality but the organ of the heart.

Death of the King and Queen

After this wonderful coming together of head and heart, Sol *et* Luna, male and female in the *albedo* phase, many alchemical illustrations next show them lying dead. Venus-love is very beautiful, but it can also bind and hold a person back on the journey. The king and queen have gone through the purgation of dying to that sort of love in order to move over to a further stage. Soon, at last, is coming the mysterious marriage, *hieros gamos*, the conjunction between the masculine and the feminine sides of ourselves that can bring into being a new life. This is what puts men and women closest to creation, to the divine: we can by our conjunction create new life. Some of us aren't able to do that physically but the promise is that we can do it inwardly, helping the creation of a quality of being, the power of love in the world, a new birth of understanding. Paracelsus, quoting alchemists who had gone before him, said that the true agent is love. We are working with that true agent as the alchemist does, returning to the womb for rebirth. Beginning to love and accept ourselves, we're able to love and accept the 'otherness' of the other, and it's in the heart of relationship that we come to this absolutely major experience. Desire and sentiment have a lot to do with the love of power, which underlies much of what we call our 'love'. But now we are working out the difference between the love of power and the power of love. So we help to create the double helix of the staff of Hermes, which doctors have taken as their emblem for the healing process.

More dreams of the *solutio*

The *solutio* isn't all about the male getting lost in the female; sometimes it's the masculine in the woman that needs to be lost in the feminine. A very intellectual woman aged thirty-six, a real father's daughter, extremely clever in her work, trying to do everything through her head, had the following dream - and she didn't know anything about the *solutio*. It was part of the healing process going on within her as her heart began to open. 'I am taken into a cave holding a flaming brand as a light' (that's her intellect, as she later said). 'The cave is all white, made of salt' (salt is one of the alchemic components of the feminine principle). 'Hundreds of children are kept down there. Cows and horses are licking the salt and are in danger of dying of thirst. I know I must save them by penetrating further down the spiral opening to a deep underground lake.' (Her intellect is deciding it's going to save all these instinctual aspects of herself, which is very important, but the dream is saying it's not the way to do it.) 'But how to get them there? The children start to laugh and dance around me. My torch goes out but the salt casts a silvery glow. I struggle to get away from them and to lead them, but am jostled and forced down to lick the salt. It is bitter at first, and then sweet like honey. I start to cry and the children, cows and horses lick me all over and comfort me with their rough tongues.'

That was a *woman*! Her dream was of going into the feminine principle, the underground cave with the pool at its centre, in among the children, the realm of the instincts, there with the cows and the horses. She was so frightened of pain and grief and despair and losing control that it took at least three years of work, plus a lifetime thrown in, for her to stop trying to lead all her instincts by the head. And as she began to weep, as the waters of her life began to flow, as the light of her brand went out and she could see a little more by the light of the feminine principle reflected from the salt, so by degrees she was healed. They 'licked her with their rough tongues'. Then she too could lick the salt - bitter, feminine - and at last open up to joy and life and love and laughter, as well as to sexuality. *Solve*, solve: the dreamer is solving her intellectual problems by being transferred to the realm of feeling and instinct.

Another woman, having heard about the pelican or swan or phoenix penetrating its own breast, told me this dream. (She was born in Africa, so 'flamingo' may have had some particular meaning for her.) 'It is dusk, with a magnificent red sunset. Then I see that it isn't a sunset at all: the sky is covered in millions and millions of flamingos. Their colour is very important, and the setting has to do with the extremes. All at once the flamingos start dropping, and I see pools all round me. I think they are pools of water, close to me, reflecting the sunset; but they aren't, they are pools of blood, the blood of all these flamingos. And they are dying; vast quantities of this blood covering the earth. And I am desperately trying to resuscitate them. And there's a very old man, really angry at what is going on, but also stopping me doing anything.'

I sensed that at a deeper level the dream was about her feeling for the earth, or perhaps a precursor of some deep experience of relating: the interacting and coming together of the red *sublimatio* and the white *solutio* experience. She said, 'For years and years I've been coming back to the feeling of complete despair, of being unable to do anything about those dying flamingos.' She felt it could have been about her tendency to be extremely open to the collective. 'After all,' we agreed, 'we don't need to save *all* of the birds of the collective - just one!' Maybe the old man was saying, 'Let it be, let the flamingos leave the earth in their own way, don't try to impose yourself between that and the collective experience.' Bitterness is cleared in the *solutio* process. 'Without bitterness' is a very strong alchemical phrase. Some people emerge the other side without any bitterness, any remorse. One man went through what could only be described as crucifixion in every realm - hands broken, feet broken, back broken. There didn't seem one vestige of hope for him. And he came out a totally joyous human being. He came through the *calcinatio*, through the *solutio*, and when I last saw him he was in the *coagulatio*, and without bitterness.

Cauda pavonis in the *solutio*

The *albedo* is like the dawn, the promise of the new Sun appearing over the horizon. Remember that dream in which the pool became cloudy and there was a milky glow, moon-fluid? This is the falling of the dew of grace, dew falling as the sap of life, as grace descending. It is the *aqua permanens,* the water that will be incorruptible and pure, the amniotic fluid of the higher womb that is to come into being. Out of the quiet milkiness at the bottom of the flask now begins the scintillating flashing of colour which gives one the heart and the guts to go on to the next stage. The flashing of rainbow colours and their starry quality suggests the beginning of the building of the rainbow bridge of the esoteric system, the bridge between spirit and matter over which human beings were said to be able to go to God. It's a sign that the movement of the *solutio* process in the flask must be coming to an end; it is once more the *cauda pavonis*.[47] One woman, separating herself from her father and at the same time struggling in a crisis with her daughter, had an image of peacocks which she felt was to do with the *cauda pavonis*. Putting it into perspective in therapy, she found that the birds were about her creativity, and she went out and bought herself some peacock feathers. 'They're holding me together,' she said. They represented hope within the midst of all the darkness of separation and transformation. And it may be that this peacock's tail is the rainbow after the storm has passed, when the light of the new Sun begins to catch the watery drops. Here is assurance of the final ending of the process, and of colour to come. Through the darkness and confusion, through the mist and the whiteness, there now emerge the shimmering colours of what will one day be the diamond body, the pure diamond itself.

---

[47] The *cauda pavonis* was said by some alchemists, as we have seen (P. 36 above), to have appeared between the *nigredo* and *albedo*, as the black went to grey ash in the oncoming white. However, a number held that it is seen again now. Whether it comes between *calcinatio* and *solutio*, or within or after the *solutio* is altogether uncertain. Jung implies the former in CW 12, para 263. However, in para 334 he says it is *within* the *solutio*, after the washing and before the whitening; and para 400 (XX), has it as a result of the eclipse of the sun in the *coagulatio*. Various notes in CW 13 imply it heralds completion of the *opus* and attainment of the goal.

End of the *solutio*

Although the alchemical process is going on for anyone who is to any degree on the journey, reading of it somehow makes us much more conscious and aware. If you, the reader, find yourself in this watery stage, if it is anything more than just a series of words for you, you can't be unchanged by it. It could help to loosen things up for you. Changes do occur in people's lives when they come in contact with this alchemy. I know that I am changed by it. That's why I address it with care and with caution. When this stage is done we will have a broken and a porous heart. The alchemic saying for the end of the *solutio* is, 'If thou knowest how to moisten this dry earth with its own water, thou wilt loosen the pores of this earth.' It's about becoming porous. From mediæval times to the age of romanticism, to be *gentle* - gentle-woman, gentle-man - was seen as a noble quality. To be porous, to melt, become more fluid, more flexible, to be able to say, 'It's both this *and* that', had the noble quality of gold, the quality to solve problems of the head (*solve*, again) by including the heart and not leaving it out.

Why throughout the process didn't the couple smash the flask? It remains a great mystery. Something kept the seal on the alembic, holding it, preventing escape. What? Mercurius? the Self? Fate? An act of love? Something is at work, and we may glimpse that this something is - meaning and purpose. A good word for it is love. There are some beautiful *solutio* statements in both the Old Testament and the New. We can go right through the Bible or the Koran and find continuous reference to these things. I'm not saying that the Bible was written as an alchemic text, but the alchemists' view was that every profound book reveals the alchemy at work within it. Once a person has something of these books under their belt, everything opens up in the most extraordinary way. In Isaiah we find, *'And the Lord shall - satisfy thy soul in drought - and thou shalt be like a watered garden, and like a spring of water whose waters fail not.'* [48] Again, *'The wilderness and the solitary place shall be glad for them; and the desert shall rejoice, and blossom as the rose.'* [49] Then, in the Song of Solomon, a statement about the four stages of alchemy: *'For lo, the*

[48] Isaiah 58, 11.
[49] Isaiah 35, 1.

winter is past, the rain is over and gone; the flowers appear on the earth; the time of the singing of birds is come, and the voice of the turtle is heard in our land.' [50]

In the New Testament John tells us about the woman of Samaria. Jesus says, *'Whosoever drinketh of the water that I shall give him shall never thirst; but the water that I shall give him shall be in him a well of water springing up into everlasting life.'* [51] John again quotes Christ: *'If any man thirst, let him come unto me, and drink. He that believeth on me - out of his belly shall flow rivers of living water.'* [52] And there's that extraordinarily obscure statement, which becomes luminously clear in the light of all this: *'Except a man be born of water and of the spirit, he cannot enter into the kingdom of God.'* [53]

---

[50] The Song of Solomon 2, 11-12.

[51] St. John 4, 14.

[52] St. John 7, 37-38.

[53] St. John 3, 5.

The Transducers

CHAPTER SIX

COAGULATIO

This is what we do on Monday morning after the heights of Sunday
The gold needs the darkness in order to be seen

Fire of Earth

Many of the later alchemists left the *coagulatio* out, or rather, they ran *solutio*, *coagulatio* and *sublimatio* together as one. As we've seen, the stages are highly variable. However, I go back to the earlier and Eastern traditions and again seek out this third stage; as modern alchemists we have to be aware of it. By its name it's that which coagulates. The colour is yellow, so it is called *citrinitas*. It still has a touch of the white *albedo*, the milky fluid at the bottom of the flask, so it's a yellow-white. This is the first hint of the gold to come, a glint of yellow-gold, moving towards what later becomes red-gold, the final gold of the *rubedo*. As the element of the *calcinatio* was fire and of the *solutio* water, so the element of the *coagulatio* is earth. This is the 'fire of earth', the trial by earth. I find it coming up frequently in therapy as a distinct stage in itself. It's also known as *fixatio*,[54] the fixing, embodying and grounding of all that we have worked through and discovered and un-learned in the previous stages. It's 'giving substance to', when matter or substance is revealed to be coagulated spirit. Very many of us know it. We need to be helped through it, because at this stage too we can feel like giving up. It sometimes seems as if we are nailed to matter. I believe that here at a very profound level we have the mystery of the incarnation. Spirit and matter are one and the same thing, the two faces of one coin, the two ends of one spectrum. The image is of the Christ nailed to the cross, fixed on that tension of opposites between the vertical and the horizontal. He becomes spirit later, but this is the stage of the fixing.

---

[54] See P. 34 *Fixatio*.

The Androgyne

We saw how by the end of the *solutio* the lovers are very often pictured as two corpses. They're lying side by side in a glass coffin at the bottom of the flask, not so much knackered as having died - died to being only masculine *or* feminine. And after the death there now appears in many of the drawings a new figure: a single torso, with male and female genitals and a double head. The two of them are beginning to come out together. This is the emergence of the androgyne, not only the physical but the spiritual marriage of the pairs of opposites. It feels like an ending; and the later alchemists did often see this end to the *solutio* as a finish, a triumph: out of the struggle comes the synthesis, the marriage where the two have become one. Surely all that is left is to move towards the *sublimatio*, the raising? It's as though a person, having come a very long way, were now ready for the sublime *rubedo* stage.

So male and female, *yang* and *yin*, [55] *Sol et Luna*, have become one in the flask, in Mercury. Mercury, or Hermes, messenger of the gods, is now linking earth and heaven, heaven and earth, spirit and matter, revealing them as one and the same thing. However, he is still very tricky. The work here is to coagulate the volatile Mercury. Nowadays we'd say there needs to be a connection between the ego or personality and the Self. Poor old ego, here it is '...*with its head all beaten around, Roasted and toasted and pulled under ground, Scrubbed up and melted and washed-out and drowned...*' and now, having been hung on a line to dry so there's nothing left, it's brought in again! With this comes the testing of how much inner and outer reality the ego can take. If it's to wake up again after having been basted and roasted and multiply washed, if it's to be allowed out to function in the external world, then how much can it stand, how much can it *with*stand, *under*stand? There is danger in waking up. It's why so many of us stay asleep. Coming back to ourselves can be very painful, as when a limb comes out of numbness and hurts like hell. 'Now I remember who I am and what I'm about. Oh the waste, the awful wastage of the years! I've wandered such a long way from myself, from home; I was lost in a labyrinth, I'd lost my thread.' Typical words are: 'heavy, bogged down, flat, bored, tired, weary, disillusioned'. As the heat is applied and reapplied we say, 'Not

[55] *Yin* and *yang* are the great feminine and masculine principles of the Taoist tradition. See Chapter 8 below.

again! What's it all been for, after all these years?' But it's the ego through which the Self is to be expressed in the external world, linking the spiritual with the material. If out of this earth comes our understanding, the Self stands with us and we withstand.

Plate 11. Six Alchemical Pictures, Later Stages

When this *coagulatio* stage is completed, we shall have the true *sublimatio*. Here already are six different alchemical ways of speaking of the completed stage ahead, each saying much the same thing. The prime themes are death and resurrection after the mystical wedding; the separating out of the opposites and their bringing together in the androgyne; rebirth and exaltation. Many of the symbols will be recognised: Mercury with his caduceus, the king and the queen, the bird pecking its own breast, the crowned eagle, the lion and the Sun. These pictures speak for themselves through their imaginative power and coherence.

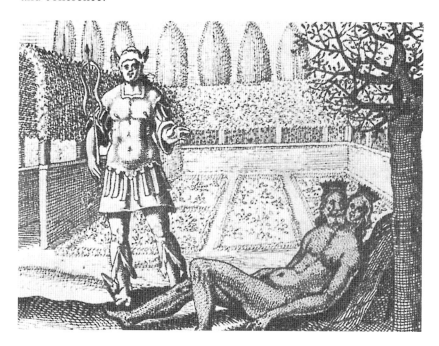

Plate 11a - Mercurius and the Androgyne

Here we see our Mercurius, recognisable by his staff and by his winged sandals or boots. His rod of Hermes is the double helix of life, the magical wand of twining snakes. This is again the healing rod, and here is the healer stepping out of the flask. The Hermes who first went into the flask - Mercury, Quicksilver - now comes out of the union of *Sol et Luna*. We recall how Mercurius is many things: he is the flask, he is the alchemist, he is the *prima materia*, he is in the tricky middle stages within the flask - and here he is emerging from it as the Philosophers' Son. With his left hand he is pointing to the figures of the king, now made one in the androgyne. They are waking up out of their death that followed the *solutio*. Of one flesh, one body, twin-headed, they're lying under the tree of life in the philosophical walled garden. This is the outcome of the early, original marriage. Though they were not winged, yet even then they had their crowns. Now is the time for the *hieros gamos*, the chymical wedding, the true, the sacred marriage which will bring into life a whole being.

Plate 11b - The Raising of the Androgyne

Here they are again, their faces changed, lying on the sarcophagus as androgyne. Now they are lifted and raised from the sepulchre. This picture is another form of the great marriage. Sapientia, winged and wise Earth, is beside them; the Great Mother, as Wisdom, is raising the single body out of the Sun and the Moon (note their heads). Remember the raven or eagle who was around when the alchemist was sitting in the split, speaking of the abyss and the need for a death? Here, that dark bird of the *nigredo* is coming down towards them as an eagle on the wing; still dark, but crowned and flying, helping to raise this married pair to their eternal kingdom. They are going to be reborn as *Sol et Luna*. This is the *hieros gamos*, the marriage in heaven, and all around them is the new Earth.

Plate 11c - Sol et Luna Reborn

So now they have been born again. Here is Sapientia walking with the baby Sun and Moon, Wisdom holding the children by the hand. Children in terms of wisdom, they have become children of earth and children of heaven. She's holding them together by wisdom beneath 'the raincloud of knowable things'. [56] The gracious dew of heaven is dropping from the clouds, the rain of divine grace falling from heaven, creative spirit descending to make the earth fecund.

---

[56] Attributed to Patanjali. See Alice Bailey 1934, P. 456.

Plate 11d - Emerging from the Flask

The flask has set them free - and out they come! The two of them climb out of the baptismal bath, out of the furnace, the *vas*, and the phoenix is beside them. This is the firebird once more, the pelican pecking its own breast and letting the blood fertilise the earth.

The next picture, Plate 11e, overleaf, shows them standing on the earth, on the ground. The two have tamed the Green Lion and overcome the basilisk. A reptile or scorpion hatched by the serpent from the cock's egg, the basilisk can blast by its breath or look. It is a beast sometimes shown as salamander or snake; here it's a cross between a lizard and a scorpion. This creature has stung itself to death in the flask and now lies dead before them. [57] And here's the alchemic tree bearing in its branches seven stages of alchemy, all now shining with gold - all those suns! The two of them are standing by the tree. Each of the seven branches has the Sun and Moon on it, incorporating

[57]   According to the Book of Azoth, Eve in Paradise was seduced by the 'infernal basilisk'. See Jung, CW 13, para 180.

Plate 11e - The Alchemic Tree

the seven *chakras*, [58] the seven levels of human experience and the seven stages of initiation.

In the last picture, Plate 11f, we see our friend the lion again; but now at the end, as flask, he's revealed as a king, a lord with stars all over him, showing that he's now a heavenly, a celestial lion. He's disgorging the Sun again, the pure gold, but now it's the eternal Sun that has arisen. The Green Lion makes things concrete. What he is regurgitating at the end is the new earth, the new world, the city of God. He also stands for the wild excesses of the ego that have needed to be tamed in this process. [59] If you look down into the water you can see both the Sun and the Moon: the original ego-sun, the one that submitted and went down into the water, is now beginning to come out of the water and if you turn the picture upside down you'll find in his

---

[58] *Chakras* are a system of seven subtle energy bodies aligned between the base of the spine and the crown of the head.

Plate 11f - The Green Lion Regurgitates the Sun

reflection a feminine face. This is yet another way of speaking of the conjunction; or it can be seen as a new ego coming up out of the water, a personality that, like it or not, has to live in the world. So the ego that was in the flask, calcified, dissolved, apparently suffocated and killed, has been coagulated and now it's coming out again. There's a wonderful, totally inclusive alchemical statement! It's the eternal Sun that now emerges, the everlasting part, and the ego becomes its agent. Again, it is the eternal *son*, the Philosophers' Son, that has come out of the personality. The ego can become an agent for the God. Now the Self pervades earthly life - 'Not my way but Thy way' - and heaven and earth, earth and heaven, are linked together.

---

[59] Exactly as depicted in Norse mythology. At the last great battle of Ragnarok, Baldur the son of Odin is slain and the Wolf Fenrir, chained from time eternal, breaks his chains and swallows the sun and all hell breaks loose. That's a bit like the 'Twilight of the Gods'. There are floods and God knows what, then out of that rise the Gimli, and the new people. There was Asgard before, and the Aesir - different Wagnerian terms. And you get the new reign, the new world, new beginning, new civilisation. But in that story it's a wolf swallowing the Sun, and he's been chained, held back. It's an exact parallel - for Lion read Wolf.

Thus these 'impregnable' pictures render up their meaning. Whatever has occurred, whatever we've experienced, whatever we are beginning to express through the processes of the flask, it needs to be made solid and actual. There's a lot here about commitment, staying with it, taking a stand. This is what we do on Monday morning after the heights of Sunday. This is where the person can become agent for the Self: God needs man.

Dreams of the *coagulatio*

A change of consciousness takes place within the *coagulatio*. People dream of razed landscapes, of things falling from on high and hitting the earth, crashing from above, anchoring, earthing, grounding. Here is a dream from a man aged forty-nine, an industrialist with cardiac problems: 'I am walking between an avenue of high pillars. I look up into clear sky and suddenly see a huge, round rock or meteorite dropping at an incredible pace. Somehow I catch it on my shoulders and brace myself to hold it. My feet are driven into the ground by its impact and my whole body is in tremor. But I stand.' It's very alchemical. He couldn't have known, didn't know, much about the alchemic process, but he withstood the impact. He woke, he said, with a great sense of strength, stability and sureness. 'I went in next day and quit my job - it felt terrific.' I said, 'Now hold on a bit, not so fast!' But he'd done it, he'd made his decision, that was it, and there's no doubt that he was right and I wasn't. He needed to do something like that. He made a drawing of the terrific impact of this weight coming in and hitting him, some rock from heaven which he held. He was driven, pushed into his ground, his body was in tremor, 'but I stand'. This was *him*, and what he did after that was him too. It was very important.

Saturn

The presiding deity of the *coagulatio* is Saturn, once more at his great work. Saturn, throughout mythology and particularly in astrology, [60] has been known as the inhibitor, the frustrator, the one who blocks and confronts and tests us all the way through till we're cleansed of the dross. Saturn is the refining fire, and now the pot goes into this new fire and a fine glaze is put on to see whether it will sustain its colour.

---

[60]   For the astrology around Saturn, see Reinhart 1996/2002. For a concise account of the Greek myth, see Pp. 4-5.

Or again, Saturn is the one who tempers the steel, striking it to see whether it rings true. He tests the quality of the gold: will it just melt away, or will it stand adamant for ever? In the *calcinatio* Saturn was the opening, the cracking up of the old earth. Here he's the grounding in a new earth. He is now the initiator, the door-opener, for this time *Jupiter* is with him.[61] Who knows, maybe the Christians had it wrong? Driving Saturn out was probably a great error. Rather than Satan the devil, was he not Lucifer the fallen angel? [62] Son of the morning, Lucifer came down to earth to live in the Underworld, and is continuously testing us with a refining fire. We know from the story that Lucifer, whose name means 'bringer of light,' pre-empted and stole power (like Prometheus, whom we shall meet later). Maybe that fallen son of light was there to tempt the strength of the strong. I suspect that, in some way whose nature I do not understand, humans are also helping Lucifer back into heaven - another heretical suggestion, but it's an important statement, very much in the Gnostic tradition. Hence the Christian idea of the Redeemer, the redemptive Christ-figure, as a medial principle, as gateway from matter to heaven and from heaven to matter again. [63]

Dangers of the *coagulatio*

So Jupiter and Saturn are here together, Jupiter with the raising and Saturn with the fixing principle. But there's a risk in having the two of them together. This is a very dangerous point of *hubris*. Will we become too high, ungrounded, unworldly, volatile, 'too good for this world' and too big for our boots? Staying with it, taking a stand, giving substance to - this is very important. If we are inflated, on cloud nine, exalted, carried up, the need is to be brought back down. We have to

---

61 Originally a sky spirit, associated with lightning and thunderbolt, Jupiter has links with the upper or intuitive mind and with our fundamental religious urge. Later the chief of the Roman gods, giver of victory, he is identified with the Greek Zeus. See Greene 1977, P. 40-41, for an astrological description of Jupiter.

62 The Concise Oxford Dictionary tells us that Lucifer is: the planet Venus when it appears in the sky before sunrise; the morning star; the light-bringer. Also that it is by a misunderstanding that Lucifer is also held to be Satan, the rebel archangel, before his fall. (In Isaiah 14, 12 the Hebrew epithet 'shining one', translated as 'Lucifer' in the Vulgate, is applied to the king of Babylon.) He is now chiefly in the phrase 'as proud as Lucifer'.

63 Of course, Christ was a much later figure; we'd had the same principle in Shri Krishna and in Odin, in the same kind of story.

be weighted with the leaden weight of Saturn, held to earth, made to incorporate it, to coagulate and through that process to give substance to spirit. However, not so weighted that we lose the lift of Jupiter. There's a lovely letter from Jung to his dear friend Richard Wilhelm. [64] He writes that he must keep on telling him that he is '*too important* for our Western world' to melt away or get ill or otherwise disappear. 'Wicked desire' should pin him to the earth so that his work might go on. Jung could feel Wilhelm becoming of the other world, unworldly, and in fact Wilhelm died not long after.

Eating problems

The alchemists taught about making the stone adamant so that it would stand. Now Saturn's lead, the thwarting of the conscious will by the desire of the inner Sun, itself becomes the initiating principle. Mercury, that free spirit, is being connected with outer Saturnian reality and groundedness. As there's a possibility that some people with anorexia are linked with the *calcinatio* and stripped down to the bone, so, for a number of others, weight problems may have to do with the *coagulatio*. These people have worked through a great deal. Now, just as they want to fly, feeling at last they have wings, they find themselves being held down by Saturn's weight. Are they holding and anchoring themselves, part-consciously helping their mercurial spirit to get itself earthed? Volatile Mercury is dangerous. Are they grounding themselves? Is it about dignity, incorporation, adding substance, adding weight? Or may they be struggling with a *resistance* to earth? Do they have an outside life which, because of their exquisite sensitivity within, is just too painful?

Alchemist as initiator

This is quite a mature stage. Many people are in their fifties by the time they hit the *coagulatio*; some come to it earlier, but really getting into this stage usually takes the best part of a lifetime. There's no doubt that it is a *magnum opus*. We may not know who we are or where we're going, but we begin at last to know who we are *not*, where we are *not*

---

[64]   Letter, 26th April 1929, the year Richard Wilhelm and Carl Jung published 'The Secret of the Golden Flower'. See Letters I, P. 63.

going - and that takes *half* a lifetime. The benign alchemist is working. That which has to die really begins to die at last. Hence the many alchemical images here of crosses and deaths and coffins. This is the end - and the end is where it starts from. It is the testing into which many are called but very few are chosen. It's the desert place, that no-place between reality. In Paracelsus's version of this stage of the initiating processes (the rites of passage, the initiation of adulthood which is what this is really about) the High Priest would say to the one applying for initiation:

> *Thine is not a wedding garment.*
> *Magic has opened thy heart and made thee known;*
> *therefore even as gold and silver*
> *must thou be refined from blemish, and tested.*
> *Seven times more severely than gold and silver*
> *is cleansed of its dross by fire,*
> *must thou be tried.*
> *This is demanded of thee:*
> *Thy transient wealth belongeth to another.*

The body

'Thy transient wealth belongeth to another.' Eastern, especially Indian, alchemists emphasise that the body and the instincts must be incorporated. They cannot be left out. Those who have been 'pushed out of the body' now need help to honour it, for it is also spirit - spirit is earth, but earth is also spirit. In his 'Visions Seminars', Jung said that individuation can only take place if we first return to the body, to our earth; only there does it become true. [65] The Self is born from the body. Individuation requires the body, the body pays the expenses and it costs not less than everything. 'An expenditure of a life is required.' This more than anything, added Jung, gives meaning to pathology: the body can no longer be left out; it has to be incorporated.[66] And it requires commitment, sacrifice. 'Sacrifice' comes from *sacer facere*, to make sacred. Nothing can be sacrificed for ever. When a great sacrifice

---

[65] See Jung 1930-34.

[66] See the address given by Jung on May 10th, 1930 in Memory of Richard Wilhelm. Cary Baynes' translation is in Wilhelm 1931, Pp. 148-149. R.F.C. Hull's translation is in Jung 1966, 'The Spirit in Man, Art, and Literature', CW 15, para 95.

has taken place, it will later return in a changed form. And then a resistant and healthy body must be ready for it, able to meet the shock of such a great transformation. Jung pointed out that this spiritual crisis may be of such dimensions that it means death, should the body be weakened by disease; for the one who was sacrificed now holds the sacrificial knife and of him who was the sacrificer a death may now be demanded. Honouring both the outer *and* the inner, we consciously assume responsibility for practical, earthly, bodily life. Those who go through the process of individuation, said Jung, certainly don't come out any younger; as a rule they age very much. The bird of wisdom settles only on a snowy roof!

But also there has to be a refining process, where the very substance of the body is raised to a higher frequency to carry the charge of spiritual energy. Otherwise there'd be an implosion (or explosion), a short-circuiting. Certain people have a quality about their substance which directly reflects the quality of their spirit. They have a delicacy, a refinement of atomic structure, an extraordinary vitality. Quite often they're not physically robust, but this vitality is a totally different thing, almost a transubstantiation. There's an actual light - a lightness in texture. It's shown in drawings and paintings as an aura or halo around the heads of saintly figures.

Illness

I do believe there is a place for illness. It's been so much part of the human condition for so long. Quite a lot of the illnesses people get at this stage, including some forms of cancer, are part of the re-atomisation required by the physical body so that it can bear pure spirit. When something is being refined and purified, it is put through fire and tension, and this applies equally to the body. Now, instead of life's getting easier, by the grace of God the heat is reapplied. Just when a client feels, 'I've gone through all of this, stayed with it, honoured it! Now I'm in the clear!' their back cracks up, symptoms emerge, they find they've got some illness. Ailments they thought they'd got rid of (or paid you to get rid of for them!) start to make their mysterious reappearance. The very effort and strain that have brought about this major achievement within the flask may have set up a process that has to go full circle. It's such an important stage. It may be that the last thing to go as the tensions are released is the symptom. At last the body, that miraculous temple of the spirit, has been able to let go of some of the stresses it had carried through the years. However, when this happens to us, not realising what it's all about, many of us go into guilt, shame and horror at what we call our pathology. Inner and outer are beginning to reveal themselves as one reality. 'Surely I'm all right now, moving towards health?' It's one of the most flabbergasting, difficult and painful things for a person to have the knowledge of the *coagulatio* - and, 'Look! Now up I come with a physical illness!'

Symptom as symbol

Traditional stories of the beggar and the leper show there is nothing too menial, too dirty, too wretched not to be full of divinity. The whole of the living spirit of God and of the Christ is here. If someone were fully through the *coagulatio* stage, everything would be known to be divine. God would be seen everywhere, in every grain of flour in the bakery. I don't know the nature of it, I don't understand it, I'm still working on it but, as I said, I think that here we're dealing with the mystery of the incarnation. It is why the god takes form, is made incarnate. This is why each human person can become God. There is no division between spirit and matter; they are one and the same thing. Illness is a brilliant and miraculous imaginative language containing within itself a symbolic, metaphoric meaning for the person to read. The holistic therapies, so well-meant, may do a great disservice here. They can be outrageous to people's pathology! Fighting against mechanistic excesses, too many of them have gone to the opposite extreme, contriving all the time towards perfect health, even partial health. They say life's *all* about healthiness, wellness. The answer is, so it is - except when it's not. There's all the difference in the world between being whole, and being free of symptoms. Biography shows that the great sages have rarely escaped physical illness. Despite the 'incorruptible body of the spirit', we're still living in a corruptible earthly body. I'm not talking now about the lesser kind of symptom, which can readily be seen as a symbol. Such a symptom probably *can* be shifted, and it's part of the client's and our work to try to move through it to a greater wholeness. However, sometimes we are faced with malformations and deformations of the body which are *not* coincident with malformation or deformation of the soul, or with people with intransigent or terminal illnesses who have been made to feel that they *ought* to be able to get themselves better. 'If only you handled your stroke differently, went on the right diet, you would be cured,' they're told, and an enormous weight of guilt is given them to add to what else they have.

Active imagination, however, can translate us again to the thinking of earlier times, where many illnesses, particularly the dire, intransigent kind, were seen to be visitations of the god. When he went into a near-schizoid episode after his break with Freud, Jung tells us that, to the extent to which he could translate his emotions into images, he was calmed and inwardly reassured. [67] This calming and reassuring is very important, the waiting on it until it coheres, coagulates, crystallises. Hold it. We don't understand, we can't know the fullness of it. But stay with it. Give it external form to help the holding. We can see illness as a time to be quiet, to be with God in the *meditatio*, the *contemplatio*, those major modes of the alchemist. And so in transpersonal work we frequently invite the body to act out the images that come up in long guided fantasies.

For yet other people, those relatively free from symptoms, it's dangerously easy to leave the body out, take off in flight, move out from the very thing that one is about. As therapists, we help them to stay with it. We've seen how people in the *solutio* feel drowned in the therapeutic process. Now, in the *coagulatio*, they fly off, they slip away. 'Fine!' they declare. 'That's it, thank you very much!' 'Well, you may not altogether like it,' we respond, 'but maybe you could stick around with this one?' 'Bye, lovely to have met you, here's a box of chocolates, a bunch of flowers!' And they vaporise themselves!

Dying

It is the same with dying: we flee it. Toe to toe and inch by inch, we try to push it away. Many in the medical profession believe it's a defeat to let somebody die. However, not so very long ago, to die was seen

---

[67] Jung 1961, 'Memories, Dreams, Reflections', P. 201.

not as somebody going whimpering to defeat, but as a privilege. Then we could listen to the one who had come from heaven to fetch us. The god was pictured as coming to take us back up the ladder created between earth and heaven, taking the person who had attained and achieved home over the rainbow bridge. And it was to be hoped they would be born to something else. Certainly, when it's the true *coagulatio*, something in us dies. It's as if the touch of the soul is too powerful for the body and, as we saw, a death is required. It is probably not a physical death. Some people feel they may die, but don't. However, others do, and this can make a lot of sense. It has been my fortunate experience to see many, many people die, and frequently there is a major breakthrough at the threshold of death. This really touches the meaning of illness. We are getting reborn, and you can't be reborn if you haven't died - once at least.

The Therapist

I suppose (to bring it back modestly and small) if we wish to be therapists we hope also to have the guts to stay in the flask, to sit in with ourselves through the air, earth, fire and water, the dry, moist, warm and cold of our own and other people's lives. It's the courage to stay steady. It's knowing how to go to heaven and down to hell with those people, how to cross borderlands between inner and outer, between illness and health, between madness and sublimity; to be with them and with ourselves, be in the agony and in the ecstasy, and somehow to hold on to the fact that it's all in the round. And, as therapists, we can help. There's very often a need here to be more active, more participative with our clients. As they are doing the actualising, we move in alongside them and help them stay there: 'Have courage and heart now, don't pull back, stay with it, be conscious, be aware, be alert.' For a time we'll be beside them. To most Western people we have to say, 'breathe in, and breathe *out*' and then, 'your body is tired; rest it'. We help them to get the flow, so that if they're moving in towards actual death, they go over the threshold as the triumphant success that it is.

I think a lot of people pass through this stage in the flask, reach this degree of maturation, as they are actually dying. Others at this point go through the *mortificatio* of dying to all that was. What yet has to come into vision is not quite with them. So we stand alongside them. We can only do that with authenticity if we know life and death ourselves, have been over the border and back, earned the right to be at the border, at the crossroads. And that means the continuous struggle to become conscious - conscious of the mystery, incorporating our own death, our own divinity, learning every inch of the way, growing more humble in the light of what it's about. Otherwise we're useless. We leave our clients, and they just walk on.

While some people need to be anchored into life, others need to be helped up and lifted. In my experience, with myself and others, an awful, yawning weariness comes over us. It is so tiring. We've come such a long way! Yet now we risk falling back exhausted, letting go, relaxing just when we have it made and need to go on, losing heart, losing enthusiasm. 'Enthusiasm' means to be inspired, 'breathed through' by a god - and we are no longer 'enthused'. As the heat is re-applied we feel, 'Oh my God, not again, after all this! I can't go on! - and just when we need to hold the tension and push through, we become flabby. It's as though we'd been plodding for ever (and we probably have) and need to be lightened. So close, and yet so dangerously far! Given an insight, we have to ground it; given an illumination or understanding, we must use it for purposes wider than ourselves. We saw with the *solutio* how people on hallucinogenic trips or those moving towards alcoholism may be looking for a new perception, seeking *spirit* through the bottom of the wine glass. The trouble is, they're trying to do it on the easy boat, the easy ticket. (Which isn't to say that some have not found their way to profound understanding through hallucinogenic drugs. I'm not against them altogether. It's the abuse of them that is the problem.) In mountaineering it's notorious: the last hundred or so feet are highly dangerous because we can see the summit, the crest; it's within our vision. We think we have it made, so we let go and relax. It's perilously easy to misjudge, miss our footing, not use the patience still required to hack out our footsteps and test our hand-holds. The danger of the *coagulatio* is that we undo our crampons, let go the rope, don't watch what we're doing - and it's a short way back!

Myth and legend

Not in the many little *coagulatios* that we go through but in the big *coagulatio* there is the sense that by this stage we have paid the coin, paid the ferryman, paid Hermes who's led us on this journey, the guide who has brought us from the overworld into the underworld and is now leading us back to the middle world. Mythology offers some very clear warnings about those who tried to get out of the flask and steal what they wanted. Although he was doing it in the name of humanity, Prometheus, stealing the fire of divinity, had to be punished.[68] He was condemned to be chained on the rock of the Caucasus, there to coagulate. And it is said that a great bird, an eagle, came each day and pecked out his liver. Each night it grew back, and the next day the bird pecked it out once more. That was his punishment. And he was punished, not for being a Titan of high courage who wanted to bring back a treasure for humanity, but for trickery and theft. He overleapt himself and pre-empted the gods. 'Doing it for another' was no excuse. It was not his to take and therefore not his to pass on. So he rose up into *hubris* and was caught into the dangers of the great test of Jupiter. That was why he was taken back into the *calcinatio*, stretched out on the great rock, until at last he was released from the eagle by Hercules. He had to rediscover the liver, said in old times to be the seat of life, the organ from which he functioned. He had to reconstitute the seat of his life because he had stolen fire that didn't belong to him.

Then there was Phaethon who took the Sun's chariot from his father Helios and was not able to handle it. Driving far too fast, he couldn't contain the instinctual drive of the chariot's powerful winged horses, so he passed too close to the Sun and was in danger of burning up, then too close to the earth, risking its being scorched. Lest his action upset the harmony and balance of the universe he was struck dead by Zeus, who lobbed a thunderbolt at him, bringing him down to crash into the River Eridanus. This too was for being pre-emptive and over-audacious.

---

68 Prometheus, son of a Titan, tricked Zeus at a sacrifice and Zeus, angry, withheld fire from the human race. However, Prometheus then went to the forges of Hephaestus and stole a brand of the holy fire. Enclosing it in a hollow stalk, he carried it back to men. Another version says that he lighted his torch at the wheel of the Sun. See LaRousse Pp. 93 & 95.

Sin and guilt

This is a very dangerous stage in alchemy. We use phrases such as 'falling short of perfection', 'recognising my own evil'. As the thread comes into our hands and we begin to move to the heart of the labyrinth, we can be caught in that profound sense of sin, guilt and shame that some of the very finest human beings feel when they recognise that they have denied the god within themselves, and maybe within another person too. Whatever isolation and abandonment we may have experienced in the past, we feel that here we abandoned *ourselves*, were isolated from ourselves. Whatever betrayals we may have received from life, we very often feel that in betraying ourselves we've betrayed God.

A disciple came to a Zen master saying, 'What is the way to release myself from bondage?' The master's reply was, 'Who binds you?' An alchemist wouldn't go into the idea of sin but ask rather, 'Why do you continue to bind God?' a particularly Eastern way of putting it. 'What is all this sin? Who is it that sins? You know that the *divine* is within. If you keep thinking you are in sin and continuing to be a sinner, then you are taking the responsibility of being one-sided. By making more darkness, you are not doing the alchemical work of releasing the divinity that is in the darkness.' The alchemist would ask, 'If you know you are a sinner, why not let the sin go?' The response is not, 'I am a sinner and therefore only Christ or whatever can redeem me.' He would go on, 'What are you going to do about the darkness? Why stay with the dark of the *prima materia* when you could be with the golden dark of the divinity? Why keep God entrapped?' That would be a very alchemical question; it is the pursuit of that kind of question that keeps us in the flask. No human being can answer it. Obviously, I do not know. I'm only saying, insofar as I understand it, what the alchemists would say about it: that God is entrapped, enmeshed.

The alchemists don't work on the assumption of a finite, finished, perfect God, always eternally there. They acknowledge the God who is also in process of becoming, a God who is growing, expanding and on the adventure of something greater. There may be beyond our planetary God a greater god yet... The alchemists see no threshold, no stopping. Within the round there are other rounds and there are other rounds beyond that, just as there are other suns behind the sun that we are learning to become; behind Helios, another sun, each sun a part of some other system! Today the language of physics, speaking of black holes, time in the round, is probably closer than almost any other to the language of alchemy.

Recognising our own sin and guilt, we turn them to gold. 'Accept your guilt - make it GILT, rather than GUILT. Make it golden.' Sin, punishment, our own shame, all have to be made golden. The devil must be included and hell and heaven brought together. We can handle our sense of sinfulness, punishment and guilt as we claim our inward authority. This is the recognition of the uses of the shadow.

False gurus and fairy gold

There are on the other hand those who, far from being ashamed, claim their inward authority by saying, '*I* don't have any sin. *I* am not guilty, the guilt's out there. I do not wish to be, or need to be, punished'. This is dangerous too. This is the false guru, the false teacher: 'Not I - I am standing in a great light, I am totally in its brilliance. All the others can carry my darkness for me!' Now, that's a stance that can make us do the splits. We're highly dangerous here. The gold needs the darkness in order to be seen. The real transformation lies in what we do with the vision, with what we've brought into being. Saturn weighs down the volatile Mercury, and yet the spirit, there within the flask, is too powerful to be held down completely. A tremendous pull-push develops, no longer horizontally but vertically. There are times when we seem to be raised up, a sudden gap appears in the curtain between the two realities and we say, 'Aha, at last I have the vision!' We have come by a very long journey and have learned, and earned, a very great deal. We have too much dangerous information to be let out. Though we haven't yet been able to create the true gold, we do have its formula in our hands. What we can do is make fairy gold, the as yet unfixed gold which will need earthing, grounding and rooting. Fairy gold can too easily lead to *hubris* and inflation.

So we believe we've got out of the flask, and now we go round fishing for souls, netting souls, cannibalising souls. We may think that we are gods, or at any rate, if there's a bit of humility left, small Titans, and go out and start 'saving the world'. We may actually push the Creator out of the way and get into the works. And so we have to be tempted, as in all the stories: Christ was tempted by the devil before he began his work; the Buddha under the Bo Tree was offered release from the wheel of rebirth and Brahma had to come and beg him to stay on this earth.

More dreams of the *coagulatio*

For us, it may be our belief in the rival systems we subscribe to that has to be challenged. For example, one woman described a dream she had had at the age of five: 'I was running along a lovely sunlit hillside amongst bushes, when suddenly a great big snake came out of the sky behind me and put horrible, brown, huge toothpaste all over my back - sickly, sticky brown stuff. I've always liked high hills and climbing - going up, escape!' The dreamer went on, 'I think the brown stuff was telling me that through this life I've had to go down, go into the earth. It's about the *coagulatio*, isn't it?' To an alchemist, yes, this is a dream of coagulating. An insightful astrologer would probably see the same thing in this person's chart; somebody else would find it in the Tarot pack; yet another would throw the I Ching; and another would find that the Cabalistic process fitted in as well. Sometimes a number of disciplines all point to a synthesis: all these systems and more, all talking about the dream in different ways. If any one of them says, 'This is the only way', or 'I have the truth, the nostrum, I have the elixir' - well, you know you're speaking to a puffer, one who blows the bellows.

Therapy

A number of people have said of psychoanalysis that it leaves out the *coagulatio* and the *sublimatio*. Much of it does have to do with the *calcinatio* and the *solutio*, and brilliant work it is. On the other hand, as a Jungian myself, I would say too many Jungians leave out *calcinatio* and *solutio* and are all into *coagulatio* and *sublimatio*. But for instance, however we look at it, the recording of dreams would be meaningless except that the people who dreamt them *went on*. The dreams are the precursors of something to follow, helping the dreamers coagulate more, take into themselves that which they have earned in service of something greater. They need it for the enhancing of their lives, and this

brings them to a deeper and more profound meaning and purpose.

Alchemy does faster what Nature takes æons to achieve. Life the Alchemist doesn't waste the experience we've had. We are cooked, and so we become more tender; more tender towards the lowly and unredeemed, towards nature and the dark - and that includes the dark in people. We must be very aware of the tenderness and understanding and strength that such people require. Those who are *still* holding on to their parents, even at this stage, fearing that any new archetypal images and authorities will lose them what they've so hardly won, need help to recoagulate themselves, to lose the original, rigid boundaries and know the opportunity of boundless freedom. If they have stayed in the flask long enough to have reached this stage, we as therapists - not to mention as clients ourselves - need to be more active, more interactive, more participative, to help the grounding process. To say, 'My goodness, you've only just started!' can help support them through it. People need encouragement to externalise all this; through active imagination, Gestalt, speaking out, acting, getting the body involved, they can give external form to the invisible to make it visible, making tangible the intangible. They can paint it and put it on the wall, anchor it in their dream books, write it in letters. We help them embody their inner experience through the arts, which are so extremely valuable, as well as through the therapeutic use of art, and we glory with them in what they've come to.

Transpersonal work

The aim now is to help those who've gone through so much *calcinatio* and *solutio* to begin to gather in, 'take delivery' of that which they have become, that which they have grown to understand. It's here that the major thrust of the work goes on. This is the transpersonal approach, and it is often left out in psychotherapy. We help people to assimilate the major complexes of their lives, and that includes the ego, but it's *in service of something greater than themselves*. In a sense, the ego is an autonomous complex in relation to the Self, and it's being revivified, re-awakened now in relation to and in service of the Self. Soon, the ego is to be let out from the flask. One of the values of the transpersonal approach in therapy is that we can see a person's

direction. Through the use of *their* imagery, through the evocative way of working with them, we can see where they are going *to* as well as where they are coming *from*. Rather than making all sorts of clever assumptions about them, we actually ask them! Some people are trapped by the flesh and definitely need a lift out of desire, while others need to have their desire *strengthened*, to be anchored back into life, incarnated, to experience the devil within themselves. I would say of these, 'They need a good vice!'

The story of Job

We've seen that much of alchemy comes through from the Bible. *'For they that walk in darkness have seen a great light.'* The *coagulatio* reminds me of the story of Job and his suffering. [69] Poor old Job was in a desert, a dry setting. And didn't he have a lot to go through - terrible things! There's much in the book about scales and measuring, gold and stones, building and gradually knocking down again. In a sense Job was 'too good for this world'. His ego was high and raised up, and even to the very end he hung in there. The gold kept coming through in small things: *'He knows me in my action and in my rest.'* At the very end, before the epilogue, it all comes right: *'Therefore I melt away, I repent in dust and ashes.'* [70] It's very exciting to take a recondite process and see it alive in this way in an old text. It's real! Here are the alchemy, the gold, the dust and the ashes. Job, more than any other, went through the processes described in the alchemical books and writings. That awe-ful refiner's fire took down his will and his authority and allowed him to challenge God and to speak for humanity in the face of God. My sense of Job's story is that it was also a prefiguring of the New Testament. Standing midway in history, he was making way for the Christ-God, so much more loving than the punitive Jehovah.

And Christ Himself: there is a gap between the two major statements of Christ in his agony in Gethsemane. In the *coagulatio* process his humanity was speaking: *'If it be possible, let this cup be taken from me.'* And he ended with, *'Not my will, but Thy will'*.[71] The gap between

---

[69]   See the book of Job, for example 23, 10: 'When he hath tried me, I shall come forth as gold.' See also Jung's 'Answer to Job' in 'Psychology and Religion: West and East', CW 11.

[70]   See Job 42, 6.

[71]   Matthew 26, 39.

needs to be left. The history of the evolution of consciousness lies between the two statements. Similarly, the two statements on the cross: *'My God, my God, why hast thou forsaken me?'* [72] (his humanity, again) ending with, *'It is accomplished, it is finished'*.[73]

A dream

I heard a very beautiful dream from someone who really had gone through it! Bereavement and trauma - she'd had the *solutio* in full blast. I've rarely met anyone who'd had more. She was aged fifty-nine when within the space of about three years she'd lost two children in a motor bike accident, the daughter riding pillion. About six months later both much-loved parents died within a very short space. She was just recovering from that when her husband became ill; and then her brother died. I'd be thinking, 'Oh God, what today? Not any more, oh Lord no more!'

And then came this superb dream - thank God! It made my heart sing for her, giving me the courage to go on being strong with and beside her, because it signalled that she was coming out of the *solutio* and into the *coagulatio* (I didn't, of course, mention that; it would have meant nothing to her then): 'I am rushing between falling skyscrapers, which are crashing down on to the pavements of London-cum-New York (she spent her time between those cities). The earth underfoot is quaking, erupting, stirring like some vast animal in birth pangs. A jagged crack appears just in front of me with flames and smoke belching up (sounding, for a horrible moment, like the nigredo). "Jump and I'll catch you!" calls a man's voice. Across the widening gap is a fireman in a silver fire-suit, smiling. I leap. I wake up feeling oddly older, more serious, very sobered.'

The earth underfoot was cracking and erupting and 'stirring like some vast animal in birth pangs' - the new earth was beginning to form for her. 'A jagged crack appears just in front of me' - and there she is with all hell breaking out from under her, flames and smoke belching up.

---

[72] Matthew 27, 46.

[73] John 19, 30.

'Jump, I'll catch you!' cries the fireman in the silver fire-suit - Mercury! The devil is here now with her, the fireman who knows how to deal with the fire. 'He is smiling. I leap,' she says. It obviously took time, but the whole process of loss and grief steadied after that. In going through all those bereavements she was moving from dependency to the ability to stand alone. Thank God! There wasn't much else left. So ultimately she became able to take the leap. It's to be hoped that not too many of us have to go by *that* tragic road. But my goodness, she had to learn responsibility for practical, earthly, bodily life - and at the same time for the inner life. She had stayed true to herself, trying to take each crisis as she came to it. The woman who came out was not the dependent person who'd gone in. Very different was the free-standing, older, more tired but extraordinarily burned-through, solid woman who came out of it. Many, many people since have turned to her. And it was all about the *coagulatio*.

What stands in the flask at the end of the true *coagulatio*? Anything that falls down to earth from a height is liable to be taken into the *coagulatio*. As in the Tower card in the Tarot, we have at last fallen off the heights of ego-principle and submitted our own hard-won authority. At the beginning, with the *massa confusa*, our ego-will said, 'By God, I'm not like everybody else!' Then we were put into the flask and dissolved down into the *solutio*, tipped every which way up. We didn't know whether we were coming or going, and there was no authority because there was nothing to hold on to. But now, with the *coagulatio*, our authority begins to be emancipated out of the mass. We become more linked with the collective. It's only now, as we've seen, that we begin to discover that it is already a different kind of authority.

The Eastern alchemists took it for granted that the body is the crucible. Their yoga and meditation systems are much the same as those of alchemy, just with different images. A lot of the true tantric yoga practices and tests have to do with the *solutio* and *coagulatio*, leading to the *sublimatio*. Those teachings all say there is no short road. It has to be worked out step by step and stage by stage. Each step needs to be made concrete, coagulated, before we can build on the next, and the next; otherwise we have a very shaky foothold. We have to mark the

footprints for others who are to follow, as well as following in those left for us. This is very important. It is the work of grounding and earthing that is greater than ourselves, the creation of the Way.

The Borderland

So begins a completely different struggle and tension. It's neither the tension outside nor the tension inside but that *between* inside and outside, as what we have become challenges what we were. The old king (who thought he was dying but rather hoped he'd get reborn) is challenged by the divine son. And for many it is a battle! We get caught into ambiguities. Very straightforward stuff ('it's good or it's bad, benign or malign, inner or outer') becomes much more subtle and we're stuck with the subtleties: better or best, loving or more loving. We're faced with all sorts of problems in which the arguments are in favour of everything and there is no straight up and down. Caught into the paradox of life, we're taught to walk the borderland, to be neither inner nor outer but to be both at the same time. This is how we may become borderlanders. These are very useful people, able to walk firmly between inner and outer reality. No shaman, high priest, healer, witch-doctor, wizard, witch, magus in full regalia, has ever been able to attain fully to their calling except that they learn to walk the borderlands between life and death, heaven and hell, good and bad, evil and divinity. They come to know that these are one and the same thing - all are energy, all are one. They know that we must face the destruction of God as much as the creation of God.

We've seen how the true alchemists, as opposed to the puffers, held that the divinity, the goal, the Self that they are seeking is already there present in matter. The alchemist, or the person who goes through these processes inwardly or outwardly, is helping to redeem the god who is also trapped in matter. Very difficult stuff, distinctly heretical, particularly in the West of the Middle Ages. As we've seen, this is what led to alchemy's becoming a secret doctrine. To reiterate: the alchemists said that man needs God - but that God also needs man. That was the difficulty. The current philosophy was that man is fallen and in sin and needs to be redeemed by God. Alchemy was highly dangerous stuff, sounding like *hubris*, like saying, 'I am God'.

Nowadays, people who go round saying, 'I am God' are put in institutions. It was probably even worse in those days.[74] The alchemists held that we *become* God. At the end such a person steps out as the Sun, is the Sun, is a luminary. But the process has taken them through all the stages of being rendered down, cleaned off, reconstituted.

In the Western world God is a 'God of love'. Yes indeed; but in the East that's not all of it. God isn't only about love. God is also wealth and wisdom and power, destruction and construction. Having the Hindu pantheon of Brahma, Shiva and Vishnu, where Shiva is as important as Brahma, must make this that much easier. The trouble is, as little human beings we cannot tolerate anything but God's being good - the Daddy God. Part of the alchemic process is the fantastic mystery and numinosity of something infinitely greater than the human mind. This is where the alchemist hits inner trouble and may well just stop. 'Thank you very much, the *mysterium coniunctionis* will have to come to me tomorrow, I cannot stand the *tremendum* of God'. This is the difference between the awe and the *awfulness* - and it can perhaps be more easily encompassed by an Eastern than a Western mind. Arjuna in the Bhagavad Gita goes out to battle. Realising that Shri Krishna is the driver of his chariot, Arjuna says, "Reveal your face to me, oh Lord, oh shining one, oh beauteous one, open your veils that I may see your face!" And Shri Krishna turns to him and pulls off his veils - and Arjuna sees the abyss and the void and hell and agony as well.

It is well known that the wise child is a sage. We need to come back 'in the round' to pick up the lost child who was in the beginning. In terms of Western alchemy this is Mercurius again. Mercury is within the *prima materia* from the start. Mercury *is* the process, he *is* the child, he *is* the eternal *puer* who will remain a child. No young human being would be allowed into the flask, but one can still be young in

---

[74]   But see the Christian mystic Angelus Silesius (b.1624). From 'The Cherubinic Wanderer' :
> *I know that, without me, The life of God were lost;*
> *Were I destroyed, he must Perforce give up the ghost.*
> *God is the fire in me, And I the light in him.*
> *Are we not, each to each, Most inwardly akin?*

Jung has the version :
> *I am as great as God, And he is small like me;*
> *He cannot be above, Nor I below him be.* (CW 13, para 117).

experience, like the apprentice chosen by the alchemist - chosen for the quality, for the future alchemist visible within the apprentice. I think certain children are born who have this property, who are all ready to step into the flask. Alchemical material is common in the dreams of children under five, pre-figuring and pre-visioning. They may even be in the flask already when they get here.

The word *religio* means to be re-tied, re-bonded. This is the binding, the tying of the bond which is no longer bondage. It is vocation, coming to our calling, hearing the voice that has called us. It's very different from 'work'. Work has become a spontaneous outpouring of the spirit and no longer feels like effort. It's duty, our *dharma*, that which we are bound to do with a different kind of bondage. We no longer do things under duress. *Yoga* is yoke, and the yoke becomes lighter as we accept it and move with it.

Joy, laughter and acceptance

So - an acceptance of fate, not in a childish way, but in accepting the nature of the three Fates. Here they are under the *aegis* of the feminine, weaving the web of fate, the fabric of creation. [75] There's the one who spins the thread, the individual thread of the lifetime. There's the one who sets the loom and measures the thread which is working through it. And then there's the one who cuts the cord, when the time comes for us to leave that particular pattern and go on to the back of the picture. Jung wrote that the greatest freedom is to do willingly that which we must. To be willing. To laugh - joy comes in here, the joy of doing that which we must do. Life's a bit like a game of snakes and ladders and laughter goes through it right from the start. A sense of humour is a sense of perspective, a sense of proportion. Without it - well! In the Christian religion it has been left out of whatever stories we read of Christ, hasn't it? He must have rolled up with laughter at the humour of some of the parables, but it doesn't come through - the dance, the joy, the laughter, the quality of the lift of it all - and also the earthing. This wouldn't need to be said in the East. It's terribly Western. We all

[75] The Three Fates are daughters of Night. Legend has it that Clotho spins the thread of life; Lachesis, who is chance, the luck we have the right to expect, measures it; and Atropos, inescapable fate against which there is no appeal, cuts it. All three submit to the authority of Zeus. Graves 1959, P. 163.

sit so hard in the saddle of life and then complain we've got piles.

In Zen they say, 'Keep walking. Stay with it. If in doubt, keep walking'. Life is a labyrinth. Losing the way but always being on the thread, finding the way through by walking - only by walking - eventually one *becomes* the way. 'If you sit, sit, and if you stand, stand; but don't wobble.' This calm acceptance of the wider framework of meaning within the universe begins to be mediated to us, and eventually brings a certain peacefulness. The more we become able to stay with it through all uncertainties, the more this calm acceptance of the inevitable comes in. We accept that we are no longer arbiters of some strange, mad creation, but part and parcel of a profounder meaning than our ego could possibly have known. We have free will to make choices but our choices are within the wider principles of something greater than ourselves. Then the goal that we were aiming at vanishes and we *become* the goal.

More dreams

One woman had a rather splendid yet hearteningly ordinary dream about the *coagulatio*. Aged thirty-four, a lapsed Catholic, she described herself as having 'a very heavy Father-complex': 'I'm jam-making - strawberries?' because it was red. 'The mix won't set; is there enough sugar? "Sit and let set," says an ancient-looking, handwritten recipe book on the long wooden workbench. So I sit down to what seems like a long wait. A runnel of red, sweet jam drips over the jar's rim across the table like a stream of blood. I dip my finger and taste it; it's curiously bitter and sweet. I realise this is some ritual, some holy action, and that I am now dedicated, there is no way back. And the jam begins to set.' The strawberries reminded her of the 'sexual lust' which had led her to three abortions, one a spontaneous one. Her associations to the recipe book: 'An old Bible or chemical textbook (she didn't know about *al*chemical), with glyphs'. The workbench, 'my father's bench (he was an engineer) but also the plinth that his coffin lay on'. Blood was 'menstruation, miscarriage, blood of the Mass, Jesus'. And she said, 'Oh God, don't say I'm going to go all religious again!' 'Again?' I asked; and this, while being about the *coagulatio*, also began to lead her to the recognition of her own religious or spiritual nature.

Coagulatio dreams often come to the elderly. Just a little while before he died, my own stepfather dreamt he was repairing an old tattered wall-hanging rug to its original beauty. It gave him great peace.

White gold

And now the heat can be gently lowered. There's an alchemical saying, 'Sow your gold in white foliated earth'. This comes about through the work of Saturn and Earth. The black earth, first rendered down to ash then whitened, now appears as white earth already seeded with the true gold: white-yellow, *citrinitas*. This gold is not to be used for the purposes of the ego, nor for the person, nor even for the individual alchemist. We cease to think so much of just our own individual nature, which is strong now as a candle embodies the flame. With our fellows we begin to serve the collective, working with and through and for the group, that which is greater than ourselves. The alchemists speak of the acceptance by that which is in the flask of wider values: purified materiality, the more incorporating view. It's the ability to deal in and with the market-place - but not with false gold. 'Always keep your gold true.' It's learning how to use the currency of our times, but always going for the gold. It's still unfixed, fairy gold, not yet the red gold; but very soon it will become true and everlasting, a different gold. Already it belongs elsewhere.

In practically all religions, all the great rituals, there's a transmutation process: water is turned into wine, wine into blood and blood into water. But more important still is the eternal Stone, the foundation stone of the New Jerusalem, the first foothold in the eternal country. Our new earth, our new Jerusalem, is coming into being. A stone is beginning to emerge from it, the stone which becomes our understanding, that which stands under us. We now have earth to stand on, the earth of heaven and the earth of earth. It holds us and becomes our corner-stone. As Jung says:

> *'God wants to be born in the flame of man's consciousness, leaping ever. And what if this has no roots in the earth? If it is not a house of stone where the fire of God can dwell, but a wretched straw hut that flares up and vanishes? Could God then be born? One must be able to suffer God. That is the supreme task for the carrier of*

ideas. He must be the advocate of the earth. God will take care of himself. My inner principle is: Deus et homo. *God needs man in order to become conscious, just as he needs limitation [a form] in time and space. Let us therefore be for him limitation in time and space, an earthly tabernacle.'* [76]

That was Jung, writing in a letter at the end of his life, speaking as a true alchemist. And someone I knew, coming towards the end of this phase, wrote a poem:

There is one other thing to say:
All man-made gods have feet of clay;
But when base metal's melted down -
Lead, orb and sceptre, self-made crown -
A naked torso, velvetting with moss,
When all's confessed to be but dross,
Wrapped in patched habit for a winding sheet -
A whole man springs from those clay feet.

---

[76]   Jung, Letters I, Pp. 65-66.

CHAPTER SEVEN

SUBLIMATIO

Here stands the mean uncomely stone,
'Tis very cheap in price;
The more it is despised by fools
The more loved by the wise.

Fire of Air

So to the *sublimatio*, the final stage, the end of the whole process. Not having been sublimated, I obviously have less to say about this. It's called *rubedo* because it has the red in it, the red-gold, the eternal gold. The element of the *rubedo* is air. This is the 'fire of air'. Everything now becomes winged. The presiding deity was originally Jupiter, and now that we are conscious that we have Uranus in our solar system, he too would almost certainly be involved. The word *sublimatio* means 'to be raised, raising' (from *sublimis*, 'high', or 'to raise or lift'). Here, 'to sublimate' is to move on from that which we have known in favour of that which has newly come into being; not (in the Freudian sense) to suppress or repress. It is about the extraction of meaning, non-attachment, the transformation of instincts - very different from the limited use of the word which makes religious images into 'sublimations' of sexual urges and God into a father complex. In this sense 'sublimation' is being raised, lifted, elevated into a higher form by an ascent, by the bridge or ladder that's being built.

If the stages followed each other in the classic run, we would by now have been burned down, abluted, absolved, cleansed and coagulated. The *calcinatio* took the ego-personality down into the flask. The *solutio* began to dissolve the opposites, the polarities of masculine and feminine, all the polarities of our lives. The *coagulatio* has been to do with the androgyne, the masculine and feminine together, Sun and Moon being brought into the presence of another sun, the Self. The *sublimatio* is the extrapolation out of the Great Father and Great

Mother. Our original parents got lost somewhere in the flask and we're now working with the great parents. Earth is raised to heaven, heaven is brought down to earth. This whole double helix that we celebrate in the Mass is part of the great *sublimatio*. Having gone through it, we would finally come out in the round. In psychological terms, I think the *sublimatio* means being able to abstract spiritual purpose and meaning from the concrete reality of every day. Although we are still in life, and the fire-by-friction of life in matter is still something that we are answerable to, it doesn't hurt so much. It has a meaning and purpose of its own. A person works *with* the hands of the healer, the hands of the potter, the maker of gold. The *sublimatio* is about the acceptance of the divinity of reality, the privilege of being part of the creative process. It takes us back to where it all began: the divine is in matter, in the darkness, in the shit, in the shadow - and when was it ever different?

We're looking here at the 'great' *sublimatio*; there are also smaller ones, as we shall see. In the Eastern tradition this great *sublimatio* means release from the wheel of rebirth. A person may choose to come back, but that's an act of choice; there's no longer a need for the refiner's fire. *Solve et coagula*, dissolve *and* coagulate, separate and yet unite. God is everywhere and ends nowhere, the wheel has turned full circle and the mandala is complete.

Plate 12. The Second Conjunction - opposite

Now the king and the queen are mating, copulating with wings. Things have changed: she's on top! The world has been turned on its head. Where we had the coming together, then the death, here is the movement towards the winged state. Now they may celebrate their 'chymical wedding'. This indicates that the agent has become love, not just lust; at last we stop blocking out joy! Though their wings are now spiritual wings, they are still in the ecstasy of love, still in the copulatory process. We don't necessarily have to give up relationships with people to have one with God. Relationship is the greatest thing of all and out of it comes a higher relationship still. In the first conjunction (Plate 10, P.97) the pair had no wings and the Sun and Moon had gone down into the waters of the *solutio* with them. Here, in the second conjunction, the Sun and the Moon aren't shown because they have been internalised and are within.

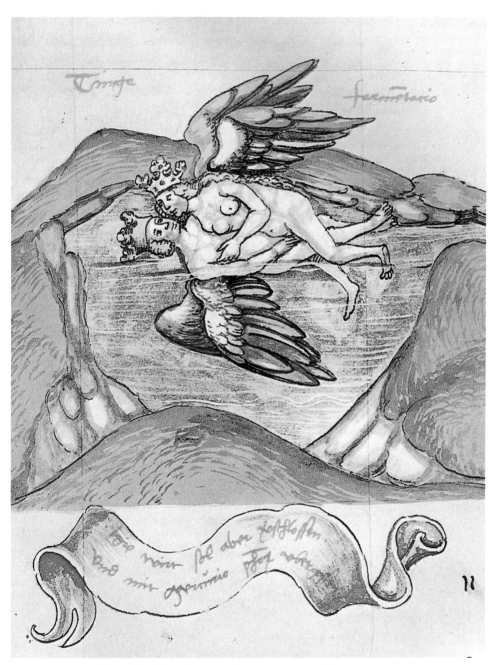

Plate 12. The Second Conjunction - *Hieros gamos*

We could say that his masculine ego has drowned in the feminine fluid and both of them have now been brought to a new birth. The two are in the new womb, a wider womb, and they are in view of the birthing channel. There is an exit, a passage out.

The picture belongs to the later, final stage of the *sublimatio*. Indeed, the *hieros gamos* has already taken place, for they rise, birdlike, beyond fire into air, lifting up on high, aiming to perceive with new eyes. The bird rising up meets the bird coming down, as foreshadowed in the six *calcinatio* pictures of Plate 5. They have risen to the top of the flask. Purgatory is above, depicting relationship and the loss of relationship, and their wings are taking them beyond their own relationship, which transcends time and space. It is the true marriage. The Divine Child will soon be born of their mating. Through their relatedness with each other (but no longer so lost in each other that they lose their meaning), they give birth to a son greater than themselves. This is a birth of understanding, a deeper lovingness, a deeper insight. It isn't just their own son that they're bringing into being but the Philosophers' Son, the final goal.

Implicit within these two *Rosarium* pictures is much about human life and human experience. The Sun and the Moon are re-enacting the creation myth: the Creative Father in heaven is relating and mating in the beginning with the great Earth Mother, and the two are rolling in the ecstasy of their joy in the marital bed, spawning creation as they go. In their interaction, their copulation, their creation dance, in the beauty of their love and passion, they seed the world with men and women. Love is indeed the redeeming principle. This is re-enacted in the heart of each man and each woman. Towards the final stages of this we are said to be in love with all life.

Dangers of the *sublimatio*

Now, since I have not been sublimated, have not gone through the great *sublimatio*, I can really only talk *about* it. But enough of us have probably had the experience in a small way to recognise the poetry of the language. We have not many but certainly a number of small *sublimatios* before we would ever hope to reach the full one (if you'd had the great *sublimatio*, why on earth would you be reading this book?). There is danger as well as triumph in this smaller *sublimatio*, as in all of these areas. We come across people who are *too* high, exalted, insightful. I think you will recognise this in yourself and in others: we tend, for every kind of reason, to be too remote, detached, too liable to take the observer view. It's a risk of being 'special' - or too aware that we're special. This is not quite the same as the *hubris* that we had to deal with in the *coagulatio*. In the *sublimatio* the specialness cuts both ways: someone who has reached this stage *is* special, this *is* the divinity, this is the gold. The art is to honour the specialness but not become exalted. People with this vision are sometimes a bit disdainful of humankind, human fallibility. The word 'cynicism' comes in here. If it hasn't been fully worked through in the *coagulatio*, it can almost become contempt. They get distressed at a very profound level at other people's inability to see their own wider vision, or at their own difficulties in trying to express in words the vision that they have. It can be very lonely and isolating, feeling that they're prophets in their own country and nobody's taking any notice of them. It is very difficult. They need somehow to see that both the ascent and the descent are necessary, and not to fall into the blasphemy that alchemy is trying to resolve. The danger is that, going for the high vision, they'll again fall into the split. Humour is one of the greatest vehicles, necessary certainly for the *coagulatio* with its 'Oh no, not again, not again!' - and it is needed here too!

Dreams of the *sublimatio*

One woman, a painter, had a dream: she came out into a clearing and found a singing stone. This stone became important to her and began to appear continually in her paintings. Her next picture showed herself as 'an exotic peacock standing on this stone'. She said, 'Nobody else was about. I was observing from the stone; I had a hunch that I must promise always to take it around with me. It's the goal - or it's the continual process.' My sense was that it also sounded like the warning of the *coagulatio*. It's both. Watch out for the specialness! The Stone is notoriously able to look after itself. In the Eastern tradition the *lapis* was said to have the power to make one able to fly, or to become invisible, or to go deep into the water, or to walk through fire unscathed. The uses of the Stone are many.

I'm not saying this next dream, dreamt by a man, a computer operator of about fifty-four, is of the great *sublimatio*, but there's certainly something coming in. I love it! 'I, as king, am on a throne, with the lot: ermine - purple - an *entourage*. A great feeling, considering everything.' (And his 'considering everything' was the roughly nine years of fairly unmitigated hell that he'd gone through.) 'The lot! Suddenly, from underneath the throne, a fireball explodes. Talk about a squib up the arse! I shoot up in the air and wake up laughing myself silly. Now everything seems in better perspective. I can trust myself to hope a little and laugh a lot more in days to come.' Here's Jupiter's 'Up yours!' to the exaltation process! And yes, after all that he had been through he did feel a certain right to relief. He really could see the funny side of this playful, beautiful joke. In the East it would be the clout round the head by the Zen master. His reaction showed that he was ready and appropriately placed, laughing at himself, a king on the throne - the ermine, the purple, the *entourage*, the lot; 'a great feeling, considering everything.' Lovely!

A gentle, lenient heat

We started with heat and we end with heat. It isn't taken off, even at this stage. However, it's said that now the alchemist can begin to turn it down and it becomes gentle and lenient, the residual heat of the flask. We are no longer burning by our own heat. In chemical terms, the solid stone is heated once more but this time, instead of going down to the base of the flask, it 'becomes gaseous, rises, and then solidifies in the upper, cooler region' - a very alchemical statement. Later, the alchemist will unseal the hermetic flask and the residual part of the process will be completed by Helios, the overhead Sun. So, a gentle, lenient heat. Again there is the danger that we will abuse it. But if we don't, if we can stay with it, if we can still go with the rendering-down process, then at a certain point what we thought was us, is no longer us.

Probably those people who do go through to a fuller kind of *sublimatio* knew about it as children. They may, even then, have felt a sense of being preordained, bonded, being a bondsman or bondswoman to something greater than themselves. They probably resisted this sense of vocation and destiny all the days of their lives. Nobody wants to take this mantle on themselves until they feel ready for it. Of course, the mantle doesn't come to them until they *are* ready, but they aren't to know that. Their struggle has very often been away from this life, to get out of it into some quiet place. They may so have given themselves to their dedication throughout their lives that they've almost lost their body. This is the chance for them and their bodies to come back together once more. This is 'body made perfect' - perfect in the sense of the Chinese or Japanese artist for whom, if anything's too perfectly symmetrical, then it's not perfect. This is not the denial of the body but the incorporation of the body, the perfection of it in the round with its light and its dark, its faults and its divinity - *that* sort of 'body made perfect'. Presumably it is the subtle body that will arise to the trumpet at the day of the Last Judgement. No alchemist would think it was this corrupt body of earth that is raised to heaven; it is the subtle-physical, transmuted, perfected body that will rise into eternity.

Transpersonal work

It may well be through symbols that we experience this. A symbol is the sublimation, the 'making sublime' of an experience, a 'click', an 'Aha!' Jung talked of the healing love there may be within ritual and symbol. It is as if psychic energy would naturally run away 'horizontally', as it were, but the symbol can entrap and canalise it and it begins to form as an image. We are then creating on a non-biological level, finding in the process free will, choice and the capacity not to be blindly driven from within. Transpersonal psychology, following on the path of Jung, has a great deal to do with this (though counsellors and therapists who work transpersonally tend too often to leave out the *coagulatio* in favour of the *sublimatio*). As we have seen, this process has its dangers, as do they all. Watch out for someone with repetitive imagery of ascent and flight and height; they may need to come to their earth. Part of the work in therapy is to reveal to them their need for grounding. Their vision, which they have very strongly, needs to be anchored. If they lift too much away from the earth and into the heights, they'll be taken back into the flask to be re-coagulated, they'll have to go through more washings and even be barbecued again in the *nigredo*. The true transpersonal has to do with both rising *and* earthing. It's through the processes of flying and grounding, flying and

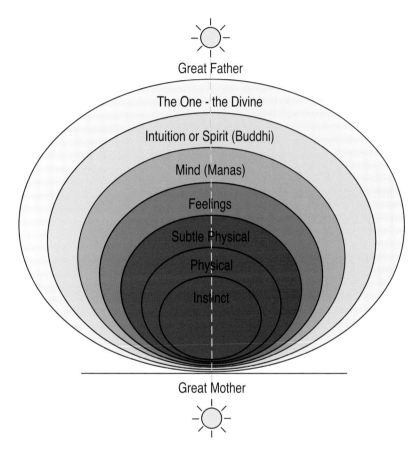

grounding again, that we go through north, south, east, west, the four quarters, the four experiences, in the round. Then we are able both to rise and to walk this earth - to have our feet firmly planted and our head also among the stars.

Figure 2 - The Great Mother to the Great Father and Back

This diagram shows seven known stages or levels. We build a vehicle at each level. If we put these on to an 'onion map' we get a vertical bridge connecting the Great Mother with the Great Father. We descend from the One, the Father, to the Great Mother. At each level, pairs of opposites marry each other. And finally the Green Lion regurgitates the Sun. The Sun is put back in heaven, the lion gives up what the flask contains - but the Sun in the sea now contains the upside-down face of the feminine. [77]

Psychologically, therapeutically, both the *sublimatio* and the *coagulatio* are required for the raising and the anchoring. It's very important for people to *have* their ground before they take off from it. A lot of people say, 'Lord, take me, I am Yours, I believe and trust in You completely.' But they're very much children and they haven't anything to offer. I assume the Lord requires truly tempered beings, not just children. 'Not my will, but Thy will.' It's very easy to trust when we've never gone through doubt and torment, pain and agony, disillusion and dissolution, lost ourselves and found the way and lost it again, been through the labyrinth, through low earth and high heaven. The one who's been truly tested and tried through the fires has stood and withstood, and now 'under-stands'. Then they have something to offer worth the taking. If therapy has any value, it's that we stand alongside somebody and help them to stay with the process. We do more than we know when we try, even in very small ways (and usually failing more than we succeed) to stay in the flask and stay with them, seeking to understand. I think - I know - it is through this that we work at levels so much deeper than ourselves, taking part in the redemption of earth. I mean this not in the Christian sense that what is fallen must be redeemed, but in the best possible sense: the making sacred of a non-sacred planet within a sacred universe.

The Returning One

At this stage the strong, fiery, energetic will that has been built to stay through the *coagulatio* has submitted to an authority greater than itself. This is about the collective. Here is the Boddhisattva, the Returning One who will step back on to the wheel of rebirth to save others. This is the path of the world saviour. Such a one has the vision, recognising themselves to be a son or a daughter of the God. As we've seen, a danger for anyone who reaches this stage is that they may go out of life and not come back, widening the gap between other people and themselves. They need somehow to be helped to stay in the house of humanity, because it is for that that they are here - to be among the

[77]   Plate 11f above, P. 113.

bridge-builders between God and earth, earth and God. Remember the Buddha under the Bo Tree? He had many visions of beauty and when he had come to illumination and seen the vision, he knew he had the opportunity to take enlightenment. He could stay ever in bliss, be ever with the gods, become a transcendent immortal. After what he had gone through, all of that lay before him. Now came the terrible temptation to stay there. 'In no way can I translate the vision if I stay on this earth.' It was an enormous test, very much of the *sublimatio*, and we saw how Brahma himself, the Great Father in heaven, had to come down the ladder, down the tree to the Buddha and beg him to remain here. Only then, having been asked to by Brahma, did he choose to come back and become a Boddhisattva, a Returning One - the myth of Buddha Maitreya: *'So long as one blade of grass cries out for light, I shall return.'*

It is the going away - and the returning. In my belief (and I feel a bit cheeky saying this) the Maitreya is already here; the returning Christ is already within the human heart. But Buddha still had to go through it, as did Christ who was tempted by the devil to stand on the mountain and rule the world from there.[78] I suppose a great Master - a Christ, a Buddha, a Mohammed, a Shri Krishna - who has achieved in whatever tradition, is very *concerned*. Not all great souls are on that line. Some do choose to join the immortals, to go to Olympus or to Valhalla and to work with creation from that level, and maybe they are no longer concerned for the planet Earth. But those who are concerned with the redemption of humankind do choose to come back. So the Buddha returned from under the Bo Tree to go about his work, and Christ came out of the wilderness. From the mountain of the Transfiguration they veil their faces and come down, and are about their Father's work on earth. In the Chinese and Japanese alchemies they end up in the market-place. All the Boddhisattvas and the Messiahs, the coming ones, have come *down*, back into work, into the market-place, into the valley - as we shall see.

New liquor

So for us, too, a continuous circuit of all the aspects of our human nature gradually grinds the Self, the Stone, into solidity as the

---

78 See St. Matthew 4, 8-10.

synthesising centre; up and down, up and down again, this circumambulation around the Self. Or maybe it is that the Self, the pure diamond body, is grinding *us*, polishing us so that we ourselves become aware of the synthesising centre? Do we have the Self, or does the Self have us? At this point it's both, and it ceases to be a problem. This is the new liquor, the heady stuff of the *sublimatio*. I came across this by Emily Dickinson [79] and it struck me that there's a little bit of the joy of release in it:

> *I CAN wade grief,*
> *Whole pools of it, -*
> *I'm used to that.*
> *But the least push of joy*
> *Breaks up my feet,*
> *And I tip - drunken.*
> *Let no pebble smile,*
> *'T was the new liquor, -*
> *That was all!*

Plate 13. Exaltatio V. Essentiæ - overleaf

For the final stage the alchemists use again the picture of our alchemical pelican, biting into its own breast at the base of the flask. It is a picture often found in churches and cathedrals and it is an alchemical symbol borrowed, for it is the Christ symbol. Alchemists of the Christian tradition took the pelican at the time to represent Christ, who broke his own heart so that his blood could flow and redeem all mankind. This is the Redeemer, the redeeming one, the Christ in our Western tradition. All great Returning Ones, Maitreyas, returning Buddhas, have given their lives and have opened up their hearts' blood for the redemption of earth. In the sacrifice of that which was in the flask, in the opening of the heart, in the ability to put oneself to death, one fertilises the earth, becomes eternal. In alchemy the intent is to let all juices flow and all seeds sprout from the heart's blood in the earth. Every one of us who manages to withstand the painful process of having our hearts opened and letting the blood flow can also water and fertilise our own earth, and the earth itself.

---

[79] Emily Dickinson 1924, 'Complete Poems'.

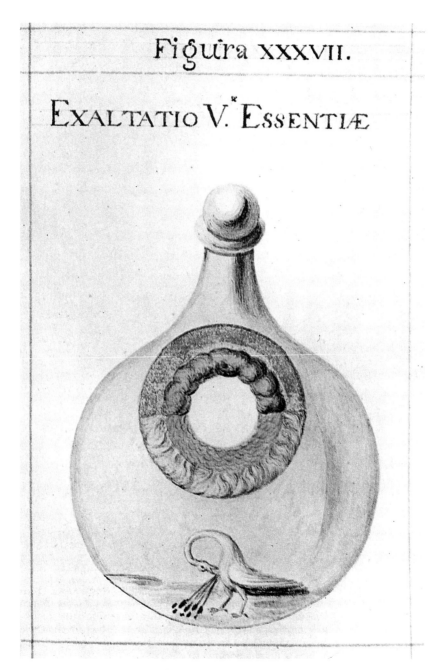

Plate 13. Exaltatio V. Essentiæ

So the golden pelican, opening its own heart and letting out its life-blood to nurture the world, has put itself to death in the flask. Shown above the bird are all the eight elements - air, fire, earth, water; dry, moist, warm, cold - coming together at the top of the flask.[80] Not only do we become friend of the elements, but in our turn we are befriended by them. All the elements are become one. We've had experience of the elements throughout the many roastings and washings, and the times we've had to go back through the *coagulatio*. Now, the four quarters are one: air, water, earth, fire; mind, feeling, sensation, intuition. In the Eastern tradition dry, moist, cold and warm, once separated as polarities, are brought into the One, and wood and metal are also incorporated. Perhaps mercury was chosen as a metal because it is both dry and moist, liquid and solid (although I suspect that the god Mercury predated the discovery of the metal - otherwise why call the metal 'mercury'?). All these things are now in the round. There is no polarity, no opposition, simply the working with the Creator on the creation as part of the creation. The one who comes out of the great *sublimatio* becomes part of the creation process.

Stay with Mercurius: he went down into the flask as the *prima materia*. He was the alchemist, he was the flask, he was what was in the flask, he was the tricky middle stages of the work, and now he emerges as the divine son of God, the Philosophers' Son. So it is completed. It really does have all these many meanings. This surely is the language of paradox!

We started from the reconciliation of the opposites. The work was begun when we recognised the separate bits that needed to be split apart in order to be reconstituted and re-coagulated; indeed, we had first to be split, in order to be coagulated. The *hieros gamos*, the true, the sacred, the chymical marriage, has brought into existence a whole being, still human enough to feel pain and joy and relate appropriately to time and space, still conditioned by God's created world, but already living in eternity. This is what it means to be in the world but not of it.

---

80   Aristotle said that the four elements are linked through their properties:
        Cold + Dryness = Earth
        Heat + Dryness = Fire
        Cold + Humidity = Water
        Heat + Humidity = Air. See Klossowski de Rola, P. 17.

Now we have become one, re-coagulated, reconciled. This is the appropriate life. This is the exaltation of the essence, the essential joy. Now at last we begin to hear from afar the sound of golden trumpets.

Squaring the circle

Alchemy was a secret art for reasons we've seen, sometimes talked of as the art of squaring the circle. As mentioned in the introduction, the sign of the squared circle was very often marked on door or wall or paving stone to tell his fellows that here an alchemist was at work. Everything is held within the circle of God. The symbol included the lower triangle of man penetrated by the higher triangle of God: will, love, wisdom penetrating mind, body, feelings to create a star. In the *sublimatio* they interact, and in each triangle the process seeks to bring the fourfold out of the threefold and put a square around it. Thus, spirit was brought out of the triangle of the body, mind and feelings of man, and often the devil was added in to the trilogy of God. Now the squaring of the circle is really beginning to emerge. As these interlock in the divine container of God, whose periphery is everywhere and whose centre nowhere, man becomes body, soul and *spirit*. So the partial man who is incomplete without God and the partial God who is incomplete without man are brought together into the form of a star. This will reveal another God and help to form a new creation. All that which was polarised and in opposition is now brought in to the square, the divine container. Somebody who had achieved that within themselves became a Master of alchemy!

The *lapis*

And now the Stone is emerging. As in astrology, and as in all the initiation processes, there is about now a kind of 'crank point' where the wheel of rebirth, which is still going round, reverses. A heat is applied, but it's a different kind of heat, gentle and lenient as we have seen. And what comes out of the flask - well, here it stands, *in* the flask! It is the Stone. Porous but adamant, it becomes the touchstone of our life and has the power, when touched, to turn things to gold, make life golden. However it is called, Elixir of Eternal Life or Pearl of Great Price, 'the Stone' is the traditional name for the goal of the alchemists. And the Stone, the *lapis*, is now here. Breathed into by

God 'so that for ever it will stand', the Stone also breathes God, or, as the alchemist would say, the god that is already within the stone begins to breathe. In the Eastern tradition they call it the Diamond Body. Diamonds are carbon at a high frequency; at a low frequency, carbon is a lump of coal. *'I the* lapis *beget the light, but the darkness too is of my nature.'* [81] The Stone can go to heaven totally untouched. It incorporates the darkness. It is completely pure because it is of God, and nothing, no pitch will stick to it, no dross remaining, no substance in it that is of hell, except that it understands all hell.

My own profound belief is that the devil and God are two faces of one thing, not split apart, and that this is what the *lapis* is. What sort of god would we have who stayed in heaven yet created a hell in which people suffered? The alchemists believe - and again this is part of the heresy - that God is down in hell as well as up in heaven. Whoever comes out of the flask in the true *sublimatio* knows how to walk all borderlands and to be in all places at the same time. That which was originally in the flask as the *prima materia*, the life experience, is still here - it hasn't gone away. It depends how we look at it. It doesn't necessarily mean that we are freed from our humanity; that is the very substance from which we can go out and be useful to the collective, knowing what it is to be struggling yet still trying to find meaning and purpose. Meaning and purpose are here; both the light and the dark are here.

This is the non-denying Stone. As seen in the flask between the *coagulatio* and the *sublimatio*, it isn't necessarily a golden stone. It's frequently a grey one - very grey and very ordinary. A great alchemist, Arnaldus de Villanova, gave a voice to the Stone:

> *I am an orphan, alone; nevertheless I am found everywhere. I am one, but opposed to myself. I am youth and old man at one and the same time. I have known neither father nor mother, because I have had to be fetched out of the deep like a fish, or fell like a white tone from heaven. In woods and mountains I roam, but I am hidden in the innermost soul of man. I am mortal for everyone, yet I am not touched by the cycle of Æons.* [82]

---

[81]   A saying of Hermes. In Jung, CW 12, para 140, which gives the source as the Rosarium Philosophorum (his Note 16 gives Tractatus aureus, Chapter 4).

[82]   In Latin, carved by Jung on the lake side of the stone in his garden at Bollingen. It is not known when Arnaldus de Villanova was born, but he died in 1313. Quoted and illustrated in Jung 1961, 'Memories, Dreams, Reflections', P. 254; and in Jaffé, Ed., 1979, Pp. 201 and 204.

I am both this, and that; I am not this, I am not that. So the alchemists say that the Stone [83] is found everywhere, wherever we look for it, but disregarded, seen only by those who have the eyes to see it. It's with us all the time - it was never lost. We're liable to bump into it on the highway. In the East there's the sense that the Stone is to be found in the market-place but we miss it because we're seeking something extraordinary. We had not realised we can take anything - the dust at our feet - and we're holding heaven in our hands. As a colleague remarked, we go searching for the Great Lotus and put our foot straight in the eye of the daisy. It's a very ordinary thing, this Stone. It's not something particular or special; it's 'of the earth earthy' and, like so many ordinary things, it *is* extraordinary. Here is Arnaldus de Villanova again, speaking of the Stone at the base of the flask:

Here stands the mean uncomely stone,
'Tis very cheap in price,
The more it is despised by fools
the more loved by the wise.

Plate 14. V. Essentia Exaltata - opposite

Now, to rejoice! All the trumpets of heaven shall resound! Here is a culminating picture of the *opus*. Now it is complete. At last the heat is turned right down, the Hermetic seal can be taken off, the eternal Sun overhead just warms the flask and that which was in it is released - released to come back. The entire flask is flamed; you can see how beautiful it is. The gold and the white have come together. The pelican, or phoenix, is now in the centre and the whole thing has gone down to the bottom of the flask. And that is the illustration of the final stage of the *sublimatio*. An Enlightened One is emerging now out of the flask, a 'twice-born' who has died once to personal life and once more in the flask, and so is now '*thrice*-born'. This is one who has voluntarily accepted incarnation and so is both of the world and of heaven. The new man has emerged from the old Adam. Child of earth, child of

---

[83] 'To him that overcometh will I give ... a white stone, and in the stone a new name written, which no man knoweth saving he that receiveth it.'. Revelation 2, 17.

Plate 14. V. Essentia Exaltata

heaven, he stands as *pontifex*, maker of bridges between earth and heaven and presumably between heaven, the cosmos and whatever lies beyond the cosmos. Such people are bridges linking our known worlds, heaven and earth and hell. They come and they go, they pass in through creation and out again, dancing back in the eternal dance of the cosmos - sons of earth and sons of heaven. Again, remember Jacob's ladder with angels ascending and descending? [84]   Instinct, body, feelings, mind, intuition, spirit - all the levels are connecting now, and thus creating the ladder. The connective link offers a two-way passage; the ladder between earth and heaven is in place. The restless wheel, the turning of the alchemic processes, is stilled. White birds ascend, rising from the material that is being heated. The circulation is complete and Spirit is released at the top of the flask. The Redeemer comes from heaven to earth and rises again to heaven.

Aflame with God

So the *ars contra naturam*, the art contrary to nature, another definition of alchemy, is finished. As the double helix is the source of all life, so all systems fall into this system. Alchemists Christian, [85] Gnostic and Eastern all said that the great privilege of being human is that we help the God of the universe to be in process of becoming. As I understand it, it's not so much that Helios, the Sun, lights the flask but, as the alchemist realises, he or she has *become* Helios and can move between heaven and hell, overworld and underworld. He *is* the god. Now it is the internal Sun that does the heating, the warming, the continuation of the process. The whole flask, the whole body is aflame with God. The Christian church went just about as far as to see the haloes around the *heads* of the saints; in the Eastern tradition the attained one is all aflame - the entire aura is full of fire. Aflame with God in the free passage between all the worlds, the person walks back into life and lives relatively ordinarily. Such a person is back in the flow and there's nothing contrary to nature about that. They can flow upstream and downstream with the river of life, go to earth, go to heaven, walk all the borderlands. Every *chakra* from the root to the crown is alive to its very base, and rising.

[84] Genesis 28, 12.

[85] The Pope is called Pontifex, bridge-maker.

The eternal Stone, the *lapis*, is now. The *lapis* stands under us, gives us our understanding and will stand and withstand. This is the eternal Stone that cannot now be destroyed. We are in the flow of life again. Here is '*the still point of the turning world*', [86] the fountain and the spring. The alchemists had pictures of the spring and the rising fountain coming from the spring, the circular fountain in the square garden. Here's Jung, talking about the *sublimatio* and I think also giving us a key as to how to help clients and ourselves: 'If you accept the fact that fate is really created by your own self,' (Self with a capital; he wrote it with a small s, but the Self these people accept as creating their fate is the one with the large S)

> - *if you accept the fact that fate is really created by your own Self, then you are in the current and then, even if the external situation is bad, you have the spring flowing within. Then you can say with the exalted, 'The soul becometh joyful', for you are in the river of life, you are joyful, you are lifted up by the river.* [87]

In the East that is known as being 'in the Tao', in the flow of things. What comes out of the flask is re-made, re-membered to a new pattern; this is what *remembering* means.

The touchstone

Alchemy is a very simplifying process. A person comes out of it more ordinary, yet where that person goes things are touched and redeemed. As alchemist, he or she now has the gold, the elixir, the touchstone. It doesn't belong to them, it just is. It's not particularly evident, just held within them. They carry it around with them. It's the kind of stone you'd find every day, not necessarily outstanding, not gleaming with gold, yet things start to change when other people touch it. Shared, it becomes theirs as well; working with the same touchstone they all have eternal life, even in this temporal world. The alchemist can leave the outer form of laboratory or oratory because it's now portable. He or she can do and be at the same time, can go out into the market-place, can put that mark on the wall - the squared circle, their recognised

---

86   T.S. Eliot 1959, 'Burnt Norton' I.

87   Out of Jung's private papers.

symbol to other alchemists, their way of advertising.[88] They are recognised by their ordinariness and their joyfulness, and by these continuous themes: to square the circle; the sacredness of each moment; to journey from One and so return to One. They don't often speak, but they are informed. They have a vast understanding, but aren't necessarily learned; are wise, though not always knowledgeable. Even tainting and tarnishing is in their presence also revealed as the true gold. The touchstone is serenity - till it changes to humour. To be able to make people laugh!

And human beings will kill them for it.

So, to reiterate, this is the *sublimatio*, the *rubedo* of the element air. The presiding deities are now winged. There's no polarity, no opposition, just working with the creator on, and as part of, creation. One who comes out of the great *sublimatio* becomes part of the creation process. Such people have come by the way of atonement to at-one-ment. As Jung said, to have produced the coin out of their own experience, to have been rendered down to their essence, is to have paid the price. He pointed out that true individuation can only take place if first the body is returned to earth. This is the point where our mortality and our immortality meet and we realise there's no split between earth and heaven. Earth-wisdom and God-wisdom seem the same. They have come together. Sapientia is now the feminine principle. 'As above so below', as inside so outside, with no split between earth and heaven.[89] All is now in the round. The Self itself pervades earthly life, earth rises to heaven and heaven comes down to earth. Of people who have reached this stage of the *sublimatio* and who are ready to come out of the flask, Jung said that they come to themselves, can accept themselves and be reconciled with themselves, and *thus* with adverse events and circumstances. He doesn't say, we note, that there *are* no adverse circumstances and events. Neither does he suggest that they're 'exonerated from', just 'reconciled', *because* they are reconciled with themselves. It was very much part of alchemy to come to yourself and discover that yourself is the Self, and the Self

---

[88] The Masons took a lot of symbolism from alchemy, as did the Rosicrucians, the Theosophists, Alice Bailey, *et al.*

[89] See the Emerald Tablet, Appendix below.

is yourself, and when was it ever different?

Befriending our own divinity, we see divinity everywhere. 'I salute the god in you, and the god in myself.' People in therapy often deny the god in themselves, the gold in themselves, and consequently in others. The gold looks ordinary. But someone who has been through the processes in the flask will salute the gold in another, and salute the gold in themselves. God begins everywhere and ends nowhere. The wheel has turned full circle many times, and now the circle, the mandala, is complete.

> He made his peace with God,
> He has sacrificed his own will,
> He has submitted himself to the will of God.

We are that which, sacrificed, is now sacrificing itself on an altar greater than itself. Yes, 'to sacrifice' - *sacrare* - can mean 'to give up'; yet also it can mean 'to make sacred'. This is the point at which we fully realise that our 'transient wealth belongeth to another'. It is not our gold, it is someone else's. The tradition of the Messiahs and the Boddhisattvas is all about this - about the transforming and redeeming one, who isn't a 'sacrifice' but is someone who helps to make sacred that which is already sacred.

Zen story

There's a story about a disciple who came many times to the Zen master saying, 'Master, I want to be taught by you, I want to be enlightened, I want to know your method'. And the master kept saying, 'Go away, go away - go away for seven years - go away for *another* seven years.' And the disciple came and said again, 'I want to - ' And the Master took him by the scruff of the neck and held his head down in his drinking bowl till the poor man nearly drowned. 'When you need enlightenment as you needed air just now, come back!' Straight Zen. Boom! It's said that the disciple was then enlightened. Well, if it doesn't kill you it might enlighten you! Which is probably true of alchemy, too. One of my favourite Chinese writers said:

> When a man lives in contact with the world and yet still in harmony
> with the light, then the round is round and the angular has angles;
> then he lives among men concealed yet visible, different and yet the

same, and none can compass it. [90]

No denial of either the world or the light, and the round is round, the angular has angles. Life is just as it is. That is a very Chinese statement. Things are just as they are. Then the person lives 'concealed, yet visible', the same only different, and 'none can compass it' nor understand the processes that have led there. Such a person is just there, of the world. This is the secret alchemist.

Hindu story

A similar statement comes out of the Upanishads of the Hindu tradition: [91]

> *'By what light does a man go out and do his work and return?'*
> *asks the king.*
> *And the sage replies, 'By the light of the sun.'*
> *'But if the light of the sun is put out?' the king asks.*
> *'Then by the light of the moon.'*
> *'And if the light of the moon is put out?'*
> *'By the light of the fire,' replies the sage.*
> *'And if the fire is put out?' persists the king.*
> *'Then,' the sage replies, 'the man will go out and do his work and*
> *return home by the light of the Self.'*

So the transformation has occurred. The alchemists said that in the final stages the hermetic flask is broken and the rest of the process goes on in the lenient and gentle light of the Sun. Their belief was that the circulation, gone through so many times, was to bring someone not only to their own salvation through God's grace (as a Christian would say, although the redemption of one's Self is certainly part of it), but to the very liberation of God from the darkness of matter, which was what they'd set about from the beginning. Again, you see the terrible blasphemy and heresy of alchemy? We are let out of the flask. This is what the shamanistic trainings and the initiation processes and the yoga systems have all been about: the person has had to go into the underworld, down into hell, up into heaven, through the oceans,

---

[90] Tzu-yang chen-jen, the 'True Man of the Purple Polar Light' (probably Chang Po-tuan, 11th century AD). In Wilhelm 1931, P. 53.

[91] Bridhadaranyaka Upanishad.

through the seas. This is what the great round has been about, the great *circumambulatio*, the circumambulation that one does on one's own feet with the continuous turning of the wheel of life. But it's interesting that the *sublimatio* therefore is not the end of the process - not *The End*. Presumably, when someone is out of the flask, they become part of a larger *opus*. Working with the creator, they become part of the Great Work, a participator in creation. This is the Enlightened One; again, the thrice-born: of the world and of heaven at the same time, child of earth, child of heaven. Such a person has in a very real sense become the Son, with the ability to move between heaven and hell, the underworld and the overworld and back again.

Another dream

To finish with a dream: 'I am sitting at a round white table outside a café in one of those typical French squares when an old man shuffles up to me (the wise person turns up as a shambling old tramp, as wise persons often do). He asks, "What shape is this square?" "It's a circle!" I say. He puts a glass of wine in the centre of the table, looks at me deeply then drinks the wine. My eyes are riveted to the blood-red circle left by the glass, bang in the centre of the table. A great sense of joy, relief, almost bliss comes over me. It has lasted now for many weeks.'

Ask a divine question and you get a divine answer: the Stone is ordinary. We can find it everywhere. Psychologically, of course, we require all the stages, and many times over. What starts in earth ends in earth. What starts in the *prima materia* ends with the return to earth, walking around the earth - but in relation to God. The *circulatio* has been not so much the bringing about of one's own salvation through God's grace, but the liberation of God from matter and from the darkness of matter. The great heresy again: not that we need to be redeemed because we're fallen and in mortal sin, but that we *are* redeemed, we *are* God, and that there is no fall. So the alchemists were burned! But maybe, too, it's not so very heretical after all. Christ descended into hell after the crucifixion. It's in the Psalms, it's in Isaiah:

Do not be afraid for I have redeemed you: I have called you by your name, and you are mine. Should you pass through the sea I will be with you: or through the rivers, they will not swallow you up. Should you walk through fire, you will not be scorched and the flames will not burn you. For I am Yahweh, your God, the Holy One of Israel, your Saviour.[92]

And it's in Eliot:

......Not the intense moment
Isolated, with no before and after,
But a lifetime burning in every moment.[93]

And, I would guess, the one who has gone through all these stages does live a lifetime burning in every moment of fire and flame.

So, those were the four processes of the *opus* of Western alchemy. Once the process has you, whatever you read begins to make sense. I could have started from a complex scroll, such as the Ripley text where the great toad explodes in its own venom and goes through stages of black and white and yellow and red, and still everything would have become clear. It's like reading a page of shorthand: once you know how, life renders itself up, but otherwise it's gobbledygook, gibberish (back to Al Gebir).

We are led on naturally now to the alchemy of the East which is so dear to my heart. Western alchemy is important, and very beautiful too. However, I do love the Eastern tradition, which seems to me to go straight to the heart of the matter without so much carry-on of words as to how it got there. We'll be looking with joy at the Circulation of the Light (which incorporates the dark) and at the Oxherding pictures.

---

92 Isaiah 43, 1-3.
93 T.S. Eliot 1959, 'East Coker' V.

PART II

The Alchemy of the East

INTRODUCTION

In the East it was accepted that the body,
like the earth, is divine

This is the *magnum opus,* the Great Work, the great tradition known in
China as 'the circulation of the light'. However much the languages of
the Eastern and the Western traditions of alchemy may vary, there are
many similarities. I'm cautious of putting two traditions together and
trying to unite systems, but there are so many cross-identifications that
I think it's worth bringing them out. What follows are my own
comments. You won't find these connections in books - none that I
know of, anyway. It would have saved me a lot of trouble if I'd been
able to find a book that linked the stages of West and East.

I'm not saying the Chinese method is better than the Western; it is just
different. It too is a mortal combat, yet it is taken rather differently -
more quietly. It's not such a struggle. However, let us not be fooled by
the tranquility of the East. It may be a quieter way of looking at it but
nonetheless it means being put to the fire, put to the test. Here is the
Samurai master, holding inside and outside in equipoise, being able to
stay with it while everything he's desired and longed for and yearned
for is taken down and gone.

East and West are absolutely agreed that it's the basic material of our
lives - the *prima materia*, the potter's clay, our life-experience - that's
put into the flask; and then the Sun-principle, which still has the divine
essence in it, is darkened and narrowed. The ego-consciousness, all
that is stereotyped, conditioned, fallible, goes down into the flask and

is plunged into the abyss. As in the West, it's accepted that the mother-lode goes into the flask, the ground of the mother, mass reaction, the past, the whole of the collective unconscious. The ground of the father also goes into the flask, needing to be rendered down by heat. This is the 'old king', the father-lode, collective consciousness, the ruling principle, all our tradition. In either case there's the sense of gathering, of freeing from the collective, as the individual steps out from the mass. And the slow process, the repetitions, the endless patience, the working at it while yet in life to become immortal, is again part of that tradition with which we're so familiar. This is like the *calcinatio*.

Next comes splitting and polarisation, the separation of hot from cold, dry from moist, masculine from feminine, the battle together and the struggle. The masculine energy of the *yang* as ego-consciousness has to go down and be darkened within the feminine *yin*, be plunged into the abyss of earth and matter, cooked and fired, divided in the water of the *solutio*, purified in the bath.

Then follows the overcoming of the lower nature by going into it, organising it differently and raising it in a process of circulation, with the use of disciplines, meditation, contemplation and the external practice of the Noble Eightfold Path of the Buddha. It is re-gathered into the air of a new consciousness where it's made adamant, eternal and fixed by fire. This is like the fire of the *coagulatio*. Freed from the smaller self, our nature comes into the loving bondage of something greater than itself.

Thus it rises, to become again the pure gold of solar fire, and the nature of lunar silver is within it. All meditation and yoga systems were set towards this end. The rituals, the contemplative life of the East, were aimed at purifying, lifting and finally coming to the raising - the *sublimatio* again. Here we find the same principle as in the West, though it's much more marked in Chinese alchemy: the need for the divinity to come down and impregnate and fertilise the womb of the Earth Mother. Then she will be fecund and give birth to that which is required by creation, so that it will again rise and come to the eternal heavens.

Theism and Buddhism

Underlying all Western traditions is the concept of a mediator sent to earth to become a walking spirit. Osiris, Attis, Wotan - Christianity, with the concept of the atonement - are about the same thing, though I believe the wrong emphasis is placed upon the crucified, not the resurrected, Christ. While the West is monotheistic ('I and the Father are one') the Eastern tradition is non-theistic. The aim is to live in accord with nature ('I and the Universe are one'). Intrinsically, both traditions honour nature, but the poor old Western alchemists had to work steadily towards what those in the East began from.

In the East, there is no mediator. Everyone can do it, everyone is divine from the beginning. Not fallen to be redeemed, we are divine to be redeemers. It is not that they don't believe in a god, but they don't personalise a god. That is the difference. Buddhists don't *worship* the Buddha, though they speak of the essence present in both gods and men. They look on the Buddha as a great teacher of the methods of arriving, becoming at one again. We have to stand on our heads and get into a different psychology altogether to understand that it was simply assumed that one *was* the Buddha. The Buddha was one with man. The Buddhist tradition doesn't kill and is so loving of life because each person has divinity. 'I salute the spirit in you and in myself.' There's no question about it.

Alchemy in the East wasn't seen as heretical, though it might have been frightening to people who thought it to be witchcraft. Since most Easterners took it for granted that spirit and matter were one and the same thing and that the earth is divine, the open and avowed wish to be one with the Buddha didn't need to be excused or justified. It was possible to talk about these things much more openly than in the West: 'We are looking for immortality - we wish to become immortal, to become one with the gods, with the deities' was a major thrust in many lives. And they believed it could be done. It was totally acceptable and there was no need to deny it.

Women alchemists

As we've seen, alchemy was pretty heretical in the West. There, the nature of the body, 'the flesh', was evil - and it was female! In the East it was accepted that the body, like the earth, is divine. Mind you, at first the Easterners too weren't so sure about women. In most of the early traditions the feminine was looked down upon. Mahayana Buddhism had three major stages and, even in the early period of Lao Tsu (the great master who most wrote and spoke of the Tao), Buddhism was very, very masculine-principled. It was Buddha and man - or man and Buddha! - who counted. They were aiming at the masculine spirit, and the feminine side was not to be talked about too much, just dealt with. In the middle stages there was more feeling towards the feminine, but even then, while they honoured the Moon, it was really all about spirit and red sulphur and the Sun (red sulphur is one of the names of the eternal Sun). For a woman to become a master alchemist and rise to heaven she would have had to be transformed and turned into a man: women had to become men in order to become Buddhas! Only much later, in the Tantric stages [94] involving sexual energies (both the use and the constraint of the seed, the sperm), does the honouring of the feminine principle begin. Female Buddhas, Kuan-Yin and Tara, start to appear in the system, and the female Boddhisattva is within the whole panoply of the immortals. [95]

An oral tradition

We don't have too much written on Eastern alchemy because again it was an oral tradition, passed from master to acolyte to apprentice, who then became a master or mistress of the art and passed it on in turn, in the knowledge that it would be honoured. No-one was entrusted with the secret unless they were felt to be highly trustworthy. Although it wasn't like the heretical tradition of the West, Eastern alchemy was not an easy art to follow. There were similar worldly problems and for similar reasons it did have to be kept secret. The ruler would discover that there were alchemists about, and torture them to get them to make gold to pay for armies and suchlike. An alchemist wasn't only

---

[94] Tantra is the yoga system that grew out of all this alchemy in the third stage of the various dynasties.

[95] However, they're not in the various wonderful paintings of the immortals, of whom there were about ten in the earliest traditions, sixteen later. As in the pantheon of Olympus, they don't appear till the very late stages.

expected to turn lead into gold; if your local duke or emperor thought you had the key to being able to fly, or become invisible, or levitate, then you were going to be burned, flagellated, screwed by the local dignitaries just the same. Chased and pushed on every hand, no wonder many Chinese alchemists were forced to go underground. This was why, as in the West, they had to use the language of disguise, often speaking of themselves not as alchemists but, more acceptably to the Chinese tradition, as scientists or artists. Otherwise, they kept quiet.

Honour

Don't forget honour. The honourable way of life, the honour of the Way, was a very great Chinese tradition. It was part of the collective. Remember the times they were living in and their culture. In most of their history, personal behaviour was extremely important. If you defiled or shamed honour, your whole family suffered for it. If you stole, not only did you have your hands cut off, but they might have theirs cut off too. Not only were you killed as a robber, but your family was imprisoned as well, if not killed. In the same way, if you were honoured then your family was honoured; be made a prime minister and your whole family would be exalted with you. In personal terms they carried great burdens. What they did very much affected those around them, so it wasn't difficult for them to realise that it also affected the universe around them.

In the following chapters we shall be looking at two of the most masterly Chinese texts, the finest traditions: 'The Secret of the Golden Flower', and the Oxherding pictures. We don't know when it was first put into writing, but 'The Secret of the Golden Flower', an esoteric text which describes 'the circulation of the light', was printed in the eighteenth century AD and found again in 1920 in Peking by Richard Wilhelm. We have seen how he translated and reprinted it, inviting Jung to write the commentary, and how Jung and Wilhelm became and remained very great friends. All that Jung had been looking at in terms of alchemy was there in this book.

Hologram

CHAPTER EIGHT

Taoist Alchemy of China

All methods take their source in quietness;
this marvellous magic cannot be fathomed

The whole of Eastern alchemy, as we know and understand it, is embedded in Taoism. Chinese alchemy stems from the Tao, the Way. Lao Tsu, its founder, was born in China in the sixth century BC, so Taoism is older than Buddhism - a very much older tradition than anything in the West. It was Lao Tsu who said, *'Those who know don't speak; those who speak don't know'*. That which is sublime cannot be expressed in words. So say all who work inwardly. However - first, to a bit of the back history of Taoist thought! Understanding the wider Chinese viewpoint helps us to see how the alchemists built up their tradition.

The Tao

Taoism itself had been flourishing in China since Lao Tsu had written about it in the sixth century BC (just think what that 'BC' means!). It wasn't necessarily devised by Lao Tsu, but certainly he rationalised it. He was one of the mystic 'al-chemists':

The Way is like something seen in a dream,
Elusive, evading one;
In it are images,
Elusive, evading one;
In it are things like shadows in twilight;
In it are essences, subtle but real,
Embedded in truth. [96]

The Way

Scientific *and* mystical, even in the early stages, it was apparent that the Eastern approaches were both outer and inner. The word 'Tao'

[96] 'Tao Te Ching', Twenty One.

originally meant 'the Way which, though stable, fixed and adamant in itself, leads from the beginning directly to the goal'. The signature in the upper part of its Chinese glyph means 'beginning', the lower, 'standing still'. It is referred to over and over by Chinese alchemists as the Right Way, the Way of heaven and of man. It is religious in origin. In the beginning is the Tao, unified, enduring, eternal, undivided. It is pure essence, the equivalent of the diamond body, or the pure spirit of the Indian tradition. From the Tao spin all the dualities of light and dark, inner and outer, life and death; and also *yin* and *yang*, the great feminine and masculine principles.

The goal of the Taoists was very much to do with release from the wheel of rebirth. Although it was understood that the 'true man of no rank' [97] would willingly come back to earth as a Boddhisattva, there was still a wish to be released from the necessity of return and they were hoping to work towards that release. We recall the final great test of the Lord Buddha - how, on Enlightenment, he wished to go back to the Tao and how Brahma begged him to stay. No longer *needing* to return, he agreed, and came back for the sake of the world. He had become the Returning One: *So long as one blade of grass cries out for light, I shall return.* He had achieved enlightenment and the right to live in the Tao; he had become a divinity.

When did all this become alchemy as such? The first direct reference we have to alchemy in China is written on a tablet from 144 BC, earlier than a lot of the traditions of Western alchemy. An emperor had ordered the public execution of anyone producing 'counterfeit gold' (an edict against 'puffers' again). Counterfeit gold? We can assume that alchemy must already have been flourishing in China before then.

The Neitan

As in the West, alchemists who sought the true gold, the true Way, those concerned with the inner elixir, 'the elixir of eternal life', were different from those looking for the mundane, untrue variety. In this tradition, an alchemist pursuing the inner goal was called 'Neitan'. The Neitan sought the qualitative, internal principles of life. Such a person

---

[97]   Rinzai said, 'In the midst of the body there lives a true man of no rank who continually goes in and out through the senses.' And see P. 221 below.

was seeking not riches but transformation into a true man of no rank, true to himself and true to the Tao. It was a golden touchstone that he was looking for, an elixir of immortality. We recall that the end result of Western alchemy was that a person could be in touch with immortality even while living in a decaying body. The Neitan too had the idea that, even on earth, he could live in a heavenly body and become the true man, dancing with life, one with the Tao and one with the immortals. He was struggling to become not just immortal but *an* immortal, to take a place in the pantheon of the gods. An immortal deity would become an ancestor and that mattered more than in the West, which doesn't honour its ancestors as does the East. The everlasting principle was very important.

We might ask: 'If the ultimate aim is to become Tao, part of a whole, isn't there some kind of error in wanting to become an immortal?' The answer is, 'Yes - both yes and no.' Certainly the Neitan was aiming for immortality; but what he sought - elixir, gold or stone - was to make him not personally but *im*personally immortal. The elixir was *within*. He called on nothing for help, not even on the Tao. He expected to do it himself. Grace would descend, Tao would descend, if he worked hard enough and stayed true enough. And he longed to do it in one lifetime. He hoped to work through the transformation, make his soul spiritual and gain immortality as an Enlightened One, while still living here on earth. His aim was to become truly in harmony with the Tao, to achieve samadhi, the bliss of living eternally in the One; and through the process he saw himself as serving creation. Trying to become a Boddhisattva, a returner, he needed plenty of time. Longevity would give him long enough.

The Weitan

Unlike the Neitan, there were also alchemists who were after the *outer* elixir. They were looking for something in the flask that could transform one thing into another, make lead or tin into gold. Known as 'Weitan', they too sought immortality. However, while the Neitan wanted to be transformed closer to the Creator, the Weitan were interested in personal rather than impersonal immortality. Scientifically, they were seeking an elixir of longevity for the prolonging of the life of the senses; and they were trying to make substances to help the sick for, like the Neitan, many Weitan were seeking power to help others. While the way of the Neitan would transform matter into spirit, the Weitan was trying to turn spirit into matter. The Neitan knew that spirit and matter were already one thing, along one spectrum: spirit is etherealised body, body is coagulated and embodied spirit. Matter going through the necessary stages will inevitably become spirit, while alternatively, that which starts as spirit and goes through the necessary stages will inevitably become matter. That wasn't a problem. Einstein came to believe it too, I understand, though he didn't to begin with; Fritjof Capra talks about it.[98] The problem was how to find the steps in between. We have both the Neitan and the Weitan within us. We can choose which way we go. It is possible to become an Enlightened One at any time. Yet maybe we need to choose the way of the Weitan because it is simply too hard to go the other way.

Science and medicine

Of course, Eastern alchemy was being practised at the time of much trading between the worlds of West and East. Larger ships were being built; people were going with caravans between Europe and Asia, particularly Russia and Persia and Arabia. So, as we have seen, there was a cross-fertilisation between Eastern and Western alchemists. During the Han dynasty, two hundred and twenty years before Christ, there was in China a tremendous flowering of interest in science. Science had arisen out of alchemy, for true alchemists both inner and outer were experimenters, with scientific heads as well as mystical hearts. In working to find the elixir, using minerals and plants, metals and herbs as ingredients, they gave rise to China's later interest in metallurgy and chemistry. Astrology, botany and zoology all flourished. Today we have physicists and chemists working with matter and substance, experimenting in the outer world, researching endlessly, very much in the alchemists' tradition. Although they are trying to bring about external magic, they often have a great love of what they're doing.

[98]   See Fritjof Capra, 'The Tao of Physics', 1975.

As we have seen, Chinese alchemists tried to discover substances that would help the sick; medicine was already well established by this period. The ability to cure diseases was very important, and a lot of them were also physicians. In modern times we are following the path of the outer elixir of China. A number of very sophisticated early texts survive, of particular interest in our times with our holistic approaches. It is delightful that a lot of complementary medicine is returning to Chinese systems of healing and medication. In a scientific way, I suppose, their search for an elixir of longevity is paralleled in what our genetic mechanics are doing now. Spare-part surgery isn't all that far from the Weitan. The question is, what do we do with it? The inner and the outer are bound very closely together. *Laborare et orare* - are work and prayer running side by side?

Bellows-blowers, magic and healing

Remember the 'puffers' who sought for gain and power by using alchemic processes to create mundane gold? Well, inevitably, these had their counterparts among the followers of the Taoist tradition, and again they were given names. Generally from among the Weitan, those who were looking *only* for an elixir of longevity were called 'bellows-blowers'. They included those who went for the restoration of youth, seeking physical immortality for themselves, as well as those who tried to use their powers for their own purposes. In the view of the Neitan, and of the true Weitan, their attempts to create earthly gold implied a lot of hot air to no end: it was fool's gold. The story of Faust in Goethe's play is very close to this.

Many of them wanted to heal through magic. However, some were concerned not only with healing but also with its opposite, the bringing on of disease. So in came white magic - and black magic too. Out he would come, the false healer. In a rural environment such a person might easily have been seen as unusual, perhaps even as a high master to be paid for what he did. He could cure people but he could also put the voodoo and the hex on them. Many such people were aiming, through alchemy, to acquire the *siddhis* - transformational and magical powers enabling them physically to levitate, to fly, to become invisible. 'Levitation' meant different things. A bellows-blower, seeking power *over* people, hoped to learn physically to rise and fly about. But the true alchemist meant by levitation the sublimation, the lift, the raising. Again, some among the Weitan had ideas about being possessed by spirits earthly or divine, and so learning to practise great powers. This communing with spirits later became the Shinto tradition of the market-place, seen nowadays in China and particularly in Japan. Very much of the outer elixir, it was often misused. It involved the use of psychism and mediumship and magical, yogic powers to hold the people. Certainly some bellows-blowers among the Weitan were able to use these powers, but they were false prophets. Feeling that the powers were really their own, they took them out into the market-place and made money from them. All right, yes, they made gold - but it wasn't quite what the Neitan had in mind!

A Neitan would disdain these *siddhis*. Out of India came the true approach: seeking the real elixir, the true alchemist didn't wish to have such powers, or, having them, he would choose not to use them. Yes, he expected to *be able* to fly, to move mysteriously from place to place, to transform substance - but he didn't do it. He would say, 'On the Way you will receive many *siddhis*. You will speak with the gods and be spoken through by them. You will be able to rise in the air, become invisible. But - you don't *do* it. If you have these powers of the market-place, you do not use them; certainly you don't hang around in them. You concentrate on losing any you may have gained until they become yours by making you immortal.' It's quite a discipline. However, the Neitan could still be scientists and work on the outer elixir, as did the Weitan who followed in their footsteps. In this tradition the inner and the outer processes were seen almost from the beginning as ways to the same end. And by no means all Weitan had the motivation of the bellows-blowers. Just as in Western alchemy, some were doing more of the *laborare* stuff while others were following the *orare*, the prayerful, contemplative processes. The bellows-blowers naturally came in at the substance end of it, seeking the false gold, the restoration of youth and a long life for the body. But both the Neitan and the true Weitan aimed to come again from the polarity to the original oneness, bringing spirit and matter together.

Meditation and contemplation

Most Eastern alchemists were not set apart; they didn't retire from the external world. They were expected to try to handle outer life, at the same time moving more and more towards the Tao. Although it was a struggle to be the householder and be about many things, they would always set aside time for the work. Certain monks (and later, nuns) were in fact withdrawn into areas where they could practise, but they were also encouraged to keep working. 'Work' was not a dirty word and alchemy was practised by extremely busy people - rulers, emperors, doctors, surgeons, teachers. Becoming a master of the Tao is about withdrawing not from the world itself but from the lure, the seduction of the world. The endless, endless hours of prayer and contemplation required - and the outer work, too! Here is a master of Chinese alchemy speaking:

> Children, take heed: if for a day you do not practise meditation, the light streams out, and who knows whither? If you only meditate for a quarter of an hour, you can set ten thousand aeons and one thousand births at rest. All methods take their source in quietness; this marvellous magic cannot be fathomed. [99]

Well, that's typical Chinese exaggeration - for all their understating behaviour they made some wonderful over-statements. Quarter of an hour's practice, and ten thousand aeons and one thousand births are set at rest - at least! But it underlines and emphasises the importance of meditation. We are not only working for ourselves; the whole universe is involved in this system. This is the true master speaking of the incessant practice of the disciplines needed to bring about the real work. It is the internal magic of the Neitan, concerned with impersonal power, impersonal creativity, serving the universe, helping others to be freed from the endless turning of the wheel of rebirth.

Names for the goal

Lao Tsu said that once the whole is divided, the parts need names. However, names tie things down. To seek after Tao is like turning in

---

[99] The master Lü Yen, or 'Guest of the Cavern', author of 'The Secret of the Golden Flower'. Lü Yen was born in 755 AD and lived into the ninth century. He derived his secret and esoteric lore from Lao Tsu, via the Tao Te Ching. In Wilhelm 1931, P. 33.

circles to see one's own eyes. Rather, walk on. It is well-known in Zen: 'In my hut this spring there is nothing, there is everything. You may stay with the master, if you understand.' Be that as it may, the Neitan called what they were looking for by a number of names, just as did the Western alchemists. Though they too sometimes spoke of the goal as the Stone, the Elixir is the most common name - the Golden Elixir or the Golden Pill of Immortality. It was known in China as the Paradoxical Language. It is the Dragon Castle on the Floor of the Sea; it is the Golden Flower discovered through the Circulation of the Light (the tradition of which we'll be looking at later). It is the Golden Castle, the Heavenly Heart, the Terrace of Life, the Field of the Square Inch in the House of the Square Foot. It is the Empire of the Golden Joy, the Land without Boundaries, the Central White Light, as well as the Purple Hall in the City of Jade. Pictorial, imaginative descriptions of that which was sought, these names were used by various alchemists to speak of the outcome of the approach of the followers of the true path.

All this is tremendously like the end product of Western alchemy. The Eastern alchemists knew that whatever is found inwardly in the flask at the end of the process can make a person immortal - make him *an* immortal. As we have seen, it can transform matter into spirit and spirit into matter. It's much easier to understand in the Eastern traditions that we too can live in a heavenly body even while our earthly bodies decay. We can be everlasting, live in rhythm with nature and in touch with immortality, even while we're on earth. The immortals are rays or aspects of the Tao. Shiva, Brahma and Vishnu are not separate, but aspects of the one god.

Immortality

We've seen how, at this level, a very high aim was to become one who serves the Tao in the world, a Boddhisattva who takes on a personality, comes back and helps those still struggling on the wheel of rebirth. But that wasn't the only aim. At a certain point a person would be drawn back into the Tao, become an immortal and lose every sort of individuality. There would be a passing over into what we translate as 'nothingness' and the Chinese tradition calls 'no-thing-ness'. This is *nirvana*, in which the personal identity is wiped out, returned beyond the individual to the central essence of the Tao which has no personality at all. The aim of Buddhist tradition is to go into *samadhi*, vanish into the Oneness and become an immortal, an aspect of the god. This is why so many in the West believe that the Eastern tradition has to do with vanishing and loss of personality. It isn't so. We get much closer to what they were talking about, not by reading the neo-Buddhists but by going very deeply into the teachings of the Buddha himself - like reading Jung instead of the neo-Jungians.

> *What makes my life good makes death good. The sage delights in early death, he delights in old age, he delights in the beginning, he delights in the end. The true man of ancient times knew nothing of loving life and hating death. He who clearly apprehends the scheme of existence does not rejoice over life nor repine at death, for he knows that these are not final.*

That's one of the marvellous quotations for all times - Chuang Tsu, at whose feet I worship.[100] Now there was a true alchemist, a Neitan! A pupil of Lao Tsu, he was speaking of the interior knowledge that the divinity is already within man - that life and death, inner and outer are one and the same. Life and immortality can become one. The aim of the Neitan is to become an *inward* immortal, seeking the elixir of eternal life which, when taken, will transform him into the true man of no rank.

How is this state to be reached? Purity of approach, as in the Western tradition, is absolutely paramount. Lao Tsu said that the art is to become the right man, for even if he chooses the wrong means, they will work in the right way for him. That's because his heart is pure and his basic impulse is right. Conversely, when the wrong man uses the right means, even the right means work in the wrong way.[101] The struggle was always for appropriate belief, intentions, speech and actions, for right livelihood, endeavour, mindfulness and concentration. 'Right' here means in favour of the Tao, in favour of life - in favour of *all* life, not just our own personal desire. The Samurai tradition, seen in Zen, comes out of this, and yoga is also close to it. The turning wheel of yoga is

---

[100] Chuang Tsu lived around the fourth century BC. Chuang Tsu was to Lao Tsu as St. Paul was to Jesus and Plato to Socrates. See 'Inner Chapters' Pp. 44 and 73.

[101] When the right man uses the wrong means, the wrong means work in the right way. When the wrong man uses the right means, the right means work in the wrong way. Anon.

very like the wheel of rebirth. The yoga systems we use are out of the Indian tradition and were all part of the turning of the light through breathing, working with the *chakras*. The Tao was the Right Way, and the Right Way was to live by the Noble Eightfold Path of the Buddha.[102] If any of us could live like that, we'd already be within the Tao. Probably even now we could become immortal!

The individual

What happens for the individual in the Chinese tradition? Obviously I lose a lot in simplifying it so much, but what the alchemy was about was this: in the beginning, as we have seen, is the undivided one, the Tao. And at a certain point the creative principle of the Tao splits and divides into the masculine and feminine principles. So in the person at conception it takes the form of *yin* and *yang*. The great separation from the universal Tao into the *yin* and the *yang* of creation begins to be personal, and we become individuals. Within us are life, fate and love, and also the essence, the divine word. So this is the Tao, the undivided oneness, in the individual in the dance of life. The feminine has the seed of the masculine within her and the masculine has the seed of the feminine within him. Male and female can dance together in a dynamic celebration of creation and life, representing the Tao. Ultimately they become part of creation, as each learns how to have something of the other within them. That which was divided returns to Oneness, to unification. It is Shiva who dances. This dance, this turning, is tremendously like the turning of the four processes of the Western tradition.

Figure 3 - The Yin-Yang Symbol - opposite

The great glyph that came out of it all was the *yin-yang* figure, a much shorter way of saying all that. We sometimes find written above it, 'Central Monad - Individual - Golden Flower' (we have a small spark from the divine seed-essence in us, the spark of the Tao, known as the central 'monad' for each human being). The Tao, the undivided Oneness,

---

102   The precepts of the Noble Eightfold Path of the Buddha:
        Right Belief, Right Intention,
        Right Speech, Right Action,
        Right Livelihood, Right Endeavour,
        Right Mindfulness, Right Concentration.

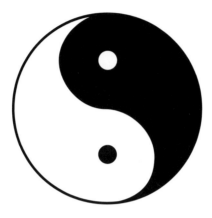

Figure 3 - The Yin-Yang Symbol

is polarising, first with *yin* on top and then with *yang* on top, and there's the struggle which, after a while, begins to be a dance. We recognise this from the *solutio* process. Tai Chi is one of the great modes of the incorporation, the dance of life. Wonderful! The dance of the Way, the dance of the gods! I have a beautiful figure of the Buddha dancing, the great Lord Ho dancing on the surface of life, as Shiva also dances. And so the dance of creation within the individual mirrors that within the universe, until the person becomes the Way even within earthly living and, walking along the Way, can come back to undividedness.

I suppose Lao Tsu was to Confucius as Plato was to Aristotle. Confucius said that one should not be sexual - one should be disciplined in an extreme way. Though he was very clear and lucid and full of uprightness and beautiful tradition, there was much of Aristotle's rigidity of morality in Confucius; whereas Lao Tsu said you can give of your seed so long as it is already given to the Tao. To love is good - but one should not possess, one needs to do it as a dance. Celibacy was not necessarily required of alchemists, only the purification of the intent of

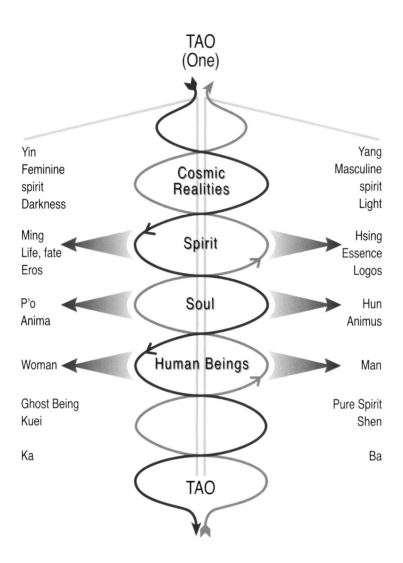

Figure 4 - The Tao

sexuality. The *alembic* was called 'the germinal vesicle' or seed container. The later Tantric tradition was about the conservation of the seed or semen, which was seen as indistinguishable from the creative seed essence of the Tao. The Chinese Book of Changes, the 'I Ching', is a treatise on alchemy.[103] In the beginning was the undivided; at the end is the undivided. The pairs of opposites are married together in the dance of the masculine and the feminine. They must be separated, and then they must be brought back together again. Fire and energy mate and copulate in this dance, this intercourse with the feminine principle. This is tantric yoga, this coming together, whether outwardly or inwardly. The retention of seed or the outgoing of seed is about the seed of the divine within us. If we live the noble, honourable life, this life, we begin to build in this *shen* side of ourselves, the immortal Self which goes back to heaven. Death cannot touch it.

Figure 4 -The Tao - opposite

This map of the Tao is adapted from 'The Secret of the Golden Flower'. It links with Figure 5, Page 184, and it is out of the tradition we are coming to, the Circulation of the Light: the One divides into two and it is the separation into the two that brings about the birth of the Golden Flower. *Yin* is of silver, *yang* of gold (the Taoists used exactly the same principle as in the West: *yin* is Moon and *yang* is Sun). *Yin* is dark, moist, cold and feminine, *yang* is light, dry, hot, masculine - and *yang* is spirit. It is tremendously like Jung's Eros and Logos, the feminine and masculine principles.

Down the left hand side is the great creating feminine principle responsible for life itself, the manifestation of the undivided one in the division of nature. Thus the Tao gives birth to the *yin* in all life. *Yin* comes into this world as impersonal life. *Yin* in all life brings about *ming*, the equivalent of the feminine soul, the Moon principle, which manifests as fate, life, matter, love of the heart - Eros-love. So it is *yin* who is responsible for the Fates (the idea of the Fates being female is very close to what later became the Western tradition); also for Eros, to whom we're all answerable. Birth, death and rebirth are all under the *aegis* of the feminine. It is linked with the Moon and Venus, like that

---

[103] See Wilhelm 1951.

which is in the flask at the *solutio* stage. It becomes more personal as we follow down the *yin* side. Each human being has a feminine characteristic called the *p'o*, or body-soul, very close to what we would now call the personal anima. (In Jung's tradition, woman *is* anima, man *has* anima, the contra-sexual side). Finally we come to *kuei*, our earth body, the earth of our body. The decaying body was very much linked with the feminine, as indeed it was in the Western tradition.

The Tao, the undivided one, also manifests as *yang*, the great masculine principle in all life, the impersonal solar principle. We move from the Moon to the Sun again. Yang the impersonal manifests for the individual at the level of spirit as *hsing*, essence - Logos. As that is made personal, becoming what we might call the animus, our own individual human masculine principle, it is called *hun*. And, as the masculine spirit-body that lives on earth and can one day go back to the Tao in heaven, it is known as *shen*, pure spirit. Though the body might decay at death, the spirit will rise, returning it to the Tao.

It was believed that if you had lived a wicked life, given way to the venal lusts of the body and fallen into desire and wickedness (all those glorious things that get you into so much trouble but make life so worth living!), then at death your whole essence would go down into and through the earth. You would corrupt and descend into the underworld, right deep down into hell. You would become a ghost-being, a ghostly ancestor, and your one aim would be to get back out of hell, back into life, back on to the wheel of rebirth to take another body - in order to have another go at the lust-pots! If on the other hand through the struggle of one or many lifetimes a person had managed after all to dominate with the *hun* side, if spirit-soul had overcome, then that person would become *shen*, pure spirit, who on death would rise and return to the Tao.[104] So, the female body would go back to the earth and to decay, while the male body would rise? We can put a question-mark here - this obviously came out of an all-male system! Later, it was realised that it's the *yin* and the *yang* together that will rise, while the body decays.

---

[104] In Buddhist teaching, the Golden Flower was held to arise from *shen*, not from *kuei*. However, in the true Chinese tradition it arose from both Yin and Yang together. See Wilhelm 1931, P.65, Cary Baynes' note.

All this equates very closely to the system in Egypt. On their sarcophagi and in glyphs you often see birds, one flying up and one flying down, just as in Western alchemy. The Egyptians held that the body, the *ka* soul, which is corruptible, goes down into the earth and decays and is part of the human condition, but the *ba* soul, the bird behind the head of the mummy, rises and goes back to its origins in heaven. The *ka* soul has to be reborn from the earth into which it has descended, while the *ba* soul is immortal. So we are continuously both mortal and immortal, and the art is to become immortal while being mortal. Simple really, if you understand it - the only problem is how on earth to do it!

In the Shinto tradition there is the belief that a wandering ghost-being looking for a body might jump the gun; trying to take someone else's body, the ghost-soul would manifest through that person. Hence the beliefs about possession, about ancestral spirits taking over a living body, and the struggle to prevent it that has to be put up by the shamans. Someone attached to the flesh (represented by the things of the feminine!) would be lured into the 'backward-flowing' - which is all that fun stuff. It's whoopee for a long time - then down he'd be taken into the *calcinatio*, into earth. There were many levels of Chinese hells. Some were about the satiation of the senses - a person had to eat so much or copulate so much that he was totally knackered and gave it up as a bad job. This was one form of Chinese torture: caught by, lured into the senses, he had to be continuously reborn until such time as, redeemed by the fire within, he could come back into the dance.

The Golden Flower

In China, by mixing silver and gold in the flask, the alchemists were bringing together *ming* (earth and matter) with *hsing* (fire and essence). Then *p'o* and *hun* interact to make the marriage of anima with animus (but using different language), till they begin to rise again to the Tao. In order to bring about the birth of the Golden Flower, to recreate Tao and get back to the original undivided principle, the person has to go through many stages. They're almost exactly the same four stages as we were looking at in the Western tradition: we are plunged into earth, into water, taken through air, through fire. We go many times through this circulation of up and down, in and out. So again, polarisation and struggle. In our lifetime, or many lifetimes, the spirit-body and the earth-body move around together and are in conflict in each person. It's the battling spirit of masculine and feminine, just as in the *solutio* pictures. *Yin* and *yang* are in confrontation and the aim is to get them to inter-relate and interact in the round in a continuous circulation - darkness with light, Eros with Logos, fate with divinity, feminine body-soul with masculine spirit-soul; until, after a while, the two begin to work together. And then at last, through processes we shall be looking at, they are brought into the mysterious marriage.

The Eastern alchemists were much more aware straight away that it's the body that is the flask. It was within the *alembic* of the body that they were trying to redeem the darkness. Matter was convertible. The body was open and available to be re-atomised and redeemed and purified. If you could achieve the quality, the refinement, of the substances of the body, you could become spirit, *be* spirit, while still in an actual body. The process consisted in breathing. It is aspiration: 'Fire and air can move our earth and water'. Even if, as an alchemist, you were moving substances around, you did it in a contemplative way, and the endless repetitions of that could eventually purify the very atoms of the substance of the physical body. So at last the dance of creation within the individual could mirror that within the universe.

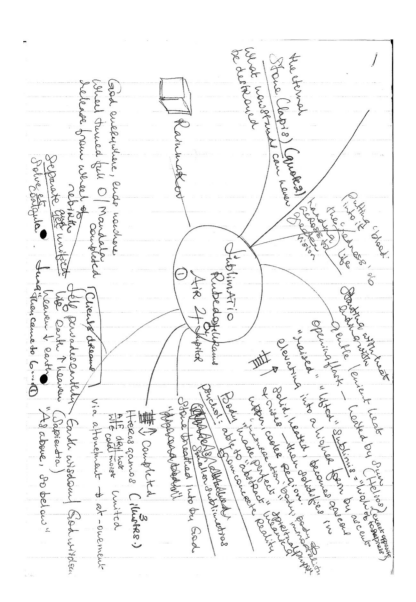

The Author's Notes

One of the pages used by Barbara Somers in the giving of these talks

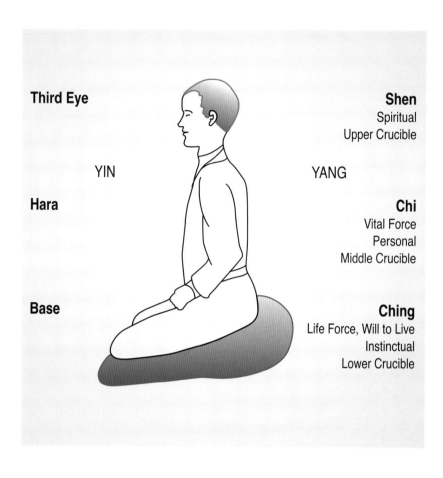

Third Eye

YIN

Hara

Base

Shen
Spiritual
Upper Crucible

YANG

Chi
Vital Force
Personal
Middle Crucible

Ching
Life Force, Will to Live
Instinctual
Lower Crucible

Figure 5 - The Circulation of the Light

CHAPTER NINE

The Secret of the Golden Flower

Watching his thoughts going across is like watching birds;
he lets them, like birds, fly over the quiet pool

Figure 5 - The Circulation of the Light - opposite

I introduce this illustration to bring in the meditator and link him with
the map of the Tao, Figure 4, Page 178. We've seen how, through the
circulation process in the Tao, the alchemical work is to bring pure
spirit to interact and relate with the feminine principle in something
like a dance. The spirit comes down through all the centres, into and
through the belly, through the root *chakra* , through sexuality. We learn
to align ourselves, head, heart, body - align the *chakra* system. Once it
is aligned then the flow can come, from the Tao to the Tao and back
again. The earth is Tao, and heaven is Tao; they're one and the same
thing, and we build a bridge.

Equally, the feminine principle begins to work in the dance to the point
where the two can come together into a marriage and then rise. We've
seen how the aim is to get back to the Tao and step off the wheel of
rebirth, rising in order to avoid becoming a ghost ancestor and having
to go back on to the wheel.

The work

The preamble is similar to that of the true alchemist of the West. The
body is itself the flask. Turned inward, the senses become the seal upon
it. The heat under it is aspiration, and the flame of aspiration sets the
light moving. All the disciplines and purification rituals of meditation
and yoga are designed to keep the process on the move, not letting the
fire go out. The adept starts by sending thought from the head to the
base of the spine, where it acts on *ching*, the life force in the lower
crucible. Thence it is sent up the back of the spine via the middle

crucible, over the crown and down again. *Yin* is breath in, *yang* is breath out. It is raised on the hiatus between in and out. Thought becomes inner fire, which begins to light the furnace. Energy learns to rise up the spine, and this is the magical road of ascent to the range of mountains beyond the head, where the immortals live. The art lies in blending the energies. The divine *ch'i*, the air, the vital force or ethereal essence, cannot be held back. [105]

Shen, the upper crucible, consists of the alter major *chakra* (or 'jade gate') and the brow and crown *chakras* with their links with the pineal and pituitary glands.[106] By this Way, the light is made to circulate through the various organs of the body. It is taken down deep into the root *chakra*, which it cleanses; then it rises through each *chakra* in turn, cleansing them all, till finally it is taken through the crown centre. All systems of yoga and meditation and contemplation involved this. There are many similarities with the Western tradition, the whole idea being that you could begin to purify and redeem the body, becoming an alchemist even in the middle of your current living. So we come to the pictures of the Circulation of the Light.[107] I invite the reader to contemplate each in turn.

Stage One   - 'Gathering the Light.'
Stage Two   - 'Origin of a New Being in the Place of Power.'
Stage Three - 'Separation of the Spirit-Body for Independent Existence.'
Stage Four - 'The Centre in the Midst of the Conditions.'

[105]   See Jung, CW 13, par 433.

[106]

Centre	Gland
Head	Pineal
Brow	Pituitary
Throat	Thyroid
Heart	Thymus
Solar Plexus	Pancreas
Sacral	Gonads
Base of Spine	Adrenals

Formulation taken from Ian Gordon-Brown, longhand notes.

[107]   The pictures of Stages One to Four (Figures 10 - 13 below) are attributed to Lü Yen. They are taken from 'The Secret of the Golden Flower', and are relevant to the Hui Ming Ching, or 'Book of Consciousness and Life', which follows it (Wilhelm 1931 Pp. 69 ff). The pictures are also in Jung, CW 13, Pp. 30-33.

Figure 6 - Stage One, Gathering The Light [108]

The element of this first picture is fire, in whose heat the separating out must occur. Attention drops to the solar plexus, where the adept's hands are. The solar plexus is now like the flask, the first alembic, where the separation of body from matter, *yin* from *yang*, *hsing* from *ming*, *p'o* from *hun* - or, in Egyptian terms, of *ka* from *ba* - takes place.

[108]   Wilhelm ibid, P. 27. Fire the element; this stage parallels the *nigredo*.

He is awaiting the parting of the body and the spirit. 'The Secret of the Golden Flower' [109] explains that the spirit, having been to some degree purified, dives down into the abyss of the abdomen to which the light penetrates. There, it cleanses the solar plexus, the root *chakra* and the sexual *chakra* with pure spirit.

The alchemist and the plumb-line

Again, listen to the poetry rather than the words of it! This stage is called 'putting the hand to it'. The process is through meditation and the aim is to make a fixed pole within the whirl of the ten thousand things,[110] from belly to heart, from base nature to crown. The meditator is drawing inward, gathering in, removing himself from the external world. The power, which is in the darkness of the *prima materia*, the past, the feminine principle, mixes with spirit, and spirit unites with the power and becomes crystallised, like the ash at the bottom of the flask at the end of the *calcinatio* stage. Keeping perpendicular, he withdraws projections and steps out of the mass. Seated on a cross-section of the tree of life, which links the underworld to heaven, he is rooted in the tree of his own life. The tree is the representative of nature and eternity. All of his life is in the flask. His slippers are left outside, put out of the holy place, for he is on holy ground. Light penetrates down through matter. His white and golden robe shows that he has moved out from 'the slag of darkness' [111] to return to the purely creative. Sitting with his whole weight on a triangular base, he has turned his senses inward. His eyes are de-focussed and turned in. Using his nose as a plumb-line, he is quiet and still. He has achieved his position.

And now comes the gathering of the light. This is the acceptance that the light is there to be gathered. All the light in the universe is being gathered into the flask, and a seal put across the senses. The man hasn't set up an outside flask; he is himself the flask. The body is the flask. In 'putting the hand to it', he is getting down to the job. He has

[109] Wilhelm 1931. Pp. 28 ff.

[110] It's said that in the beginning was the One, the Tao, which became the thousand and one things, or the *ten* thousand and one things, severally described.

[111] Wilhelm ibid, P. 26.

steadied his breathing and is gazing at the tip of his nose. Everything is turning inwards. He looks very simple and serene here, in comparison with those pictures of the nigredo of the West. Yet the struggle is great. It is a gathering of *inward* light - but it is by that very light that we become most aware of the darkness, within and without. Bright lights throw dark shadows. This is the recognition of the shadow. He allows and lets go of all the rush of the world, withdrawing projections, stepping out of the mass. He is dying to the ten thousand and one things; he is going down into the darkness. It is hard to step away from the ten thousand things. Watching his thoughts going across is like watching birds. He lets them, like birds, fly over the quiet pool.

Conserving the light

So with us: beginning to become alchemists, we gather in all that we are, leave life outside, take our shoes off and settle. Wearing robes that are appropriate, whether actual or internal, we set ourselves apart, step out of the mass. Our life-experience is brought in as the potter's clay; whether outwardly with the endless repetitions of the true experimenting scientist or inwardly with the endless repetitions of an internal philosophy, it's still the same thing. The senses are not turned outward. We don't come out of our meditation because we hear a bird sing or see a beautiful young man or maiden walk in front of us, or suddenly notice the perfume of the flowers. All these things need to be sealed in the flask so that the fire will continue to burn. It takes many hours to come to this quiet place. We too are emancipating ourselves for something greater; part of the collective, we're taking responsibility *for* the collective.

'One must forget both body and heart. The heart must die, the spirit live.' So said the master. The heart is now dying into something. In the Chinese tradition, the Eros-life, the lust-life, the desire-life was said to live in the heart, together with earth and matter. They saw the heart not as higher aspiration but as the place where *ming* lives - life, fate, Eros. It is the heart that is drawn out into the seduction of the world, the seduction of the senses. The heart is the body of desire and it's the heart which must die for the spirit to live. Now the light, instead of being spilled out, is gathered in. The constant searching for the Self, which has been projected on to things outside, has meant a spilling out to something. Now, the essence is no longer spilled out and dissipated all the time; rather, it's drawn in with the light to nurture the Divine Child within.

So the master forgets both body and heart. Now he begins to breathe. Whatever the thoughts are, they're taken out of the head and down the front and to the base of the spine. This is an everlasting circuit, reversing the flow of life: it goes down, back, up and over, till the process ceases as breathing and happens naturally. He *is* the flask, and he is now well and truly *in* the flask. He raises the breathing. He breathes in the lower crucible, between the base and navel *chakras*, the sexual centre. The *yang* raises the breath from the root *chakra*, up behind the spinal *chakras* and through each one: the sex centre, the hara, the solar plexus, the heart, the throat, the alter major and brow, and at last the crown centre. On the *yin*, the breath descends: the crown, (the pineal gland); the third eye, (the pituitary); the throat, (the thyroid); the heart; the solar plexus; the hara; and from the genitals to the root *chakra* again. Thus there is a continuous circulation, raising the fire, taking it over, allowing it to descend. It is about both breath and visualisation. We noted a plumb-line in the picture. He is concentrating attention on the vertical line from the bridge of his nose.[112] The aspiration, the dedication, the application to do it constitutes the fire under the flask. The question is, how not to be pulled off by confusion. It may take many years. There is a difference here between the Neitan and the Weitan, and it lies in his motive. The reader might contemplate the picture for a little while.

---

[112]   Wilhelm 1931, P. 39.

**Figure 7 - Stage Two,
Origin of a New Being in the Place of Power** [113]

Here the element is water. This stage has parallels with the *solutio*. In contemplating this picture we have to accept that many years must have gone into reaching stage two. 'Only after a hundred days of consistent work, only then is the light genuine; only then can one begin work with the spirit-fire.'[114] A hundred days in Chinese means a very long time. It is concentrated work. Such concentration turns 'the mill-

113   Wilhelm ibid., P. 37.
114   Wilhelm ibid., P. 39.

wheel of light' to distil its essence. The idea of the mill-wheel is very Chinese - the flow of water and the wheel turned by the Buddhist law and doctrine. This is both the beginning and the end of the *solutio* process, where all the senses are inward. Its aim is 'the origin of a new being in the place of power'.

The alchemist and the dragon

The meditator is sitting on the phoenix feathers of the earth-dragon, the ground-dragon. This is the Ouroboros, the plumed serpent, equivalent perhaps to the Green Lion, the beast of desire, soon to be slain.[115] He is sitting on nature, and the shy dragon of heaven, the log of his life, becomes the potentially divine dragon. Seen in colour I think it might look something like a coiled serpent with peacock feathers, reminding us of the peacock's tail, the *cauda pavonis*, coming up between the black and the white stages. Now he is really getting down to the work. He is giving birth to something. He is stripped down and much more naked than he was before. His very simple robe is white, pre-empting the golden; it's open and his breast is bared. He's more vulnerable, more open to the flow of energy. The belted cord of truth from his waist is touching the earth, whereas before only his slippers were on the ground. Now he has no shoes, showing that the need for protection and for the personal have gone. His top-knot is out from under the protective headgear of stage one, preparing the crown *chakra* for the inundation of light. And what is beginning to come in the place of power? He is holding in his hands 'the origin of a new being', a small Buddha sitting cross legged in the flame there, all in peacock feathers. He's already beginning to give birth to the Self, the Tao, the Baby Buddha.

The method

Raising the energy to *shen* is the aim. Focus is required for *shen* energy to awaken. Still he is only half-cooked. The fire must not go out, and the bellows must be applied. This is the place of power where the elixir is beginning to be distilled. He has gone through great torment, and yet he looks very peaceful. He keeps silent about the work: 'Don't let the

---

[115]   This is rather like St. George with the vanquished dragon of desire. There are pictures and effigies of Kuan-Yin standing on the dragon of desire, holding its jaw bone. Many of the divinities and immortals in wall-hangings are seated on the dragon of desire.

flask leak!' Sitting quietly, he fixes the heart on 'the centre in the midst of conditions', the solar plexus. As we've seen, 'the heart' is matter, is desire. Yet it is also the feminine principle, *yin*, and now it wishes to be raised to heaven. Of the heart the alchemist says:

> *One closes the lips and breathes inwardly. Breathing is at this place.*
> *The nose smells no odours. Smelling is at this place.*
> *The ear does not hear things outside. Hearing is at this place.*
> *The whole heart watches over what is within. Its watching is at this place.* [116]

So, concentrated work. The heart is now involved. As in the *solutio* (when in the first early stages of the marriage they were working together to bring into conception the Divine Child in the flask), darkness and light, the masculine and the feminine, struggle within the crucible.[117] Seeds of peace already lie within the conflict, and seeds of war within the peace. *P'o* and *hun* are no longer in combat but, each giving up their own power, they're beginning to work together in favour of the 'new being in the place of power'. And because of all the disciplines of stage one, something begins to happen in the abdomen in this place of power. We saw how such concentration lets flow the water that turns the mill-wheel. All the senses are now turned inward to this place, where a different order of being is heard. Breathing has turned in. The alchemist is said to become the mother hen sitting on the eggs, waiting for what will occur. So he remains in the darkness, waiting for the true light. Here are flames and peacock feathers. The fire-shape, leaf-shape that he holds in his hands indicates also the fire in the belly. Into the solar plexus, instead of the original 'slag of darkness' a new being is beginning to come.

The Chinese say that, when the darkness is at rest, the light begins to move. In therapy, we help clients to look at the shadow, extricate themselves from the seduction of the external and revalue their own internal world. It is then that the light within them begins to move in the darkness. They are not denying the darkness but taking the darkness with them. We recall how, in the Western tradition, the Stone

---

[116]   Wilhelm, 1931, Pp. 38-9.

[117]   See Plates 7 and 8 above, where the masculine and feminine were first in combat and then worked together to tie the feet of the dragon.

says, 'I the *lapis* beget the light, but the darkness too is of my nature'. This is the interaction of light and dark in order to bring about a different light.

The time of the living midnight

It is also a place of death, as in the *albedo*. Everything has been taken into the place of power deep down in the unconscious. The place is the centre, that place of death to past experience, where body and heart are dying to the senses and to the outside world. The senses are stilled and the poise of light is within the unconscious. Life, fate and eros-love begin to be purified. Adepts call this 'the time of the living midnight'.[118] Strong ego-will and strong desire are being taken down into the abyss of darkness. Instead of the bright light of ego-consciousness, at the living midnight we have a different luminary or luminous principle coming into being. This again is like the *solutio*, lit by the Moon. Now, when darkness is at rest and struggle is no longer such a struggle, the light begins to move.

Danger

And it's seductive! Again, this is a time of high danger. One Westerner commented dreamily, 'I have a feeling of sinking into a very deep, dark blue - like the night sky, like the spaces between the stars - I'm going through a very deep, deep dark place - and yet there's a great rest in that dark, a rest that's like no other rest.' I suspect that the danger of this place is like that of the *solutio*: it's so blissful that one could stay there, blissed out in a swoon of ecstasy, and never move on. To fail is to go into the abyss, to be overwhelmed by the dark waters 'the other side of the Moon'. A person may become a ghost-being trapped in untamed *ching*, ultimately to fall down into the hell of endless rebirth. *Embrace doubt as you would your concubine*, say the alchemists. Yet, as the raft sinks, will the adept drown in loss of certainty? This is why aspiration is needed; we can get caught in the abysmal waters, in the feminine principle, in the seduction of the *yin*, in the beauty of the spaces between matter - and between spirit, too.

---

[118]　Wilhelm 1931, P. 60.

This is where the Neitan and the Weitan move apart, the latter showing himself in his real colours, while the true alchemist goes steadily after the internal gold. The bellows-blower begins to develop those *siddhis* and he thinks he's got there. This is astral glamour - and how seductive it is! 'Ho Ho! Look, I can make light!' and there he is with devotees hanging on to his feathers. This is all very dangerous. Therapists put their fees up, falling into the counter-transference of thinking they actually have something to offer. But also this is where we, as devotees, begin to become real disciples. There may well follow a period when the master withdraws, becomes unfriendly, criticises us, beats us. It may all take *another* seven years. This is designed to stop us depending on anything outside, even on the master. It's about becoming our own master, our own midwife, and it's very painful. We may belong to a group of devoted, dependent children - and now we will be forced out. The master may do something bad, he may betray us, may be seen as wrong. The loving master is stiffening up the process to wean us, stop us grabbing the nearest tit and sucking hard for the rest of our lives! This is love.

Return of the Sun

An emergence from those waters is a baptism. To succeed at this point is to see the first rays of another light appearing above the dark waters. When day is reborn out of night at dawn, it's as if it had been washed by the night, cleansed. There is a rather *wet* feeling about that. Just before dawn and similarly at twilight there is a blending-time: trees are different, bird-song is very quiet (and there are many Chinese poems on that). I think we are seeing the dance of creation. The Tao, the emergent Sun, rises above the abysmal waters, as out of the living midnight the Sun is reborn. The water, instead of drowning us, becomes the amniotic fluid of the new birthing, and already in the drawing we see the child, the new being, coming out of the first *coniunctio* within the heart. How still, how quiet everything becomes when we just contemplate these pictures!

Figure 8 - Stage Three,
Separation of the Spirit-Body for Independent Existence [119]

The alchemist and the Divine Child

This has to do with the element earth, like the *coagulatio* - with making it adamant. It's quite a stage. The alchemist is seated on a triangular base. It's the dead dragon that's under him now, for the

[119] Wilhelm 1931, P. 47.

dragon of desire has been slain and he is sitting on laurel leaves - or are they phoenix-feathers? However, this isn't yet the rising phoenix; it's just death. He has lost his little head-dress. His robe covers him again. The work is done. He puts his robe across his breast because, although open, he's no longer so vulnerable. He is aware of and moving towards another presence in his life and in all things, and he is robed in that presence. His robe is closed also for the warming and nourishing of the spiritual embryo within. Like the gentle, lenient heat of the West, this allows the process to cook in its own way. He is now completely committed to the work. He can see the mountain. Staying in touch with this world, yet aware of another Self within, he is in the dance of the Tao, answerable to something else. His heart is growing more compassionate towards both nature and the human condition. He is moving towards becoming a master. The Divine Child is now to be born in this gentle heat.

Where stage one was about 'putting the hand to it', this third stage is called 'the releasing of the hand'. In the early stages he began to walk the Way; now he is to become the Way. Then there were tension and discipline; now is the time for release. Here is the pearl, the elixir, the new birth, the embryo. The test of the adept is to stay there, to see the powers he has attained die. He is relinquishing some of the control and the discipline in favour of something greater. Letting go of the doctrines, the alchemist begins to *become* the doctrines; he releases them *by* becoming them. It's a dangerous point, though gentler, easier and more relaxed than the Western way. It's the choice for each of us. We have to let go of our handholds and do it for ourselves. This stage is the beginning of the entering of the Tao. The alchemist is not quite there, but close to it. Eventually he will not need a meditation posture, for where he is, there Buddha is.

'The separation of the spirit-body for independent existence' means that, though not separated from the body, he is on the way to becoming immortal. However, as with the *coagulatio*, it demands an enormous amount of work. He can still be easily distracted by the senses, by the ego, and if *ch'i* and *ching* stop breathing and the fire goes down, he'll fall off the wagon and have to start again. The message is: 'Keep walking. In all circumstances, keep walking.' Breathing begins to raise fire from the solar plexus and take it up through the heart to the third eye, till eventually what was in the solar plexus rises out through the crown of the head. From out of the concentrated work emerges the Golden Flower - life, the elixir, the pearl, the 'essence of the holy embryo', whatever he wishes to call that which he is seeking.

It is also possible for the energy to go downwards, through the crown of the head to the root *chakra*, so that the whole body becomes a vehicle for the flow of life. This begins here in the true marriage of *p'o* and *hun*, bringing about the Golden Flower on to which the Sun of the Tao can shine. The Flower in turn reflects the Sun: 'As above so below'. The master alchemist said that when the light circulates, it mixes naturally; the elixir is made spontaneously and the performance of worldly tasks at the same time is not a hindrance. 'I do willingly that which I must.' In the early stages this is a difficulty: how, through the disciplines, do we have the light circulating all the time, yet also live in the external world? In the *coagulatio* particularly, we experience the reluctance of the body - of matter - to involve itself, to go down and become earthbound, go back on the wheel again. Spirit wants to take the body *up*. But we must have our feet on the earth while we're incarnate. Between earth and heaven is a battleground where matter fights against the rising movement of spirit.

Exhaustion

This struggle must have taken many forms in the lives of Eastern alchemists. I guess that a lot of monks would have left their monasteries and many of those who'd been in the Samurai, Zen or martial arts disciplines would have found the pace just too much, too long. However, the alchemist who did not abandon the Way might by now have enough powers of healing, miracles and mediumship to be quite useful. We saw how the danger was, again, that he would come out of the flask too soon. Having the siddhis, sensing the ability of the spirit-body to fly, to 'lift', to make itself invisible, the Weitan might step now out into the market-place and start levitating, using those powers *against* the Tao, against life, claiming power for himself. Lower psychism would have become possible. We also recognise here the aeonic tiredness and exhaustion of the *coagulatio*. We are thrown down continuously. We lose our tempers, catch ourselves out. It's an up-down, in-out struggle. We get up to fall, we fall to struggle up again. We're there - and then, we're not there. Here in the labyrinth are to be found exhaustion and illness, for as we grow freer we become more bound. We are in voluntary bondage to the true Self.

However, towards the end of this stage, if he continue through, the true alchemist can live in the world and yet not be of it. He can be 'spiritual' within it yet able to deal with it, walking the earth as a free man while yet entering into voluntary bondage to the Tao - or, as I would say, to the Self. Wherever he goes he finds the air of home. Withstanding, understanding, standing by a principle of something greater than himself, he has brought into being the separate existence which yet sub-stands and walks with us. That separate existence is now beginning to live in the world. Every worldly affair is a Buddhist work, says the Zen master. Like a gem, he stands out even in the mud; like pure gold he shines even in the furnace. Along the endless road of birth and death he walks, sufficient unto himself. In whatever associations he is found, he moves leisurely and unattached.

Figure 9 - Stage Four - **overleaf**
The Centre in the Midst of the Conditions [120]

And so we contemplate the picture.

The feather of truth

The element is air, and now we have come to the equivalent of the *sublimatio*. With the earth under his feet the alchemist can move to this final stage, this centre in the midst of the conditions. His senses are so illumined that, as we can see in the picture, each serves an immortal. See his crown, and the flames around his head? His crown *chakra*, now fully opened, is a lotus of light, his body is aflame in this *rubedo*. He's holding the feather of truth and immortality as a fan.[121] The fan is used to keep the fire burning and the light circulating. He's sitting on a winged sky-dragon, a serpent eating its own tail like the Ouroboros. He is holding the three-knotted cord of *ching*, *ch'i* and *shen* in his left

---

120   Wilhelm 1931, P. 57.
121   In some traditions his other hand holds the peach of immortality.

Figure 9 - Stage Four,
The Centre in the Midst of the Conditions

hand. Everything has become one. He is now the Tao. At this fourth stage the master alchemist will say, 'You may cease to meditate - let *it* meditate you. You may cease to *try* to live - let life live you.' The aspiring, smaller self is met by the descending fire; the two have come together to form an adamant.

> *Light overcomes all darkness, light is in the abyss.*
> *Creative light meets creative light,*
> *They unite inseparably, and unceasing life begins.*
> *One steps off the wheel of rebirth.*
> *Of this it is said:*

Clouds fill the thousand mountains.
The Moon gathers up the ten thousand waters.
The child comes home to live.
This is the method of finishing. [122]

Light overcomes all darkness. Light is in the abyss. Light is now in both the lower system (the root, the sexual *chakra*) and in the solar plexus. Light is also rising out of the head - all these divinities are rising out of him. His senses are transfigured. Each sense puts him in touch with an immortal, who is in touch with immortals, who are in touch with immortals; and each of *those* would have others, if you follow me! It's the realisation that beyond the individual lie creation and the Tao, and beyond the Tao lies another creation, and beyond that another and another, and that there is no end to it.

As well as the alchemist, each of the five figures is holding a feather of immortality in the form of a fan. (They could just as well use the feathers for quill pens; it depends - first get your feather, and then you can use it for what you will.) These fans are made of the feathers of the phoenix to which they have attained. I link this with the Egyptian process, in which the soul is taken to the gods Thoth and Anubis in the underworld to be measured against the single, very light, feather of truth, the only thing that will balance against the world. Recall how, if you outweighed the feather, you had to go back and have another crack at life; otherwise you could be taken onward and allowed to go to the realm of the gods. This is very similar, but now he is *holding* the feather of truth and immortality. He is in the Tao, in the unity.

Till now the alchemist has been working against personal nature. Now he is working *with* nature, with the flow of the Tao. He is by now a master of mineralogy, metallurgy, herbs, medicine, magic. He is the true gold. Where he is things start to happen. We know that a true magician would not make his powers evident (though this is where the danger of the false magician still arises). So he lives among men both concealed and visible, different yet the same. This is the invisibility he was looking for - no more worry about being invisible in order to gain power over people. He's there, obviously, yet not seen to be an immortal. That is the

---

[122]   Poem by Po Ming, Suzuki 1987.

great aim of the Chinese alchemist: that he should be ordinary! The extraordinariness of the ordinary is one of the high realisations of the Chinese system. 'Creative light meets creative light; they unite inseparably, and unceasing life begins.' He has become a divinity while remaining very human. It has involved the work of many lifetimes, as well as this one. He too has struggled in the flask, developed the ability both to go up and to come down, to circulate the light till he became adamant, became the elixir, became what was sought. As in the sublimatio, once a person is here, he can be about his Father's business in the world, becoming a true man of no rank, staying naturally with the principles of the Noble Eightfold Path because there is no other way to live, no other way to be. He has nowhere to go from here. He is in the Tao because he was never out of the Tao. 'Where is God not?'

'Clouds fill the thousand mountains, the Moon gathers up the ten thousand waters, and the child comes home to live. This is the method of finishing.' Death to the small self, rebirth to the Self. The light is circulating. At physical death he can now move on, taking the etherealised body up - or down - to the Tao. He can go into the temple and into the market-place at the same time. Or he can step off the wheel of rebirth and come back voluntarily into the world as a Boddhisattva. 'So long as one blade of grass cries out for light, I will return.'

Light is circulating

We recall the Chinese saying about the man who claims nothing and yet is true to the Tao. When a man lives in contact with the world *and yet* still in harmony with the light - at the same time - then the round is round, the angular has angles. He doesn't try to change the order of things, because everything, as it is, is in the Tao. If it's round it's round, and he wouldn't deny it. That's how it is. He doesn't argue with it. He doesn't distress himself in trying to make the angular round or the round have angles; he just accepts what is. Nature is as it should be, life is as it should be, the Tao is everywhere. Again, 'the still point of the turning world'.[123] Light is circulating, the Tao has found another experiment. Remember the Biblical saying about becoming a shining light set on a hill - not bleeding under a bushel! He doesn't go around

---

[123]   T.S. Eliot 1959, 'Burnt Norton' I.

broadcasting that he has the light; he just broadcasts the light. Alert, alive to heaven and to earth, he is always in touch with divinity, for he has himself become a touchstone. He moves leisurely and unattached, unstained, with something to offer both God and man. *Nirvana* means simply reporting for duty.

Reversing the light

Just before the Buddha was finally and totally enlightened, a beautiful girl, a spirit, came to him and gave him a golden bowl full of milk-rice. He drank the milk-rice and threw the golden bowl on to the river - on to the Tao. And it floated away *up*stream. That, says the story, was the sign that he had become the Enlightened One. One of the major ideas out of the tradition of the circulation of the light is that the light can flow backwards, from above down. Whereas the majority of people are struggling to keep the light going forward, the master by degrees is able to turn the wheel backwards. *Ars contra naturam* becomes the art that flows *with* nature. It's the ability to throw a golden bowl on the river and have it move upstream; to walk *across* the grain of life, *with* the grain of life, simply flowing in whatever way life is flowing. My understanding of this is that I *don't* understand it. It's a very profound mystery. I would link it with the initiation processes. The master learns to send back the light. He isn't just following the endless turn of the wheel of rebirth. He is still caught into the pull of involution, but he has stepped out of the herd, begun to step off the wheel, though it is still turning. Aspiring to get into the flask, he causes something to crank to a stillness. Astrologically, there's a point at which the wheel reverses. At that point he moves from the lower to the higher wheel.

So that was the Book of the Golden Elixir. The essence is in those four pictures. The whole thing has been a movement of light in the round, from above to below, from below to above, denying neither. It's exactly the same principle as in the West: the light was already in the darkness. Going down, it has brought the darkness up, and the darkness has allowed the light to become clearer. It's more visible *because* of the darkness. Next we'll look at my favourite of all traditions, the Japanese   tradition.

1. Searching for the Ox

CHAPTER TEN

The Oxherding Pictures

Sitting quietly, doing nothing, spring comes
and the grass grows by itself.
Lao Tsu

Art is a natural outcome of the realisation of the One, and so we come to the Oxherding pictures of Suzuki.[124] In the light of the Golden Flower, the bull or ox is both the *prima materia* and the goal, the lower and the upper crucibles at the same time. The aim is for vertical rather than horizontal living. At the beginning the young oxherd withdraws his sense-reactions from the past, faces his own resistances and focuses on the ox. The pictures show a tiny figure with a huge ox or bull. Trying to focus on the ox, he aims not to be dragged out in all directions.

Picture One - Searching for the ox - opposite

In this first picture the young boy, the oxherd, the personality, has woken up from his sleep in the solar plexus area where he has been unconscious. He is far from home. 'Where am I?' Not yet in the flask, he's looking all around him. 'Where has the ox gone?' This is a stage both celestial and earthly, about both beginning and end. The boy stands for the ego. The ox is both the Self being pursued and the nature in which it is locked, on which we have to work in order to bring out the Self. It's reminiscent of our old friend the Green Lion, who is both the *prima materia* and *also* the Stone at the end. The commentary by Chu-hung: [125]

The boy is not on intimate terms with the ox, because the oxherd himself has violated his inmost nature. The ox is lost because the oxherd has been led out of the way by his deluding senses. His home is receding farther away from him, and byways and crossways are

124   Painter: probably Shubun, Zen priest, 15th century. Originals in Kyoto.
125   Commentary: Chu-hung, 1585 edition.

*ever confused. Desire for gain and fear of loss burn like fire, ideas
of right and wrong conflict.*

It's because he himself has violated his inmost essence that he is not
yet on intimate terms with the ox. This is not meant to be punitive, it's
just a fact. We too violate our divinity to start with. We're a long way
from home. The ox is lost; so too is the boy. He doesn't know where
to go. He'll get lost again in the future, but never like this. He is
searching for the ox, but his senses are attuned still to the outside
world; desire and fear burn like fire and he cannot tell right from
wrong. His senses delude him completely and so he forgets. But his
ears are alert. Po Ming the poet says of this picture: [126]

Alone in the wilderness, lost in the jungle,
The boy is searching, searching.
The swelling waters - the far-away mountains - the unending path.
Exhausted and in despair, he knows not where to go;
He only hears the evening cicadas
Singing in the maple woods.

Here is the longing, the yearning that comes when we're a long way
from home in a far country. The need to return from the endless wheel
of rebirth draws the prodigal. His home is the source and it is receding
from him; he is a long way from the Tao and from his own essence.
We've been here too, many of us. This is the worldly person, lost in
error, projecting out and looking for something in someone else. We
are seeking for salvation, an answer, a meaning. Only later do we
become devoted to finding the Way.

Ripe for therapy! Caught in the crossways and byways of life, full of
desires and fears, uncertain as to what is appropriate and what is not,
many people come into transpersonal work feeling they've come from
a far country. The tribe they've somehow been caught in is not their
tribe and they've had to learn a language which is not their own. The
joy with which they catch the traces! Now they begin to recognise
others of their own kind. Great faith and great courage are required -
and great doubt: faith to keep walking on the Way; courage, the
fearless will to detach and remain in the fire; doubt, because faith

[126]   Poems by Po Ming, in Suzuki 1987.

without doubt gets us nowhere. Again, 'embrace doubt as you would your concubine'.

Picture Two - *Seeing the traces* - **overleaf**

'Aha, now I can see his footprints!' Now the oxherd has noticed the traces. In the commentary Chu-hung says:

> By the aid of the sutras, and by enquiring into the disciplines, he has come to understand something; he has found the traces. He now knows that vessels, however varied, are all of gold, and the objective world is a reflection of the Tao. Yet he cannot distinguish what is good from what is not. His mind is still confused as to truth and falsehood. He has not yet entered the gate. He is provisionally said to have noticed the traces.

Though still confused, still unable to tell good from evil, the boy is by now on the thread. The sutras, sacred verses from the Buddhist texts, give the disciplines and rituals that begin to put him into the flask. By the aid of these stanzas of the sages, by the disciplines, by enquiring here and there among the doctrines, he has come to understand something. But it's still only provisional. The sages don't have *his* ox, though they may well have their own. False gurus will say, 'I've got the gold. You should have my gold too!' However, we mustn't herd someone else's ox; we are not only allowed but required to have our own. And, since we can't avoid the world and its temptations, we may well have to follow misleading voices in order to learn discrimination. The true master will kick the pupil for any sign of adoration. Respect is what it's about. 'Never mistake the finger pointing at the Moon for the Moon itself.'

So he now knows that the objective world is a reflection of the Self, that gold is in every human being, that the world reflects the Tao. Yet good and evil, truth and falsehood are still confused. Again, a lot of us pay lip-service: 'Oh yes, I know the divine is everywhere!' However, it's one thing to 'know' it, quite another to *reveal* the divine that is everywhere. He hasn't yet entered the gate, but he's on his thread. We can see his ears that were earlier listening to the cicadas, and his eyes that are now beginning to focus. Po Ming's poem here says:

2. Seeing the Traces

By the stream and under the trees,
Scattered are the traces of the lost.
The sweet-scented grasses are growing thick;
Did he find the way? However remote,
Over the hills and far away, the beast may wander,
His nose reaches the heavens and none can conceal it.

The boy is beginning to realise that it's the Self he's pursuing and that the ox, who's pregnant [127] now and about to be seen wandering in from far places, is something other than he'd thought! The Self is everywhere; again, the boy only *knows* it - he hasn't yet come to the experience of it. The fact is, we have to wander everywhere, by the stream and under the trees. That's how we seek the scattered traces of the lost. Driven by confusion and doubt, searching from teacher to teacher, therapy to therapy, we are looking for healing, looking for the one who will help us *not* to have to get into the flask at any deep level. I don't think anyone consciously wants to get into the flask. But, although we can't find our ox, we are drawn by the traces. 'What makes your heart sing?' The call is strong - the divine longing, the divine thirst. 'His nose reaches the heavens and none can conceal it!' Joy will long outlast will. We are becoming more focused, more courageous; the mountains are now visible. 'Aha!' we say. The prodigal, satiated by the excesses of the world, is being drawn home.

Picture Three - Seeing the ox - overleaf

It's the ox himself. Not just the footprints but the disappearing rear end - in the West the backside of a saint is rarely shown! Now at last the boy sees him and off he goes, running very fast. The boy and the ox are alike. So far, it's the boy who has been seeking the ox. He doesn't yet know that the ox is looking for him, too. The Chinese commentary on this picture is:

> *The boy finds the way by the sound he hears. He sees thereby the origin of things, and all his senses are in harmonious order. In all his activities it is manifestly present; it is like the salt in water and the glue in colour. When the eye is properly directed, he will find that it is no other than himself.*

---

[127] 'Pregnant', sic. (Ed.)

3. Seeing the Ox

The boy is now in the flask, in pursuit of what he's looking for. By Picture Three he's lost sight of the mountains again. Now he can focus on his prey. The idea is to follow, to 'see' by listening, finding the way by the sounds he hears, until he understands that they are made by no other than himself. First, sound - and only then, sight. He has a rope for a tether. He can only either run very fast, or stay still, but always he has the rope. We recall the elephant and the seeker following each other round the spinney. We too go round and round in circles, until at last they begin to become spirals. This is the stage where we say, 'I've got it - I've made it - I have it!' only to discover that we haven't. 'Master, I am enlightened!' 'And what are you going to do with it?' comes the reply.

His listening has begun to prove true, showing the boy the origin of things. All his senses are in harmonious order - for the moment! As in the picture of the gathering of the light, everything is turned inwards towards the pursuit of the ox. For us too, in all our activities the Self is manifestly present. It is everywhere. We are learning discrimination. After all, we can't *see* the salt in the sea, nor the glue in paint or in Chinese ink. The commentator is telling the oxherd, in case he doesn't know, that when the eye is properly directed, he will find that the Self is - himself. This ties in with the saying, *'If therefore thine eye be single, thy whole body shall be full of light.'* [128] In the poem Po Ming says:

On yonder branch perches a nightingale, cheerfully singing.
The sun is warm and a soothing breeze blows.
On the bank the willows are green.
The ox is there all by himself;
Nowhere is he to hide himself;
The splendid head decorated with stately horns,
What painter can reproduce him?

This Tao, this ox, his splendid head, his stately horns - so lovely he's beyond description! Obviously the painter *can't* reproduce him, which is why he has painted the backside of this beautiful creature. Things are exactly as they are, nature is in harmony with itself and the bird of the soul is singing. The cheerful nightingale is the soul-spirit of the night.

[128]   Matthew 6, 22.

4. Catching the Ox

The ox is there all by himself in the warm sun on the green willow bank, soothed by the breezes. 'Nowhere is he to hide himself.' He's no longer only the ox of desire, the ox of body, matter and heart. He too is in pursuit of the Self.

Picture Four - Catching the ox - opposite

'Got him!' And this time he has; he's caught him by the end of his nose. The boy has at last got hold of the ox, attached a nose-ring with a tether and is hanging on to the rope. He really has a job on his hands now. We too have caught the ox by whatever is our own tradition, by the necessary doctrines. And we lose him and lose him. It's the pressure from the outside world that makes it so very hard to keep our hold on him. Endless disciplines are required, endless heatings of the fire. This is the point where the doctrines and the right paths become deeply, deeply important. It's so easy to get caught here; the pull of the outside world is still very strong. It's wild, untamed nature on the far end of the tether, all our passions and concerns. The ego has to submit and puts up huge resistance. This is training *after* the breakthrough - not leading to it, but after it.

I know another most wonderful version of Picture Four, where it's the ox that's spinning round and round on the spot and the boy on the far end of the tether is whirling in a huge circle. Again, it's the circulation of the light. High through the heavens he goes, down through north, south, east, west - under water, through mountains, into abysses - spun round in the circumambulation of the Self, holding on for grim life and death to the tether. It's beautifully done here in this picture, which looks quite calm by comparison. And from this particular lovely tradition, here are Chu-hung and his commentary:

> Long lost in the wilderness, the boy has at last found the ox and his hands are on him. But owing to the overwhelming pressure of the outside world, the ox is hard to keep under control. He constantly longs for the old sweet-scented field; the wild nature is still unruly, and altogether refuses to be broken. If the oxherd wishes to see the ox completely in harmony with himself, he has surely to use the whip freely.

He has found the ox, yes, and his hands are on him, yes. As in the picture of the gathering of the light, he's putting or 'setting' the hand to it. Now the ox has become both the Self and the senses. This is the threshold ox. Longing for his old sweet-scented field, for what he's known, for the familiar and the easeful, his wild nature is still unruly and altogether refuses to be broken. And so the ox with his longing for wild nature goes around the spinney, flinging the boy round and round as he goes.

A person can all too easily be pulled out of the flask at this point, and back into the ten thousand and one things. The whip is the mortal combat with ourselves that was more gently enacted in the pictures of gathering the light, and the origin of a new being in the place of power. The whip, the bridle and the halter are the disciplines, the meditation and the yoga practices. I don't think they mean the kind of flagellatory stuff of so much of the mediæval Church tradition. Rather, it's the continuous repetition of the mantram, the breathing, the shedding process. It's living each day in the nature of itself, letting go of the day at its end, living more and more fully in the Tao. It's acting *as if* we were in the Tao, in this wholeness. In therapy we help people to stay with it, to stay in the flask, to recognise that what is dying is also bringing something into being. Po Ming here:

> *With the energy of his whole being*
> *The boy has at last taken hold of the ox;*
> *But how wild his will,*
> *How ungovernable his power!*
> *At times he struts up a plateau*
> *When lo! he is lost again*
> *In a misty, impenetrable mountain pass.*

So with all his energy the oxherd is holding on to the ox, who's still wild and unruly and full of desire. There's pain in this picture. The curved horns are reminiscent of the horned Moon. The boy is caught by the ox. The pull of the outside world is strong and he has to hang on very firmly. As in the *solutio*, things get misty. The ox struts up the hill, only to be hidden once more. There he is and there he isn't. All the yoga teachings, all the disciplines, breathing systems, dietary practices, are here. This is both the *nigredo* and the *solutio*. The ego resents our meditation practice and stops us from staying focused. The mind is used by the personality which, with its lines of thought, continuously interferes. We let them go, like the flight of birds over the pool.

Picture Five - Herding the ox - overleaf

Now, the ox is following the boy! The picture shows a small figure in a great tension of concentration leading the huge bull-like ox by his nose-ring. We can imagine how he might have stopped him, managing to place a knee on the bank on either side of a lane to slow down his headlong progress. He is not to loose the main string. He could still get distracted and taken out of the Way. This is a very difficult stage. Picture Five and still having trouble! There is still considerable tension and conflict. We've come so far. Many years have gone into the conscious work of the disciplines of the senses, and though we won't be projecting quite so much on to the outside world now, it's easy to be a bit pompous about what we know. We start pushing the doctrine and the dogma at other people, forgetting that we're in the process ourselves and supposed to be holding on to our own ox. Instead, we're in danger of rushing around trying to hold everybody else's. We do need to take the work and the endeavour seriously; but we do *not* need to take ourselves with much earnestness. We get extremely dedicated and self-flagellating. Humour is often missing. The idea is for people to laugh *with* themselves. Helping them to keep the heat up is far easier than helping them to ease it off. We need both to rest *and* ride, walk and be at ease, breathe in and breathe out. Perhaps we need to be a bit cracked, a bit eccentric, before we can re-centre.

In the text, the oxherd is quite soon to become a man; but here he's still a boy, still herding the ox. We can see that the body of the ox is growing slightly whiter, both dark and light, a mixture. The ox is manifesting Tao. Its eye is now on the boy, watching his motivation. Will he keep walking, sustained not by the ox but by the Way, the Self? So the commentary:

> *When a thought moves, another follows, and then another; an endless train of thoughts is thus awakened. Through enlightenment, all this turns to truth; but falsehood asserts itself when confusion prevails. Things oppress us, not only because of an outside world*

5. Herding the Ox

but because of the self-deceiving mind. Do not let the nose-string
loose; hold it tight - and do not wobble.

Thoughts move and more thoughts follow in an endless train. Keeping
quiet and calm in the outside world is one of the difficulties of this
stage of meditation and yoga practice. The pull of the world in the
middle stanzas is in many ways more difficult than it was in the
beginning. It comes up and challenges, as Maya challenged the
Buddha before his Enlightenment and as the devil came to Christ. At
first, anything we learn in any discipline - becoming a therapist or a
lawyer or a musician - comes easily. It's in the middle stage that there's
confusion. It's no longer easy. We're caught between thinking and
spontaneity. 'I've got it - but I haven't got it. I see - no I don't!' It's to
be hoped that by the third stage it will again come easily and
spontaneously, but this is about that middle bit, when we both have it
and don't have it. It's like the transition stage in labour; the mother
feels, 'My God, if I could go back! Why did I, how could I, ever get
into this?' And so, no doubt, does the baby. If you're *in* the flask, there
is no turning back.

But in truth we are oppressed less by the outside world than by the self-
deceiving mind. It is a bit like coming out of the *solutio* into the
coagulatio. The mind does need to come back and waken up again. We
begin to ask questions, we doubt, get confused and tangled in
falsehood. Here the ox is the self-deceiving mind. We are required to
hold on to the nose-string (and what, for us, is the nose-string?). 'Hold
tight!' is the message, 'and don't wobble.' Enlightenment will turn it
again to truth. The trouble lies with the wobbling. The Chinese
describe the razor-edge path we are walking. 'If you sit, sit; if you
stand, stand - but don't wobble'. It's also said in Zen, 'Keep walking.
Don't think too much, don't feel too much. Keep walking.' This is
why, here in Po Ming:

The boy is not to separate himself with his whip and tether,
Lest the animal should wander away into a world of defilement.
When he is properly tended he will grow pure and docile;
Without a chain, nothing binding,
He will by himself follow the oxherd.

The boy (notice it's *with* his whip and his tether) is to separate himself

6. Coming Home on the Ox's Back

from neither the world nor from the ox. Whip and rope are necessary lest he stray. We're not to let the doctrine and the dogma stand between ourselves and the living process that is coming into being, or the ox may wander into defilement. Eventually the ox will follow, even with no tether.

Picture Six - *Coming home on the ox's back* - opposite

With the sixth picture we're moving towards the end stages of the *coagulatio*. He has mounted the ox and is riding slowly homeward. The ox too, can rest. He will not be enticed away now. All things merge in 'no thing'. The empty person is riding the empty ox. This is the completion of the struggle with ego. Mounting the ox, riding life, he is coming home to the Self. The commentary is:

> *The struggle is over. The man is no more concerned with gain and loss. He hums a rustic tune of the woodman, he sings simple songs of the village boy. Saddling himself on the ox's back, his eyes are fixed on things not of the earth, earthy. Even if he is called he will not turn his head; however enticed he will no more be kept back.*

Looking neither to right nor left, he's playing the flute. Now he is carried by the ox. He is in the call of the Tao. The struggle with the will-nature is over - though not completely over by any means; he's not yet there, but he's in the pull of it. That he comes home riding the ox shows that he has overcome the tendency to wildness, to spilling out. Now it won't spill over, it's held. All lusting and rapacious thoughts have died down. Motivated by the values of the heart, he is no longer passionate but compassionate. He is no longer holding the tether to the nose-ring on the ox, who is walking peacefully along. No longer the boy, 'the man' isn't occupied now with loss or gain. Coming home to his true Self, he is concerned with simple and natural things. Humming rustic tunes, playing songs of innocence, he has straddled the ox, fixed himself to it. His eyes are no longer fixed on things of earth and nothing will stop him, whatever happens. The ox is looking at the Moon; the man, no longer distracted, will keep going now.

Nonetheless this is a dangerous stage. It looks like attainment - in a sense it *is* attainment. He's got his own being under control. There's not much further to go in most of the later Chinese traditions, which stop

7. The Ox Forgotten, Leaving the Man Alone

with the picture after next. (However, this particular tradition goes on and by now only half the journey has been made.) The temptation is to get off and begin teaching others and then we'll have yet another sorcerer's apprentice. The poet says:

> *Riding on the animal he leisurely wends his way home.*
> *Enveloped in the evening mist,*
> *how tunefully the flute vanishes away.*
> *Singing a ditty, beating time,*
> *his heart is filled with joy indescribable.*
> *That he is now one of those who know - need it be told?*

So he rides peacefully home in the mists of evening. The flute vanishes away because he has *become* the music, and therefore needs no instrument. He sings, he beats time, his heart is filled with indescribable joy. He is now one of those who know. But there are further stages.

Picture Seven - *The ox forgotten, leaving the man alone* - opposite

The small figure by the little hut is looking up at the setting Moon. His knees look uncomfortable. In other sets of drawings the ox moves from dark to light throughout these pictures, becoming by now pale-coloured. But here there's no ox at all. The whip and rope and ring are inside the hut. I miss the ox! Yet the ox is within, transcended. You don't need the raft after you've crossed the river.

The dawn is coming. Once again he can see the mountains. Soon the red Sun will be rising out of the abyss. In blissful repose within his thatched dwelling he has abandoned them all. All merge in *no-thing*. This is the stage of the Little Hut Initiation. The light is circulating. Fire burns between eyebrows and heart, for the circulation includes the heart. As Rinzai said, in our bodies lives a 'true man of no rank who continually goes in and out through the senses: let him penetrate you.' The commentary is very obscure:

> *The Dharmas are one and the ox symbolic. When you know that what you need is not the snare or the set net, but the hare and the fish, it is like gold separated from the dross, it is like the Moon rising out of the clouds. Then one ray of light, serene and penetrating, shines even before the days of creation.*

Seen with the third eye, the duties and disciplines of life have all become one. Now he realises that all the doctrines, all the *Dharmas* or teachings, even the ox itself, are symbolic. They are metaphors for something else. He doesn't need the mode of catching the hare but the hare itself. The hare, or the fish, is the source; the snare is merely the dogma. He doesn't want the controlling principle but the living spirit; not the doctrine but the essence. Then the gold is separated from the dross and the Moon rises from the clouds. One serene ray of light, shining even before the days of creation, can now penetrate him.

There's much loneliness in this picture. There is no-one there. It would be all too easy for him to put his hands together now and look for one to worship. The danger is, he may come to worship and adore the Moon and the mountain. There's a risk in that - it'll be the ego that's worshipping those things! Where the Bible has, 'In the beginning was the Word', and 'I am that I am', the often-used Zen koan asks, 'And what is the face you had before you were born?' Now we begin to find that face, and discover that beyond the Golden Flower we have been working on, beyond the central monad, is the Tao. All we have done, all the disciplines, the doctrines and the dharma, are no longer important. Even the ox itself is only a symbol for something greater than itself. Po Ming's poem:

> Riding on the animal, he is at last back in his home
> Where lo! the ox is no more.
> The man alone sits serenely;
> Though the red sun is high in the sky,
> He is still quietly dreaming.
> Under a straw-thatched roof are his whip and rope
> Idly lying.

At this point he's no longer of this world. The dream is of the next, all struggle forgotten. The disciplines and the doctrines that have supported and aided him are no longer needed. After all, when you're in the donkey-cart you might as well put down your bundle on the floor. The tether and the whip are inside the square hut, also forgotten. He's beginning to move into *sublimatio*. Is he able to hold the aloneness of that high space, and allow it to penetrate him? If so, then something happens. The all-one leads to being 'alone', which leads to separation - but finally it brings him back to all-one. He will never be lonely again.

Picture Eight -
The ox and the man have both gone out of sight - overleaf

This is my favourite! The picture is just a glow, a mixture of the red-gold of the Sun and the silver-white of the Moon. A lot of the traditions stop at this point, as if it were the end. But even after this he needs to stay with it, for it's not too late for him to be a Weitan - he may *still* be only half-baked, even now! The commentary:

> *All confusion is set aside, and serenity alone prevails. Even the idea of holiness does not obtain. He does not linger about where the Buddha is; and as to where there is no Buddha, he speedily passes by. When there exists no form of dualism, even a thousand-eyed one fails to detect a loophole. A holiness before which birds offer flowers is but a farce.*

There's a great humour in this. The boy is now fully man. All is empty, though not empty in the usual sense. There is no dualism, only serenity. The Buddha outside is not the Buddha; there is no Buddha, there is no non-Buddha - there just *is*. There's neither sacred nor profane, neither holy nor unholy. The ox and the man are both gone out of sight. He has been penetrated and has vanished. All is in the round. All is worship: samadhi, orison, rapture, bliss, nirvana. The mirror is clear, the heart shines brightly. There are no images, nothing to be awakened, no hut, no moon, no mountain, no ox. And there's no himself either. There's no thing. This is not 'nothing'; it's no-thing-ness rather than nothingness. It's beyond the opposites, where the Way ends in the untreadable and language in the ineffable. There's no word. He goes like air and wind. To claim to be holy, 'a holiness before which birds offer flowers', is just a farce. Bird and flower are both the god; how can the one offer the other, and to whom? Forget the doctrine, forget the dogma, forget the Buddha - forget what you went out for. Simply be in the Tao. Po Ming's poem:

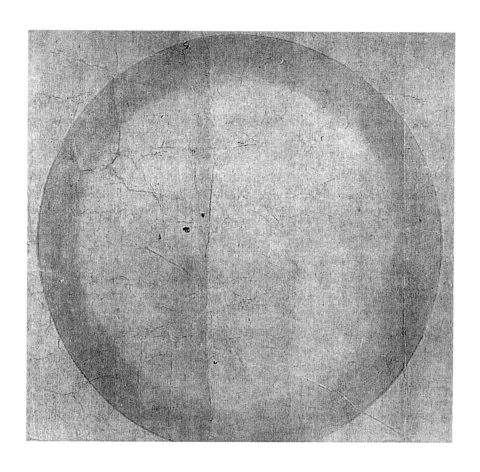

8. The Ox and the Man have Both Gone out of Sight

All is empty.
The whip, the rope, the man, and the ox.
Who can ever survey the vastness of heaven?
Over the furnace, burning ablaze, not a flake of snow can fall.
When this state of things obtains
Manifest is the spirit of the ancient Master.

All is void. There's no cold, no moist, no earth; cold and hot are one and the same, dry and moist, inner and outer. No descent into death and the ghost world is possible now. The spirit of the ancient master is now manifest. He has found the Tao. To stop here, as do many of the later traditions, may be the call. This is the farthest stage most of us could dream of. But the Returning Ones have to come back. 'Chop wood, carry water.' The river has become the river again.

Picture Nine -
Returning to the origin, back to the source - overleaf

I love this picture because it goes on. See the spray of cherry blossom? There's a dragon enmeshed in the roots, though it doesn't show up very well. This is now the tree of life. The ox has been the Tao all along. Man, nature, the Tao, all one. A tree by a river, a bird flying, a mountain behind. 'I see that which is creating and that which is destroying.' The commentary:

> *From the very beginning, pure and immaculate, the man has never been affected by defilement. He watches the growth of things while himself abiding in the immovable serenity of non-assertion. He does not identify himself with the Maya-like transformation going on about him. Nor has he any use of himself, which is artificiality. The waters are blue, the mountains are green; sitting alone he observes things undergoing changes.*

He is back here now. The water is indigo, the mountain emerald. He never has been affected by defilement. The pure essence always was the pure essence; when was it ever anything else? The gold was never, anywhere, anything but gold. It just appeared to be. He quietly sits and watches things happening. It is like the story of the Rainmaker [129] who

---

[129] See Appendix. The Rainmaker story is also told in Somers & Gordon-Brown 2002, P. 252.

9. Returning to the Origin, Back to the Source

sits in his little square hut and puts himself in order - and the whole universe puts *itself* in order. The will of the Divine has broken the sacrificial cross, which means the struggle of the small self. It has been turned into the equal-armed cross of acceptance of the will of God. Then that cross too is broken, to be formed up again in the equal square, then the cube. The Hut initiation is one of the most familiar in the East, with the little four-square hut, the equal-sided cube, in which the great one sits. Po Ming's poem:

To return to the Origin, to be back at the Source -
Already a false step, this.
Far better it is to stay at home
Blind and deaf and without much ado.
Sitting in the hut, he takes no cognisance of things outside.
Behold, the stream is flowing, whither nobody knows;
And flowers are vividly red - for whom are they?'

Returning to the origin, coming back to the source - a false step! Even that isn't true! We don't need to go anywhere. We're not back, because we never left. Better stay at home, 'blind and deaf and without much ado'. Why make a fuss about it? Sitting in the four-square hut (the transformation of the Rainmaker's hut) his senses are turned in. He is perceiving and listening. He hears things outside, but for him they are not the important matter. The stream flows - where? It's the 'is-ness' of things; the stream of light, the stream of the Tao, is flowing, and it just *is*. I don't wish to argue with that. The flowers are vividly red; so, the *rubedo*. Who are they for? The gold is there again - but for whom? All that effort, all that discipline, all that work, the pursuit of the ox and the following of the traces - for whom? They belong to the Self; they are for the Buddha; they are, of course, for the Tao.

In the beginning -
  trees are trees, rivers are rivers, mountains are mountains.
At the middle -
  trees are not trees, rivers are not rivers,
  mountains are not mountains.
At the end -
  trees are trees, rivers are rivers, mountains are mountains.

'Don't push the river, it flows by itself.' Alert, aware, watchful, we use

10. Entering the City with Bliss-Bestowing Hands

the breath to cool our own parsnips. *It moves, it* sits. The spool of our lives has been going round one spindle; now it's going round another. We come home to nature, and the stone starts the angel's wing. Lao Tsu said: 'Sitting quietly, doing nothing, spring comes and the grass grows by itself.' Or again, *'complete simplicity, costing not less than everything'*. [130]

Picture Ten -
Entering the city with bliss-bestowing hands - opposite

So he returns, blissed out, full-bellied and substantial, into the market-place. He is the Tao, the Way in action, and all is transformed in his presence. And he is in the world. Here is the image of the old, fat man and the single spray of cherry blossom. The commentary:

> *His thatched hut gate is closed and even the wisest know him not. No glimpses of his inner life are to be caught, for he goes on his own way without following the steps of the ancient sages. Carrying a gourd he goes into the market-place; leaning against a staff he comes home. He is found in company with winebibbers and butchers; he and they are all converted into Buddhas.*

In both traditions the alchemist comes back with the Stone, with the elixir - back to the market-place. The wisest do not know him, and can catch no glimpse of his inner life. Now he treads his own way, no longer following the ancients. He has become the true man, become Buddha. The gate to his thatched hut is closed. The keeper of the gate keeps it shut till there's someone ready to pass through. Entry is both inaccessible and accessible. With the gourd of emptiness he goes into the market; leaning against a staff, which is the Tao, he comes home.

The Eastern way sounds easier than the Western, but it isn't. 'What did you do with the life I gave you?' Some people become hard, with a strength born out of endurance, but no bird flies - there's no meaning. Defensive, they lack a dimension. Although this is not contemptible, it isn't enough. (Perhaps they live in the dragon castle on the floor of the sea, rather than in the purple hall of the city of jade?) Others become more childlike, more spontaneous; they widen and expand. The man is

---

130 T.S. Eliot' 1959, 'Little Gidding' V.

become the holy fool, innocent, spontaneous, childlike, at play. He is like the river, the atom, energy, life. He's at home everywhere, in heaven and in hell. He speaks with resonance and is silent with resonance, too. He is indeed blissed out! He is in the market-place now with his basket of eternity and his staff of knowledge. Here is the poem:

Bare-chested and bare-footed,
He comes out into the market-place;
Daubed with mud and ashes,
How broadly he smiles.
There is no need for the miraculous power of the gods;
For he touches, and lo!
The dead trees are in full bloom.

No concealing veil thrown across his face, here he is bare-breasted, bare-footed, porous, open and vulnerable. He can keep company with butchers and winebibbers, as Christ kept company with money-changers and rogues and harlots. He and they are all converted into Buddhas. The outcome of the *sublimatio* stage, so far as we understand it, is the attained one, the Enlightened One. Such a person will come back. He doesn't deny the market-place but has dealings with this world, because he can no longer be touched. Nothing can defile him. He is gold that cannot be tarnished. He sees the gold everywhere, the Tao everywhere, the essence everywhere. He has become the touchstone. He *is* the elixir; he is the golden pill; he is the immortal who heals wherever he moves. Wherever he goes, others reveal their divinity; wherever he is, everyone is Buddha. But let us not overlook the hard work that went into the process. He's still daubed with the mud and ashes of the *prima materia*, the disciplines, the letting go of his own will, the purification which that signifies. And how broadly he smiles! 'Ever blissful, I use no magic to extend my life; and before me, trees spring to life.' No longer needing the miraculous power of the gods, his touch brings the dead trees into full bloom. Beat that!

And for us? How does all this come into our lives? We remember to bring with us our talisman, our symbol of the inner Self and of its wisdom and compassion. Here are five points:

Respecting and honouring nature, people and life.

Focusing the senses, doing tactile things. Gazing at the bamboo before we paint it, and becoming it. Paying attention and coming totally into the present, absolutely in the Now.

Keeping on walking, whatever comes. Never letting go of the Way nor losing the traces. We are inevitably walking between pairs of opposites, and that's not just because of our own stupidity - it's by being human that we are caught in the pull of contradiction.

Befriending the dragon, not killing it. Tying its feet or putting a tether on it, till both we and it are dancing the Tao. Don't kill anything, walk between things; then they aren't so frightening.

Dancing the Tao. Being present, now, with joy; being the holy fool, playful, in the round, with laughter popping the bubble of inflation. Finding the rhythm to walk the middle way till it dances after all. The man and the ox become one. He finds the Self. And the Self finds him.

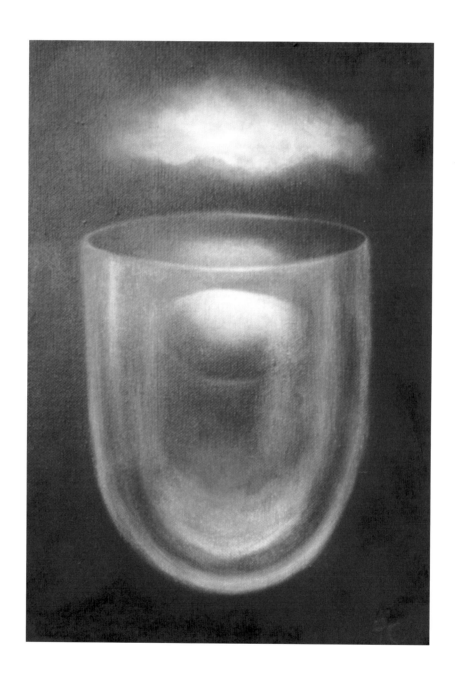

Holding.

Appendix I

THE RAINMAKER

Jung was very fond of the lovely story of the Rainmaker, one of the greatest we have. Like a creation myth, it is found in most cultures; wherever it is set, it is a good story.

In some far country, there was a time of great drought. The people and the dignitaries were very concerned because crops were failing and animals dying and they desperately needed rain. They'd heard of a famous rainmaker who would probably be able to help. So he was called from wherever he was, to come and do something about it. Fearing that he would be terribly expensive and want most of the exchequer, they were somewhat startled, even taken aback, when an ordinary, simple, unpretentious little man shuffled into their presence. 'Somebody like this can't possibly be a great rainmaker!' Anyway, being desperate, they asked, 'What do you need ? - anything, any kind of equipment - you need it, you just ask.'

The little man took a sniff of the air and said, 'I will have a hut in the field. Then just go away and leave me alone! That's all I ask.' So he was given a simple, square hut, and he went into it, stayed there three days and three nights, and the rains came. When he came out, they were all there to meet him. 'What did you do, what happened...?' 'Where I come from it smells good,' he replied. 'I didn't like the smell of this place, so I went into the hut and put myself in order, and of course the rains came. I'm going home now.'

To be the rainmaker, to have the power to draw everything into order again, is to go into that little four-square hut, into the centre of the elements, and then, if there's a need for it, of course the rain will come. If it had been the sun that was needed, he'd have gone into his hut and put himself in order, and of course the sun would have shone. Simply going into that little four-fold place is to set everything in order again, so that there's no polarity. We put ourselves back in harmony with life as it does things, not exalting ourselves above it, nor falling below it, nor missing the opportunity to stand alongside it. I presume 'putting ourselves in order' means trusting the process, honouring something greater than ourselves. And I suppose most traditions, most philosophies, most religions have said little more than that. 'Put yourselves in order, honour the gods, live the appropriate life - and remember to dance!'

Appendix II

THE EMERALD TABLET OF HERMES TRISMEGISTUS (TABULA SMARAGDINA)

Alchemy, according to its legendary father Hermes Trismegistus, is called 'the operation of the Sun.' Hermes Trismegistus was closely linked with the ancient Egyptian Thoth, god of mathematics and science. A Hellenistic figure also, he is the model for the mediæval Mercurius. His Emerald Tablet, the Tabula Smaragdina, is accounted the *Magna Carta* of Alchemy and is one of the very oldest texts of the hermetic tradition. The earliest known form is in ninth century Arabic, probably a translation from a Syrian source of the fourth century, which may in turn have been based on a Greek original. Its writing is said to have been overshadowed by the god Hermes. (See Klossowski de Rola, Page 15, and Fabricius, Page 214.)

> *It is true without lie, certain and most veritable, that what is below is like what is above and that what is above is like what is below, to perpetrate the miracles of one thing.*
> *And as all things have been, and come from One by the meditation of One; thus all things have been born from this single thing by adaptation.*
> *The Sun is its father and the Moon its mother.*
> *The Wind has carried it in his belly and the Earth is its nurse.*
> *The father of all the perfection of all the world is here.*
> *Its force or power is entire if it is turned into earth.*
> *Thou shalt separate the Earth from the Fire, the subtle from the gross, softly, with great ingenuity.*

It rises from the Earth to the sky and again descends into the Earth, and receives the force of things superior and inferior.
Thou shalt have by this means the glory of all the world. And therefore all obscurity shall flee from thee.
And this is the strength strong of all strength. For it shall vanquish anything subtle and anything solid penetrate.
Thus the world is created.
From this shall be and shall proceed admirable adaptations, of which the means is here.
And in this connection I am called Hermes Trismegistus, having the three parts of the philosophy of all the world.
It is finished, what I have said of the operation of the Sun.

BIBLIOGRAPHY

Alice Bailey 1934, 'A Treatise on White Magic', Lucis Press Ltd., London 1997.

Fritjof Capra 1975, 'The Tao of Physics', Wildwood House, London.

Chuang Tsu, 'Inner Chapters', tr. Gia-Fu Feng and Jane English 1974, Wildwood House, London.

Emily Dickinson (1830 - 86) 1924, 'Complete Poems'. Little, Brown, Boston 1924; Part One: Life XXXV, Bartleby.Com, New York 2000.

T.S. Eliot 1959, 'Four Quartets', Faber & Faber, London.

Johannes Fabricius 1976, 'Alchemy: the Mediæval Alchemists and their Royal Art', Rosenkilde & Bagger, Copenhagen 1976; Diamond Books, London 1994.

Robert Graves 1959, 'New LaRousse Encyclopaedia of Mythology', Hamlyn, London 1979.

Liz Greene 1977, 'Relating: An Astrological Guide to Living with Others on a Small Planet'. Coventure, London.

Dorsha Hayes 1972, 'The Bell Branch Rings', Wm. Bauhan, New Hampshire 1972. Dragons Teeth Press 1986.

Aniela Jaffé 1979, 'C.G. Jung, Word and Image', Princeton/ Bollingen Series XCVII: 2.

C.G. Jung 1930-34, 'The Visions Seminars' Vols.1 & 2, Lectures given 1930-34, Spring Publications, Zürich 1976.
C.G. Jung, Collected Works (CW). Routledge & Kegan Paul, London & Henley: Vol 5, 'Symbols of Transformation', 1911-12, (1952).

Vol 11, 'Psychology and Religion: West and East', 1938, (1940).
Vol 12, 'Psychology & Alchemy', 1944.
Vol 13, 'Alchemical Studies', 1929.
Vol 14, 'Mysterium Coniunctionis', 1955-56.
Vol 15, 'Psychology and Literature', 1930.
C.G. Jung, Letters. Volume I, 1906-1950; Volume II, 1951-1961, Routledge & Kegan Paul, London 1973.
C.G. Jung 1952, 'Answer to Job', CW 11, 553-758. Also published separately, Routledge and Kegan Paul, London 1954.
C.G. Jung 1961, 'Memories, Dreams, Reflections', Flamingo, London 1995.

Franz Kafka 1915, 'The Great Wall of China', in 'Metamorphosis and Other Stories', Penguin, Twentieth Century Classics, London 1961. Dover Publications 1996, tr. Willa and Edwin Muir.

Stanislas Klossowski de Rola 1973, 'Alchemy: The Secret Art', Thames & Hudson, London 1973, 1991.

Lao Tsu, 'Tao Te Ching', tr. Gia-Fu Feng and Jane English 1973, Wildwood House, London.

Lü Yen, in 'The Secret of the Golden Flower', tr. Richard Wilhelm 1931, Routledge & Kegan Paul Ltd., London 1962.

Sylvia Brinton Perera 1932, 'Descent to the Goddess: A Way of Initiation for Women', Inner City Books, Toronto 1981.

Melanie Reinhart 1996/2002, 'Saturn, Chiron and the Centaurs: to the Edge and Beyond', CPA Press, London.

Kenneth Rexroth, quoted by Paul J. Stern in 'C.G. Jung: the Haunted Prophet', W.W. Norton & Co. 1976.

Angelus Silesius (b.1624), 'The Cherubinic Wanderer', 2 translations unknown.

Barbara Somers & Ian Gordon-Brown 2002, 'Journey in Depth: A Transpersonal Perspective', Archive Publishing, Lincolnshire 2002.

D.T. Suzuki 1987, 'Manual of Zen Buddhism', Grove Press/Atlantic Monthly Press, USA.

Marie Louise von Franz 1959, 'Alchemy: an Introduction to the Symbolism and the Psychology', Inner City Books, Toronto 1980.
Marie Louise von Franz 1969, 'Alchemical Active Imagination', Zürich 1969, Spring Publications, Dallas 1979.

Arthur Edward Waite 1884, (tr. and ed.) 'Paraclesus: the Hermetic & Alchemical Writings of Philippus Aureolus Paracelsus, Called Paracelsus the Great', J. Elliot, London 1884. Universal Books Inc., New York. Holmes Publishing Group LLC., 1989.
Arthur Edward Waite, 1888, 'Lives of the Alchemystical Philosophers', London 1888. John Watkins 1955. Ams Press 1989.

Frances Wickes 1963, 'The Inner World of Choice', Coventure, London 1977.

Richard Wilhelm 1931, translation of 'The Secret of the Golden Flower', Routledge & Kegan Paul Ltd., London 1962. CG Jung's commentary included; see also CW 13.
Richard Wilhelm 1951, translation of the 'I Ching or Book of Changes', (1923), Routledge & Kegan Paul Ltd., London 1951.

INDEX